I0100783

Environment, Economy and Judiciary

Editors

Dr. Mamta Sharma   Dr. Hukam Singh

Dr. Upendra Singh

Pustak Bharati
Toronto Canada

Editors : Dr. Mamta Sharma
          Dr. Hukam Singh
          Dr. Upendra Singh

Book Title : Environment, Economy and Judiciary

Cover Picture : By Dr. Anil Kumar Chhangani, D.Sc

Published by :
Pustak Bharati (Books India)
180 Torresdale Ave, Toronto Canada M2R 3E4
email : pustak.bharati.canada@gmail.com
Web : www.pustak-bharati-canada.com

Published for
Raj Rishi Government Autonomous College,
Alwar, Rajasthan, India

Financial Assistance
Rashtriya Uchchatar Shiksha Abhiyan
(RUSA-2.0)

Copyright ©2023

ISBN : 978-1-989416-90-7

ISBN 978-1-989416-90-7

© All rights reserved. No part of this book may be copied, reproduced or utilised in any manner or by any means, computerised, e-mail, scanning, photocopying or by recording in any information storage and retrieval system, without the permission in writing from the editors.

Preface

"Our planet is slowly dying, and if we don't do anything about it soon enough, it would eventually begin to deteriorate and everything would be used. The world would become a barren place without any resources. We need to cater to the needs of our planet, and we need to change our life styles so that it becomes beneficial to the planet. We need to become much more eco-friendly, so that no harm is dealt to the planet by our existence. Many people don't realize that they waste large amounts of energy and other resources in various unnecessary things that could otherwise be saved."

This series of books is an extension of the 3 days international conference on **Multidisciplinary Approach Towards Sustainable Development and Climate Change for A Viable Future (ICMSDC-2022)** held from 12th-14th August 2022 at Raj Rishi Government Autonomous College, Alwar, Rajasthan.

We are very happy and delighted to publish our series of books which are accumulation of research papers of knowledgeable experts in the field of sustainable development and climate change.

Climate change is the most significant challenge to achieving sustainable development, and it threatens to drag millions of people into grinding poverty. At the same time, we have never had better know-how and solutions available to avert the crisis and create opportunities for a better life for people all over the world. Climate change is not just a long-term issue. It is happening today, and it entails uncertainties for policy makers trying to shape the future.

There is a dual relationship between sustainable development and climate change. On the one hand, climate change influences key natural and human living conditions and thereby also the basis for social and economic development, while on the other hand, society's priorities on sustainable development influence both the greenhouse gas emissions that are causing climate change and the vulnerability.

Climate policies can be more effective when consistently embedded within broader strategies designed to make national and regional development paths more sustainable. This occurs because the impact of climate variability and change, climate policy responses, and associated socio-economic development will affect the ability of countries to achieve sustainable development goals. Conversely, the pursuit of those goals will in turn affect the opportunities for, and success of, climate policies.

With these books, we aim to reach to as many people as we can, and spread awareness about sustainable development and climate change and its in-depth analysis through our didactic research papers. We hope that the thought with which ICMSDC-2022 was executed is taken forward through this series of books and the inception of an idea of saving the environment is rooted in the minds of our readers.

The articles in these books have been contributed by eminent research scholars, scientists, academicians and industry experts whose contributions have enriched this book series. We thank our publisher, Pustak Bharati, Toronto, Canada for joining us in this initiative and helped in publishing this series of books.

Finally, we will always remain indebted to all our well-wishers for their blessings, without which ICMSDC-2022 and series of these book would have not come into existence.

Financial Assistance provided by Rashtriya Uchchatar Shiksha Abhiyan (RUSA-2.0) is gratefully acknowledged.

Dr. Mamta Sharma
Dr. Hukam Singh
Dr. Upendra Singh

Contents

1. Chemical Pollution : An Unavoidable Debauchery

Dr. Mamta Sharma*
Dr. Hukam Singh**
Dr. Upendra Singh ***

Introduction

Environmental toxicology is a multidisciplinary field of science concerned with the study of the harmful effects of various chemical, biological and physical agents on living organisms. Ecotoxicology is a subdiscipline of environmental toxicology concerned with studying the harmful effects of toxicants at the population and ecosystem levels. Rachel Carson is considered the mother of environmental toxicology, as she made it a distinct field within toxicology in 1962 with the publication of her book Silent Spring, which covered the effects of uncontro-lled pesticide use. Carson's book was based extensively on a series of reports by Lucille Farrier Stickel on the ecological effects of the pesticide DDT. Organisms can be exposed to various kinds of toxicants at any life cycle stage, some of which are more sensitive than others. Toxicity can also vary with the organism's placement within its food web. Bioaccumulation occurs when an organism stores toxicants in fatty tissues, which may eventually establish a trophic cascade and the biomagnification of specific toxicants. Biodegradation releases carbon dioxide and water as by-products into the environment. This process is typically limited in areas affected by environmental toxicants. Harmful effects of such chemical and biological agents as toxicants, from pollutants, insecticides, pesticides, and fertilizers can affect an organism and its community by reducing its species diversity and abundance. Such changes in population dynamics affect the ecosystem by reducing its productivity and stability. Although legislation implemented since the early 1970s had intended to minimize harmful effects of environmental toxicants upon all species but still more of the strict regulations were needed.

The environment has been taken care of in general, and the issue of pollution in particular, and at various levels, whether on the public

1

formal education institutions or the non-formal education institutions. In spite of the great interest in environmental education programs, the reality of this situation is still that environmental care and importance are modest and insufficient to affect the desired effect in developing environmental awareness.

The world has known since the beginning of the twentieth century a set of developments in the relationship of man to the environment, as this century was marked by a set of transformations that caused severe impacts on the environment. The most notable of these transformations are the massive industrialization that the whole world and the developed countries in particular have known, in addition to the massive demographic explosion. These transformations have caused serious environmental problems, perhaps the most important of which is pollution that has affected all aspects of life. This is what imposed on those concerned with the environment, health, education and information in society, shedding light on the environment, providing environmental education that develops awareness of community members, alerting them to the dangers of environmental pollution, and most importantly, directing their behavior to caring for and preserving the environment. The topic of pollution and environmental studies has received the attention of specialists and international public opinion, so there are numerous seminars and conferences dealing with environmental issues and problems. Everyone has been warned that the fundamental solution to the current environmental crisis requires a major change in human attitudes towards their environment, and educational institutions must achieve this through environmental education curricula that provide an environmental culture that results in changes in behavior (Park, 1988). As the curriculum contains environmental educational experiences helps to broaden learners' perceptions, and increases their knowledge of how to deal with the environment. The issue of pollution is one of the most important study topics included or that must include environmental educational concepts, which one must acquire and adhere to.

Detour :

Chemical pollution is defined as the presence or increase in our environment of chemical pollutants that are not naturally present there or are found in amounts higher than their natural background values. Most of the chemicals that pollute the environment are man-made, resulted from the various activities in which toxic chemicals are used for various purposes.

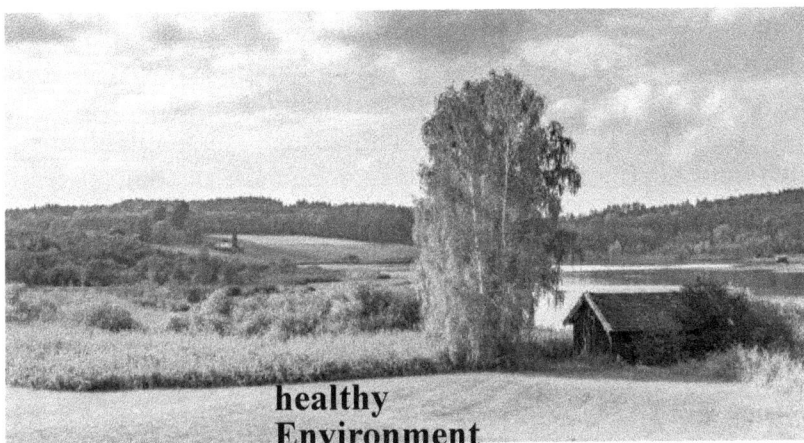

healthy
Environment

The chemicals in their gaseous, liquid, and solid states that are characterized by their efficacy, toxicity, or explosive potential, or to corrosive events, or that have other characteristics that could result in a risk to the environment and public health, whether alone or when related to other materials. There is no doubt that the industry is one of the most important sources that produce chemical pollutants in our world today due to the multiplicity of industries and the tremendous progress in the industrial application of modern science, which is known as technology and is considered the most chemical pollutants resulting from industry have the ability to accumulate in the body of living thingsIt reaches toxic degree.

Sources of Pollution

pollution is divided into two types:

1. natural pollution and 2. industrial pollution.

Natural Pollution: pollution is the source whose source is due to natural phenomena that occur from time to time, such as volcanoes, thunderbolts, and storms that may carry huge amounts of sand and dust, and damage crops, so natural pollution is therefore sources of natural origin, and there is no income for man in it.

Industrial Pollution : Industrial pollution results from human action and activity, and finds its source in man's industrial, service, and entertainment activities, etc., and in his increasing uses of modern technology manifestations and its various innovations. It responsible for the emergence of the pollution problem in our time, and reaching this degree The serious threat to life and the survival of man on the surface of the earth, and among the most important sources of industrial pollution: industrial and commercial waste and what is emitted by car exhaust, and factory chimneys that leave toxic (chlorine, fluorine and carbon) compounds, and others.

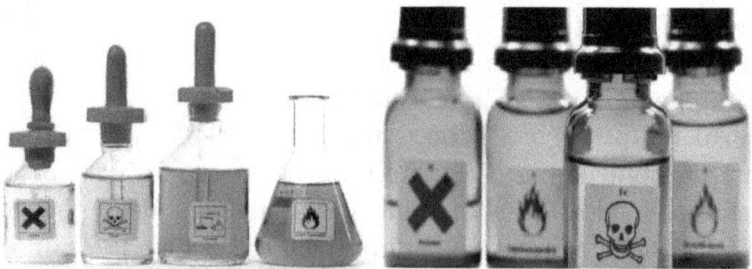

Chemical Substances Effects of Human Healthy

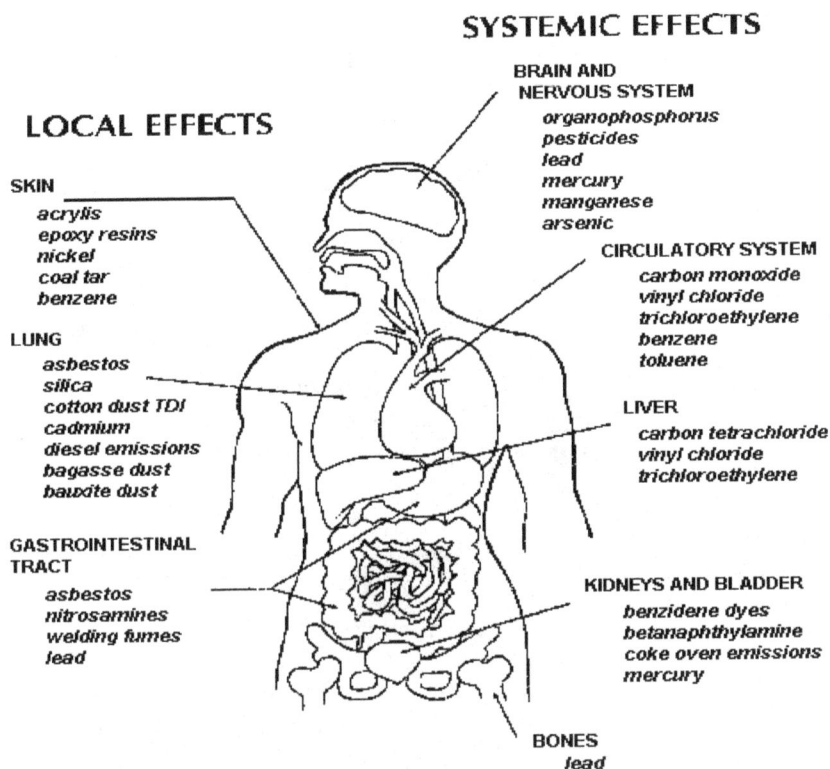

SYSTEMIC EFFECTS

LOCAL EFFECTS

SKIN
acrylis
epoxy resins
nickel
coal tar
benzene

LUNG
asbestos
silica
cotton dust TDI
cadmium
diesel emissions
bagasse dust
bauxite dust

GASTROINTESTINAL
TRACT
asbestos
nitrosamines
welding fumes
lead

BRAIN AND
NERVOUS SYSTEM
organophosphorus
pesticides
lead
mercury
manganese
arsenic

CIRCULATORY SYSTEM
carbon monoxide
vinyl chloride
trichloroethylene
benzene
toluene

LIVER
carbon tetrachloride
vinyl chloride
trichloroethylene

KIDNEYS AND BLADDER
benzidene dyes
betanaphthylamine
coke oven emissions
mercury

BONES
lead

The severity of industrial pollution depends on several factors, including :
1. The area from which industrial pollutants are emitted
2. Time period for pollution.
3. The degree of concentration of pollutants.
4. Physical, chemical and biological properties of pollutants.
5. The ability to decompose and assimilate in the environmental environment in which it is placed.
6. Toxicity relative to humans and other organisms

☐ The general pollutants classified according to the property of harmful substances or products into environment to :

(Water pollution, Air pollution, Soil pollution, nuclear pollution and Biological pollution)

Health effects of pollution

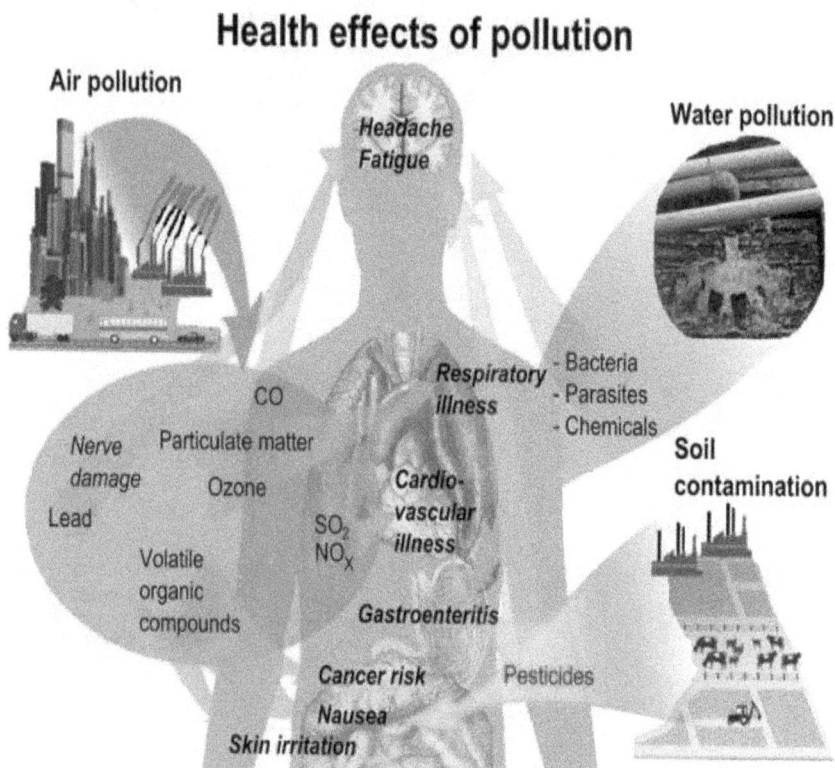

Air pollution

Headache
Fatigue

Water pollution

CO

Respiratory illness

- Bacteria
- Parasites
- Chemicals

Nerve damage   Particulate matter

Soil contamination

Lead   Ozone   Cardio-vascular illness

SO_2
NO_x

Volatile organic compounds

Gastroenteritis

Cancer risk   Pesticides

Nausea

Skin irritation

Main Types of Chemical Pollution : These chemicals can react with tissues in the body and change the structure and function of the organ, cause abnormal growth and development of the individual, or bind with the genetic material of cells and cause cancer. One of the central tenets of the study of such effects (toxicology) is that the dose of a chemical determines its overall effects and that most chemicals can be dangerous at high exposure

1. **Inorganic Pollutants** : Inorganic pollutants are released into the environment due to activities of mining, industry, transportation and urban activities. Environmental risks associated with inorganic pollutants vary widely due to several complex interactions at both intracellular and extracellular levels. Toxic heavy metals and

metalloids interact quite strongly with soil constituents as compared to salts of alkali metals, rate of which however, depend on the element and their speciation.

2. **Organic Pollutants** : More of organic compounds used in industry and medical field there are we exposure in daily life, They're used for drugs and cleaning applications and as solvents in a wide range of products such as fuels, paints, inks, preservatives and pesticides
, therefore causes more pollutions, So can have serious impacts of human health. and many can be absorbed through intact skin and absorbed into the bloodstream; and may be have more major route of entry into the body.

3. **Nuclear (Radiation) Pollutants**:

Radiation warning symbol(nuclear power plants)

Radiation pollution means the leakage of radioactive materials into one of the components of the environment, such as water, air, and soil. It is considered one of the most dangerous types of environmental pollution in our time, as it is not seen, smelled, does not feel. Without any resistance, and without any indication of its presence, and without first having an effect, and when radioactive materials reach the cells of the body, they cause visible and hidden damage that often leads to human life, and radioactive contamination may occur from natural sources such as radiation from outer space and gases Radioactive mounting from the cortex Z, or from industrial sources of nuclear power stations of atomic reactors and radioactive isotopes used in industry, agriculture, medicine or other.

Radioactivity is toxic because it forms ions when it reacts with biological molecules. These ions can form free radicals, which damage proteins, membranes, and nucleic acids. Radioactivity can damage DNA (deoxyribonucleic acid) by destroying individual bases (particularly thymine), by breaking single strands, by breaking double strands, by cross-linking different DNA strands, and by cross-linking DNA and proteins. Damage to DNA can lead to cancers, birth defects, and even death.

4.Biological Pollutants: Biological or biological pollution is considered one of the oldest forms of pollution known to man, and this pollution arises as a result of the presence of visible or invisible living organisms such as bacteria, fungi and others in the environmental medium such as water, air or soil, so the mixing of disease-causing organisms with food that The person eats it, the water he drinks, or the air that he inhales causes biological pollution, which leads to disease.

The effect of chemical pollutants on human health There is no doubt that the human body is poisoned by chemical pollutants if exposed to it, and poisoning is the occurrence of a demolition in the biological composition of some parts of the body and acute poisoning occurs as a result of exposure to toxic gases for twenty-four hours, while chronic poisoning occurs as a result of exposure to pollutants for a long period of time intermittent. Man can control solid or liquid chemical pollutants for easy identification, collection and disposal in remote places. As for gas chemical pollutants, they are rapidly spreading and some cannot be seen, which is difficult to collect if they are spread. There are three ways by which gas pollutants enter the human body and are:

- Through the respiratory system when breathing.
- Through the digestive system when eating foods and drinks.
- Through the skin, especially in the injured areas

Industrial Pollutants are divided into three types :
1. Solid pollutants, which are those pollutants resulting from many industries, such as dust resulting from the cement industry, for example.
2. Liquid pollutants such as the solutions of the chemical materials that the factories throw into the waterways.

3. Gas pollutants such as gases and harmful smoke from industrial chimneys and oil refineries.

Most important organs of the body affected by toxic pollutants are the kidneys and liver, where pollutants accumulate, as the skin and eye sensitivity are a sign of the presence of substances with an unhealthy effect in the atmosphere, and the fear of the effect of chemical pollutants on human health is not limited to the surrounding pollutants but rather leads to fear of using Chemicals in the various products that a person uses daily and that are included in food and drink items such as preservatives and flavors added to food. The World Health Organization issues lists of these materials to stop use in the food industry in the countries of the world.

Hazards of Environment Pollution

1. Poisoned marine organisms, which may cause their death, thus affecting the food chain in the ecosystem.
2. Damage to living organisms that live on Earth, whether they are microorganisms, plants or animals, as it loses soil fertility, and may lead to desertification.
3. Global warming occurs, which may cause environmental disasters, such as: global warming, as well as melting ice in the Arctic and which causes the percentage of water on the earth to rise, and thus drown.
4. It leads to a hole in the ozone layer, which leads to an increase in theharmful UV rays reaching the earth, which affects human life.

Gases pollutants such oxides of salver, carbon, and nitrogen as well as the chloroflurocarbon compounds are broken by UV radiation releasing chlorine and fluorine free radical those react woth ozone of stratosphere cause decomposed it:

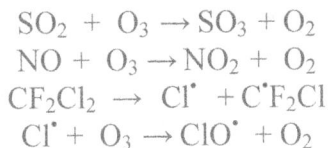

$$SO_2 + O_3 \rightarrow SO_3 + O_2$$
$$NO + O_3 \rightarrow NO_2 + O_2$$
$$CF_2Cl_2 \rightarrow Cl^{\bullet} + C^{\bullet}F_2Cl$$
$$Cl^{\bullet} + O_3 \rightarrow ClO^{\bullet} + O_2$$

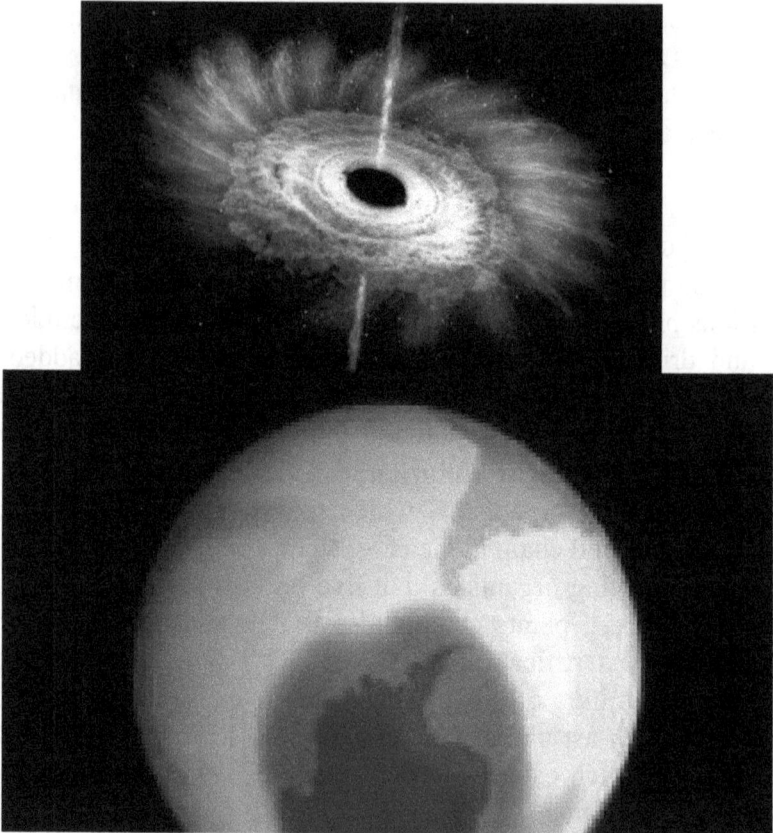

5. Acid rain causes corrosion various impacts and buildings due to the rise in the proportions of some gases.

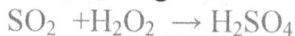

$$SO_2 + H_2O_2 \rightarrow H_2SO_4$$
$$4NO_2 + O_2 + 2H_2O \rightarrow 4HNO_3 \quad CO_2 + H_2O \rightarrow H_2CO_3$$

The Effects of Chemical Pollution

Chemical pollution can be caused by a variety of chemicals from a variety of sources and can involve a variety of health effects from simple digestive problems to chemical intoxication and sudden death by poisoning. The effects are usually related to the exposure to high amounts and accumulate of chemicals in body. Chemical pollution leads to various serious diseases, generally by consuming poisonous food, drinking highly contaminated water, or breathing contaminated air.

Chemical intoxication can have severe health effects that may trigger immediate symptoms and diseases or delayed effects which may appear after weeks or months since the exposure occurred. This is based on the type of pollutants and on the amounts to which you are exposed. **CAUTION, never assume that all is OK if no health effects appear immediately!**

Chemical compounds intoxication are organic or inorganic chemicals that are the main causes of chemical pollution. The most common chemical pollutants are those compounds used across large areas and which are persistent, meaning they do not easily degrade in nature. Examples are most pesticides, herbicides, insecticides used in agriculture and gardening, as well as chlorinated solvents used in many industrial processes and dry-cleaning activities.

The chemical industry is another example in this sense, mainly because it is usually linked to polluted waste streams. In fact, the waste streams from chemical industry are now strictly controlled and treated before being released into the environment. But this was not always the case in the past and many rivers and surface water bodies were contaminated by the numerous waste streams coming from various chemical plants, as well as other industrial sources. Even though measures were taken to reduce this type of pollution, its effects are still visible.

Chemical intoxication is caused by exposure to chemical pollutants and can have immediate effects or delayed effects, which may appear after weeks or even months after the exposure occurred. Severe chemical intoxication may cause the death of the person that inhales an increased quantity of such substances.

Household Chemicals involve a variety of chemical products and mixtures that can easily become chemical pollutants when released into the environment. Even the everyday detergents are chemical compounds that may pollute our environment! Read the labels of detergent products to confirm that they contain a variety of potentially hazardous chemicals. Such : (Pesticides, Fertilizers, Preservatives, Colorants and Flavor of Food and Cleaning substance and Drugs).

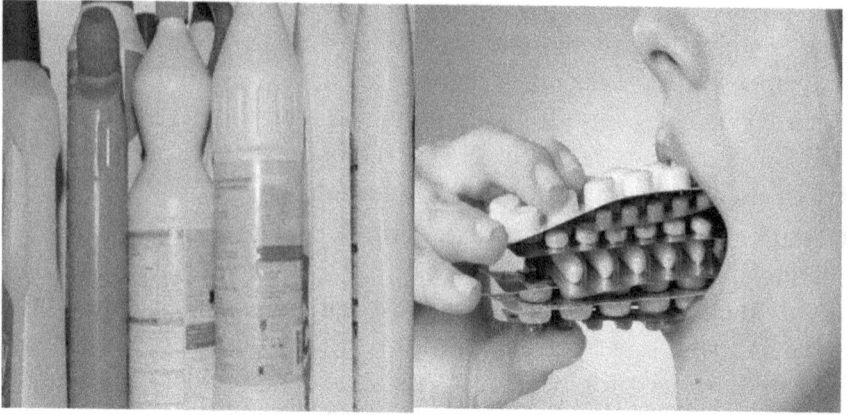

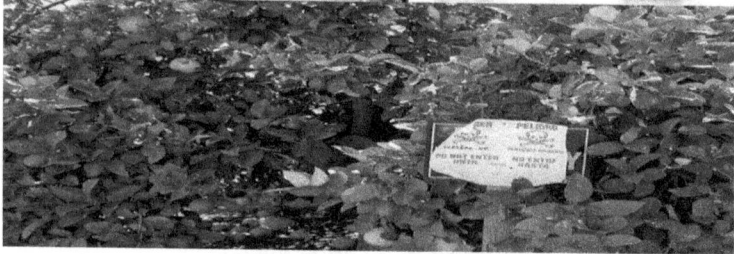

Containers labelled with chemical hazard warning signs

Pesticide Risk of the Health and Environmental

Pesticides have been commonly used to control pests causing release the pesticides component into the environment. The intensive use of pesticide leads to an increased risk of contamination of the environment and harmful effects on variety biological, food security, and water sources. The released pesticides into the environment and their impacts of the ecosystem and human health, such DDT, dieldrin, and other toxic have more affected of the healthy, because transfer to the humans by the foods of animals and plants.

Methods of Prevention of Environmental Pollution
Take preventive precautions.
1. Maintaining hygiene in its various forms, including: personal hygiene, clean working environment, water, and soil.
2. Ensure the correct use of pesticides.
3. Waste disposal and disposal in the right way.
4. Getting rid of rodents and insects and eliminating them permanently.

5. Noise reduction.
6. Continuation in afforestation and erection of retaining walls inorder to reduce the capacity of air pollutants.

Control of Pollutant Release and Transfer Register (PRTR) Substances

PRTR system: This system is for the control of chemical substances that are harmful to human health or the ecosystem. Under this system, businesses ascertain the amounts of harmful chemical substances they have released into the atmosphere, water, or soil, or transferred tolocations outside of their business facilities, and report this data to the national government. The national government then uses this data and estimates to summarize and disclose volumes of chemical substances released or transferred.

Report of Amounts of PRTR Substances Released or Transferred

(Contain manganese, chromium, nickel, and lead as alloy substances)

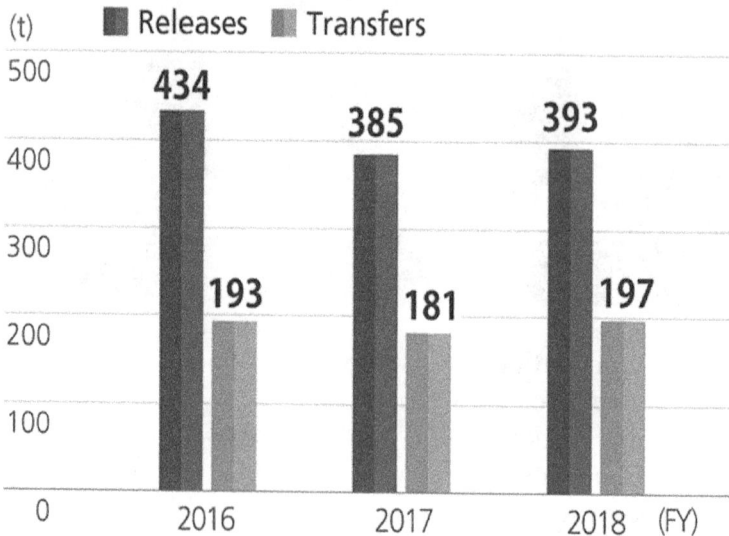

Symbols of Handling, Releases, and Transfers of PRTR Substances

No.	Substance	Amount Used (kg)	Amount Released (kg)	Amount Transferred (kg)
412	Manganese and its inorganic compounds	2,535,608	0	21,200
300	Toluene	771,721	190,919	47,785
80	Xylene	203,756	18,742	1,899
87	Chromium and chromium(III) compounds	178,801	0	28,294
273	1-dodecanol	165,089	84,320	52,808
296	1,2,4-trimethyl benzene	159,894	66,436	23,955
53	Ethyl benzene	67,158	2,541	191
374	Hydrogen fluoride and itswater-soluble salts	61,335	1,557	14,029
71	Ferric chlorides	49,985	0	0
297	1,3,5-trimethylbenzene	30,531	19,596	1,331

No.	Substance	Amount Used (kg)	Amount Released (kg)	Amount Transferred (kg)
88	Hexavalent chromium and its compounds	29,814	0	124
308	Nickel	29,168	0	0
302	Naphthalin	7,948	195	52
407	Polyoxyethylene	5,882	5,746	80
392	n-hexane	4,676	1,859	661
438	Methylnaphthalene	4,604	23	0
321	Vanadium compounds	3,618	0	0
304	Lead	3,297	0	0
133	Ethylene glycol monoethylether acetate	3,245	26	0
207	2,6-Di-tert-butyl-4-cresol	2,598	833	1,765

No.	Substance	Amount Used (kg)	Amount Released (kg)	Amount Transferred (kg)
245	Thiourea	2,125	0	2,125
411	Formaldehyde	1,118	26	5
277	Triethylamine	1,101	62	16
	Total	4,323,070	392,882	196,320

Common Substances
- Formaldehyde
- Mercury
- Lead
- Asbestos
- Hazardous/Toxic Air Pollutants
- Per- and Polyfluoroalkyl Substances (PFAS)
- Pesticide Chemicals
- Polychlorinated Biphenyls (PCBs)

References:
Source of knowledge is the internet and it is highly acknowledged.
- Environmental chemistry
- Emerging pollutants
- Chemical pollutants
- Environmental health

*Associate Professor (Zoology)
**Professors
***Associate Professor (Chemistry)
Raj Rishi Government (Autonomous) College
Alwar, Rajasthan 301001,India.
email : mamta810@gmail.com ;
drhukamsingh63@gmail.com ;
dr.usingh09@gmail.com

2. Natural Occurrence of Aflatoxin In Sunflower

A. S. Kolhe

Abstract

Sunflower seed, cake, and oil samples were collected from the market. Aflatoxigenic fungi were screened for in seeds and cakes. Mycoflora's A. flavus was the dominant species. All A. flavus isolates produced AFB1, but only isolates 21, 4, 2, and 1 also produced B_2, B_2+ G_1, and $B_2+G_1+G_2$, respectively. A. flavus toxigenic potential ranged from 0.1 to 1.5 ppm. To check for the presence of aflatoxin, all samples were examined. Aflatoxin types were checked in samples that were positive for the BGYF test. Aflatoxin B_1 concentrations ranged from 20 to 153 ppb in cake, 10 to 60 ppb in seeds, and 10 to 60 ppb in oil (Trace to 10 ppb).

Keywords : *Mycoflora, Aspergillus flavus, Aflatoxin, sunflower.*

Introduction

Sunflower (*Helianthus annuus* L.) is one of the fastest growing oilseed crops in India popularly known as "Surajmukhi." Six states with Karnataka in the lead are the major producers of sunflower in the country. Karnataka with a production of 3.04 lakh tonnes from an area of 7.94 lakh hectares followed by Andhra Pradesh, Maharashtra, Bihar, Orissa and Tamil Nadu, that provides animal feed and cooking oil. sunflower industry is an important contribution to the economics of India. Small-scale sunflower farmers make a living by selling sunflower seeds to processors, who extract cooking oil and produce seed cakes, which consist of the seed residue following extraction of oil. Sunflower oil is popular as healthy cooking oil due to its health benefits while the meal is used in animal feed industry. Among sunflower products, meal is the most traded in world market. Whereas humans eat roasted and salted seeds as a nutritious snack food, the cakes are used as animal feed for chickens, dairy cows, and goats., which serve as a reliable source of animal feed for livestock in India. The oil cake from decorticated seed is fed to cattle. Besides direct threat of aflatoxicoses to human being due to ingestion of aflatoxin contaminated food, indirect poisoning can not be ruled out because of the consumption of various animal product such as milk, milk product and poultry products, presence of Aflatoxin M_1 and M_2 have been noted in the milk of lactating cattles and woman (Allcroft *et. al.,*1968;Coulter *et. al.,*1984;Wild *et. al.,* 1987). Peoples of western part of India are exposed to greater risk due to heavy consumption of peanut and other oil seeds which are high risk substrates for aflatoxin producing fungi and aflatoxin production (Dwarkanath *et. al.,* 1969; Nagarajan and Bhat,1973; Basappa *et. al.,* 1977; Kolhe, *et. al.,*1994; Verma, *et. al.,* 1996; Kolhe and Chaudhari,2011; Chaudhari and Kolhe,2017) However, total aflatoxin concentrations in sunflower seeds and cakes produced in Tanzania have not been analyzed or reported leaving questions such as to what magnitude of the risk to human and animal health from consumption of sunflower products. Therefore, the aim of the present study was to survey total aflatoxin levels in sunflower seed, oil and cake samples.

 It is necessary to know the incidence of aflatoxigenic fungi and aflatoxin contamination. The present investigation is an attempt in that direction.

Materials and Methods

Samples of sunflower viz., seed, cake and oil were collected from different marketing centre of Jalgaon District, Maharashtra, stored in polythene bags until used. Isolation of mycoflora was done by agar plate methods using peptone, glucose, rose bengal agar medium containing streptomycin .(Booth,1971). Fungal colonies formed were identified and percent incidence of each fungus was calculated.

The isolates of *Aspergillus flavus* were screened for their aflatoxin producing potentials in SMKY liquid medium (Diener and Davis, 1966). Ten days old culture filtrates were extracted with chloroform(v/v) and qualitatively analyzed for different types of aflatoxins on TLC plates (Reddy et. al., 1970).

For analysis of aflatoxin contamination in seed, cake, and oil. The sunflower samples (seeds, cakes and oils) were examined under U.V. light for BGYF test (Fennell et. al.,1973). Powdered (seed and cake) were extracted with methanol : water (6:4 v/v)and sodium chloride (Anon,1975). Oil samples were extracted according to

Jones (1972). The aqueous methanolic extract was defatted using n-hexane followed by its extraction for aflatoxin with chloroform which was processed for qualitative analysis of aflatoxin on TLC plates (Reddy et. al., 1970).

The TLC plates were air-dried and observed under long-wave UV light(360nm) for aflatoxins (B_1,B_2,G_1&G_2). The aflatoxins were also chemically confirmed by spraying trifluoroacetic acid and 25% sulfuric acid. Each spot was scraped separately, dissolved in chilled methanol and subjected to spectrophotometric measurement at 360 nm using a temperature controlled using shimadzu UV160A Spectrophotometer (Nabney and Nesbitt,1965).

Result and Discussion

Table:-1 Mycoflora associated with sunflower (seed & cake) and their percentage incidence.

Mycoflora	Percentage incidence in seeds	Percentage incidence in cakes
Aspergillus flavus	28	49
A. niger	23	26
A.ochraceous	13	14
]Aspergillus sp.	10	1
Alternaria sp.	-	1
Fusarium sp.	13	1
Mucor sp.	4	2
Penicillum sp.	5	1
Rhizopus sp.	4	5

Table-1 records different fungi (in %) isolated from safflower seeds and cakes. It is obvious that aspergilla outnumbered other genera viz., *Alternaria, Furasium, Mucor, Pencillum and Rhizopus sp.* Among *Aspergilli, A. flavus* was dominant on seeds(28 %) and cakes (49 %). *Aspergillus flavus,A. Niger and A. ochraceous* emerge as most common infesting fungi. After *Aspergilli*, the most common infestant was *Fusarium, Penicillum, Mucor and Rhizopus* on seed and *Rhizopus, Mucor, Fusarium and Penicillium.* on cake followed by *Alternaria sp.* (isolated from cake).Jackson (1965) have reported a large and varied groups of fungi comprising over 250 species belonging to genera associated with groundnut seeds and fruits. The variation in association pattern is quite logical because of the different in their chemical composition which probably is the main reason for variation in colonization by different types of fungi.(Christensen and Saur, 1982)

Table : 2. Aflatoxin producing potentiality of *A. flavus* isolates and Aflatoxin contamination in the samples of seed, cake and oil.

Number of A. flavus isolates or samples screened	Positive to BGYF test(only samples)	Number of toxignic isolates or Contaminated samples(%)	Types of aflatoxin produced				Range of Aflatoxin Bl Concentration
			B_1	B_1+B_2	$B_1+B_2 +G_1$	$B_1+B_2+ G_1+G_2$	
41 isolates	-	28(68.29)	21	4	2	1	0.1 to 1.5 ppm
15 seed samples	15	9 (60%)	13	12	-	-	10 to 60 ppb
24 cakes samples	24	18 (75%)	11	4	2	1	20 to 153 ppb
20 oil samples	8	4(20.00)	2	2	-	-	Trace to 10 ppb

Isolation of *A. flavus* obtained from seed and cake were tested for their aflatoxin producing potentials in SMKY liquid medium (Table -2). Results revealed that only 28 amongst 41 were toxic. Though all isolates of *A. flavus* were AFB_1 producers, the isolates 21, 4,2& 1 additionally produced B_2, B_2+ G_1 and $B_2+G_1+G_2$, respectively. Toxigenic potential of *A. flavus* varied between 0.1 to 1.5 ppm. Results clearly indicate that all *A. flavus* isolates are not toxic producers, similar results reported by Raper and fennell (1965) also reported that all *A. flavus* isolates are not toxigenic. In 1965, Hiscocks noted that some isolates of *A. flavus* produced either B or G toxins, but majority of them produced both toxins. None of the isolates produced B_2, G_1 and G_2 in absence of BI (Lillehoj *et. al.,* 1977). It has been suggested that toxigenic nature of the isolates is possibly governed by their genetic make up (Ciegler, 1977). Mold growth and toxin formation require a moisture content of the substrate greater than 14 % and a temperature of approximately 25 %. Reduced oxygen content diminishes aflatoxin formation (Diener *et al.,* 1987). In Present investigation, range of aflatoxin B_1

Concentration was found in cake (20 to 153 ppb), seed (10 to 120 ppb) and oil (Trace to 31 ppb). Variable amount of aflatoxin in them is obviously due to the nature of the fungal strains as well as, the environmental condition leading to aflatoxin production (Sinha, 1980;Bilgrami and Sinha,1987) .

Out of 15 seed samples screened, all gave BGYF test under UV light but only 9 samples contained detectable amount of aflatoxin B_1 and $B_1+ B_2$, some of the seed samples had AF B_1 as high as 60 ppb.

Twenty oil samples screened for aflatoxin contamination, 8 gave BGYF test positive under UV lamp but only 4 samples had contain aflatoxin B_1 ranging from trace to 10 ppb. Aflatoxin contamination in cake, twentyfour samples screened all gave to BGYF test positive under UV lamp. But extraction studied revealed that 18 were contamination with aflatoxin. Quantitative studies revealed that 11, 4, 2 and 1 samples were contaminated with B_1, B_1+B_2, $B_1+B_2+G_1$ and $B_1+B_2+G_1+ G_2$,respectively. Some of the samples which were positive to BGYF test were not positive to very minute concentration of aflatoxin. The BGYF test usually used to detect the presence of *A. flavus., A. parasiticus* and aflatoxin contamination (Fennell *et. al.*,1973). Maximum amount of aflatoxin B_1 (153 ppb.) was present in cake followed by seed (60ppb.) and oil (10 ppb). Banu, and Muthumary (2010) were reported among the 23 different sunflower oil samples were tested, 10 of them showed positive results to AFB1 and the remaining 13 showed negative results to AFB_1. The loss of food grains under storage depend on various factors which vary from place to place under changing environmental conditions. The type of microorganism dominating in grains and nearby atmosphere and also condition of food grains particularly the moisture contain and chemical composition are very important factors the losses of food grain in some country such as India and certain countries in Africa and South America may be 30% of the total annual harvest (Neergaard,1977). Some isolates that produce aflatoxin under cultural conditions, fail to do so under natural conditions. This could be due to unfavourable and changing conditions and the effect of interaction with other microorganisms. Besides, genetical factors might also be responsible for the variations in aflatoxin production by different strains of A. flavus (Maggon et al., 1969; Ciegler, 1977)

Aflatoxin contamination in oil cakes is due to production of the toxin primarily by *A. flavus* when oil is extracted from oil seeds, part of aflatoxin goes into the oil while a portion is retained in the oil cakes, which is served as animal feeds. Another factor that causes aflatoxin contamination is poor, humid storage condition. Consumption of contaminated cake by animals may result aflatoxicosis.AF B_1 is the major AF contaminant of foodstuffs and consequently AFM_1 would be expected to be the prevalent metabolite in milk. Aflatoxin M_1 is of particular importance as it is highly toxic and appears in cattles milk within 12 hour after consumption of aflatoxin contaminated feed.

Conclusion :

According to our findings, sunflower seed and cake samples averaged about 15 (seeds), 24 (Cake), and 20 (Oil) detectable amounts of aflatoxin B_1, with sunflower cake having the highest levels. Aflatoxin detection is a severe problem because it could have a negative impact on consumer health. As a result, management is urgently needed, and exposure to aflatoxin at any level is not thought to be safe for people.

Acknowledgement :

The authors are grateful to Dr R J Verma, Dept. of Zoology, Gujarat University, Ahmedabad.for Laboratory Facilities. and also thankful to Dr. M. D. Friesen of the International Agency for Research on Cancer. Lyon, France for providing samples of pure aflatoxins.

Referencs :

Allcroft, R., Roberts, B. A. and Lioyd, M. K. (1968).Excretion of aflatoxin in a lactating Cow.*Food Cosmet.Toxicol.* **6 (5)**: 619-625.

Anonymous (1975). In Offical Methods of Analysis (Ed. Horwtiz, W.) *Assoc. Off. Anal. Chem.*, Washington D.C. Sects, 26-014-26-018, PP.465 – 466.

Banu, N. and Muthumary, J .P. (2010) Aflatoxin B_1 contamination in sunflower oil collected from sunflower oil refinery situated in Karnataka. *Health*, **2**(8): 973-987.

Basappa, S. C., Sreenivasamurthy, V. and Rajalakshmi, D. (1977). Analysis of Aflatoxin in groundnut and its Product .*Indian J. Tech.* **15**:311 – 313.

Bilgrami, K. S. and Sinha, K. K. (1987). Aflatoxin in Inidia:1. In Aflatoxin in Maize (Eds. M. S. Zuber, E. B. Lillehoj and B. L. Renfro). A proceeding of the workshop. CIMMYT, Mexico.D.F.,PP. 349-358.

Booth, C (1971). Fungal culture media.In methods in microbiology (Ed., Both, C.)Vol. **4**. Academic Press, London. PP. 49 – 94.

Christen, C. M. and Saur, D. B. (1982). Mycoflora.In Storage of cereal grains and their products. Christen Ed[n] American Association of cereal Chemist. St. paul. PP. 219-240.

Ciegler, A. (1977). Factors controlling aflatoxin production.In mycotoxins in Human and Animal Health.Pathotox Publishers Inc. PP. 609 – 624.

Chaudhari, S.B. and A.S.Kolhe (2017) Assessment of Aflatoxins and Aflatoxigenic Fungi Associated with Oil Seeds from Jalgaon district Maharashtra. *EDU WORLD*. **8**(6):357-362.

Coulter, J. B. S., Lamplugh, S. M., Suliman, G. I., Omer, M. I. and Hendrickse, R. G., (1984). Aflatoxins in human breast milk .*Ann. Trop. Paediatr.*, **4(2)**: 61-66.

Diener, U. L. and Davis, N. D.(1966). Aflatoxin Production by isolates of Aspergillus flavus. *Phytopathlogy* **56(12)**:1390 – 1393.

Dwarkanath, C. T., Sreenivasamurthy, V. and Parpia, H. A. B.(1969). Aflatoxin in Indian peanut oil. *J. Food Sci.* Technol. **6(2)**: 107-109.

Fennell, D.I, Bothast, R.J., Lillehaj., E. B. and Paterson, R.E. (1973). Bright greenish yellow fluorescence and associated fungi in white corn naturally contaminated with aflatoxin. *Cereal chem.* **50**: 404 – 414.

Jackson, C. R.(1965). A list of fungi reported in peanut pods and kernels. Uni. Georgia College Agric. Mimco. Series NS.**234** P.6.

Jones, B. D. (1972). Methods of aflatoxin analysis G 70 Tropical products Institute London. 58P.

Hiscocks, E. S. 1965. The importance of molds in the deterioration of tropical foods and feedstuffs, p. 15-26. In G. N. Wogan (ed.), Mycotoxins in foodstuffs. The MIT Press, Cambridge.

Kolhe, A. S.and S. B. Chaudhari (2011). Aflatoxin Contamination in Sesamum indicum L. (Til). *Journal of Research and Development.* **1(10)** : 23-27.

Kolhe, A. S., Verma, R. J. and Dube, H.C. (1994).Aflatoxin Contamination in Oil Cakes. *Indian phytopathology.***47(3)** : 270-272.

Lillehoj, E.B., Fennell, D.I. and Kwolek, W.F. (1977). Aflatoxin and Aspergillus flavus occurrence in 1975 corn at harvest from a limited area of Iowa. Cereal Chem., 54: 366-372.

Mayura. K ., Basappa. S.C. and Sreenivasamurthy. V. (1985). Studies on some factors affecting aflatoxin production by *Aspergillus flavus* and *Aspergillus parasiticus. F. Food Sci Technology.* 22(2): 126-129.

Maggon, K.K., Vishwanathan, L., Venkitasubramanian, T.A. and Mukerji, K.G. (1969). Aflatoxin production by some Indian strains of *Aspergillus flavus* Link ex. Frie. *J Gen. Microbiol,*59(1): 119-124.

Nagarajan, V. and Bhat, R. V.(1973). Aflatoxin production in peanut varieties by *Aspergillusflavus* link and *Aspergillus parasiticus* speare. *Appl. Microbiol.* **25(2)** : 319-321.

Neergaard, P. (1977). Seed pathology. *Macmillan Press Ltd.* London U.K., P.P. 282-297.

Raper, K. B. and fennel, D. I. (1965).The genus *Aspergillus.*The Williams and Wilkins Co., Baltimore, Maryland, pp 686.

Nabney, J. and Nesbitt, B F. (1965). A. spectrophotometeric , method for determining the aflatoxins. *Analyst,* **90 :** 155-160.

Reddy, T V, Vishwanathan, L, and Venkitasubramanian, T. A.(1970) Thin layer chromatography of aflatoxins. *Anal Biochem.***38(2)** :568-571.

Sinha, K. K.(1980). Aflatoxin contamination in some proteinaceous seeds. *Biol. Bull. India* **2** : 76-77.

Verma, R. J., Kolhe, A. S. and Dube, H. C. (1996).Aflatoxin Contamination in different varieties of peanut .*Indian phytopathology.* **49(1)**: 62-66.

Wild,C.P., Pionneau,F., Montesano, R., Mutiro, C. F. and Chetsanga, C. J. (1987).Aflatoxin deceted in human breast milk by immunoassay .*Int. J. Cancer*, **40**:328-333.

Department of Zoology,
Arts and Science College, Bhalod Tal.-Yawal,
Jalgaon, Maharashtra
email : kolheajaykumar4@gmail.com

3. International Environmental Law in Promoting Sustainable Development : A Critical Analysis

Dr. Sheikh Inam Ul Mansoor

Abstract

The intersection of "international environmental law" and "sustainable development" has been a topic of debate and discussion for several decades. While "international environmental law" provides a framework for addressing global environmental challenges, "sustainable development" seeks to balance economic, social, and environmental priorities for a more equitable and sustainable future. This research paper critically analyzes the effectiveness of "international environmental law" in promoting "sustainable development", with a focus on challenges and opportunities for improvement.

The literature review provides an overview of "international environmental law" and "sustainable development", highlighting the historical development and challenges faced in promoting "sustainable development" through "international environmental law". Despite the growth of "international environmental law", implementation challenges, limited political will, and lack of accountability have hindered its effectiveness in promoting "sustainable development". However, the review also highlights opportunities and potential for improvement, such as the rise of transnational environmental law and the importance of cooperation and collaboration between stakeholders.

The methodology section outlines the research design and approach, data sources, and collection methods used in this study. The paper employs a qualitative research design, including a comprehensive review of the relevant literature, as well as analysis of case studies and examples of successful and unsuccessful implementation of "international environmental law" for "sustainable development".

The critical analysis section examines the relationship between "international environmental law" and "sustainable development", analyzing the effectiveness of "international environmental law" in promoting "sustainable development". The analysis demonstrates that while "international environmental law" has made significant contributions to addressing global environmental challenges, it has fallen short of achieving "sustainable development" goals. This section also provides case studies and examples to demonstrate the challenges and opportunities for "international environmental law" in promoting "sustainable development".

The challenges and opportunities section identifies and discusses the limitations and criticisms of "international environmental law" in promoting "sustainable development", including the limited political will, weak implementation, and lack of accountability. This section also highlights opportunities for improvement, such as strengthening the legal frameworks for promoting "sustainable development" and enhancing stakeholder engagement and collaboration.

In conclusion, the paper synthesizes the findings from the critical analysis and challenges and opportunities sections, providing recommendations for policymakers, practitioners, and future research. The recommendations include strengthening the legal frameworks for promoting "sustainable development", enhancing accountability and enforcement mechanisms, and promoting stakeholder engagement and collaboration. The paper contributes to the ongoing discussion on the relationship between "international environmental law" and "sustainable development", highlighting the challenges and opportunities for improving the effectiveness of "international environmental law" in promoting "sustainable development".

I. Introduction

One of the most important problems the world society is now confronting is environmental deterioration. The natural balance of the earth and human well-being are in danger due to the rapid industrialization, urbanization, and population expansion that has resulted in higher pollution, deforestation, and climate change levels.[i] Policymakers, scholars, and activists have pushed for the adoption of "sustainable development" techniques that strike a balance between economic, social, and environmental concerns in order to solve these issues. An important instrument in this effort is "international environmental law," which offers a framework for resolving global environmental issues and advancing "sustainable development."

This study paper's main goal is to evaluate how well "international environmental law" promotes "sustainable development." In order to better understand the difficulties and potential for enhancing "international environmental law's" ability to support "sustainable development," this article will analyse the link between the two concepts.

To answer these research questions, this paper will begin with a literature review of "international environmental law" and "sustainable development", highlighting the historical development and challenges faced in promoting "sustainable development" through "international environmental law". This section will also examine the role of international institutions, such as the "United Nations Environment Programme" (UNEP), in promoting "sustainable development" through "international environmental law".

The literature review will draw upon recent scholarship to provide a comprehensive understanding of the relationship between "international environmental law" and "sustainable development". For example, Biermann[ii] argue that "international environmental law" has made significant contributions to addressing global environmental challenges, but has fallen short of achieving "sustainable development" goals. Similarly, Tams[iii] highlight the challenges of implementing "international environmental law", particularly in developing countries where institutional capacity and political will may be lacking.

After the literature review, the research paper will describe the methodology used in this study, including the research design and approach, data sources, and collection methods. This paper employs a qualitative research design, including a comprehensive review of the relevant literature, as well as analysis of case studies and examples of successful and unsuccessful implementation of "international environmental law" for "sustainable development". The case studies and examples will be drawn from various regions and sectors, including climate change mitigation, biodiversity conservation, and sustainable energy.

The critical analysis section will examine the effectiveness of "international environmental law" in promoting "sustainable development". This section will analyze the relationship between "international environmental law" and "sustainable development", highlighting the successes and limitations of "international environmental law" in achieving "sustainable development" goals. For example, Vihma[iv] argues that "international environmental law" has been successful in promoting transboundary cooperation and addressing global environmental challenges, but has fallen short in addressing the root causes of environmental degradation, such as unsustainable consumption patterns.

To support the critical analysis, this research paper will provide case studies and examples of successful and unsuccessful implementation of "international environmental law" for "sustainable development". For instance, Fuentes[v] provides a case study of the role of "international environmental law" in promoting sustainable fisheries management in the Pacific Islands, highlighting the challenges of balancing environmental protection with economic development. Another example is the "European Union's Circular Economy Action Plan", which aims to promote sustainable consumption and production patterns by improving resource efficiency and reducing waste.[vi]

The challenges and opportunities section will identify and discuss the limitations and criticisms of "international environmental law" in promoting "sustainable development", including the limited political will, weak implementation, and lack of accountability and transparency. This section will also explore potential opportunities for improving the effectiveness of "international environmental law" in promoting "sustainable development", such as strengthening international institutions, enhancing public participation and awareness, and promoting the integration of environmental and social considerations into economic decision-making.

To support this analysis, this research paper will draw upon recent scholarly works and reports, such as the "United Nations

Development Programme's" (UNDP) 2021 Human Development Report, which emphasizes the need for transformative change to achieve "sustainable development" and calls for stronger environmental governance and regulatory frameworks. The section will also analyze case studies and examples of innovative approaches to implementing "international environmental law", such as the use of market-based instruments, public-private partnerships, and community-based conservation.[vii]

This research paper will argue that "international environmental law" has made significant contributions to addressing global environmental challenges and promoting "sustainable development". However, the effectiveness of "international environmental law" in achieving "sustainable development" goals remains limited by various challenges, including weak implementation, limited political will, and insufficient accountability and transparency.

II. Overview of "International Environmental Law" in Promoting "Sustainable Development"

"International environmental law" plays a critical role in promoting "sustainable development" by establishing legal frameworks, principles, and norms that guide human activities and interactions with the natural environment. This section provides an overview of "international environmental law", including its historical development, key principles and norms, and its role in promoting "sustainable development".

"International environmental law" has evolved significantly over the past few decades, reflecting growing concerns over global environmental challenges such as climate change, biodiversity loss, and pollution. The earliest forms of "international environmental law" emerged in the 19th century, with the adoption of several treaties and conventions addressing specific environmental issues such as marine pollution and protection of migratory species.[viii] However, it was not until the 1970s that "international environmental law" began to emerge as a distinct field of law, marked by the adoption of several landmark international environmental agreements such as the "Stockholm Declaration and the Convention on International Trade in Endangered Species of Wild Fauna and Flora" (CITES).[ix]

Since then, "international environmental law" has continued to evolve and expand, with the adoption of several major international environmental treaties and agreements such as the "United Nations Framework Convention on Climate Change" (UNFCCC), the "Convention on Biological Diversity" (CBD), and the "Paris Agreement".[x] These agreements have established legal frameworks and principles that guide national and international efforts to address global environmental challenges and promote "sustainable development".

III. Key Principles and Norms

Several fundamental ideas and standards that shape the creation and application of global environmental treaties and state environmental legislation constitute the basis of "international environmental law." These include the "sustainable development" principle, the "common but differentiated responsibilities" principle, the polluter pays principle, the precautionary principle, and the notion of "polluter pays."

According to the precautionary principle, it is inappropriate to put off taking cost-effective actions to stop environmental deterioration when there are risks of significant or irreparable damage to the environment.[xi] This idea emphasises the need of taking proactive and preventative steps to save the environment and stop irreparable damage. According to the polluter pays concept, people responsible for causing pollution or environmental harm should pay for the costs associated with repairing the damage.[xii] The need of internalising the costs of environmental harm is emphasised by this theory, which also calls for motivating polluters to switch to more environmentally friendly methods of production.

According to the concept of common but differentiated duties, wealthier nations, who historically have made the largest contributions to environmental problems worldwide, are more responsible than emerging nations for addressing these problems.[xiii] In order to address major environmental problems and advance "sustainable development," this idea emphasises the need for equality and fairness.

The "sustainable development" principle states that economic growth should be pursued in a way that meets present needs without jeopardising the ability of future generations to satisfy their own desires.[xiv] In making decisions and formulating policies, this idea emphasises the necessity of striking a balance between economic, social, and environmental factors.

IV. Role in Promoting "Sustainable Development"

By developing legal frameworks and standards that direct national and international efforts to solve global environmental concerns, "international environmental law" plays a crucial role in advancing "sustainable development." International environmental accords set similar aims and objectives, enable the sharing of knowledge and best practices, and give countries a platform for collaboration and coordination.

By establishing systems for tracking and reporting environmental performance, facilitating public involvement and awareness, and fostering the inclusion of environmental and social factors into economic decision-making, "international environmental law" also plays a significant role in promoting environmental governance and accountability.[xv]

Despite its potential contributions to promoting "sustainable development", the effectiveness of "international environmental law" remains limited by several challenges. These challenges include limited political will and financial resources, weak enforcement mechanisms, and the lack of universal participation in international environmental agreements.[xvi] Addressing these challenges requires sustained efforts to strengthen the legal frameworks, improve institutional capacities, and enhance public awareness and participation.

V. Analysis of "International Environmental Law's" Effectiveness in Promoting "Sustainable Development":

Despite the critical role of "international environmental law" in promoting "sustainable development", its effectiveness remains limited by several challenges. This section analyses "international environmental law's" effectiveness in promoting "sustainable development" by examining the challenges and opportunities for enhancing its effectiveness.

One of the main challenges facing "international environmental law's" effectiveness is the lack of universal participation in international environmental agreements. While several international environmental agreements have been adopted, not all countries have ratified or implemented them. For example, the United States, one of the world's largest emitters of greenhouse gases, withdrew from the Paris Agreement in 2020.[xvii] This lack of universal participation limits "international environmental law's" effectiveness in addressing global environmental challenges, particularly climate change.

Another challenge is the weak enforcement mechanisms of international environmental agreements. While many international environmental agreements have provisions for enforcement, they often lack the necessary teeth to ensure compliance.[xviii] This is because states are reluctant to subject themselves to international legal proceedings, particularly if doing so would harm their economic interests. As a result, non-compliance with international environmental agreements is common, limiting their effectiveness in promoting "sustainable development".

Another key obstacle is the lack of funding for putting international environmental accords into action. Many poor nations lack the financial means necessary to put environmental regulations into place and abide by international environmental treaties.[xix] Due to this, just a few nations are now responsible for environmental protection, which limits the ability of "international environmental law" to advance "sustainable development."

Additionally, the effectiveness of "international environmental law" is limited by the lack of political will to implement environmental policies and comply with international environmental agreements. This is particularly true in countries where economic growth is the primary focus, and environmental protection is seen as a hindrance to development. In such cases, environmental policies are often seen as a luxury rather than a necessity, limiting their effectiveness in promoting "sustainable development".

Despite these challenges, there are opportunities for enhancing the effectiveness of "international environmental law" in promoting "sustainable development". One such opportunity is through the use of innovative financing mechanisms. "For example, the Green Climate Fund, established under the United Nations Framework Convention on Climate Change, provides financial resources to developing countries for climate change mitigation and adaptation projects."[xx] Similarly, the Global Environment Facility provides financial resources for projects that address global environmental challenges, such as biodiversity loss and land degradation.[xxi] Such financing mechanisms can enhance the effectiveness of "international environmental law" by providing the necessary financial resources for implementing environmental policies and complying with international environmental agreements.

Another opportunity is through enhancing public participation in environmental decision-making processes. Public participation can increase awareness and accountability, leading to better environmental policies and more effective implementation of international environmental agreements.[xxii] For example, the Aarhus Convention, adopted in 1998, provides for public participation in environmental decision-making processes.[xxiii] Such provisions can enhance the effectiveness of "international environmental law" by ensuring that environmental policies reflect the needs and priorities of the public.

VI. Case Studies and Examples

Case studies and examples of successful and unsuccessful implementation of "international environmental law" for "sustainable development" are essential in evaluating the effectiveness of "international environmental law". The following examples highlight the challenges and successes of "international environmental law" in promoting "sustainable development".

The "Montreal Protocol," a global agreement to gradually phase out the manufacturing and use of ozone-depleting chemicals, is one successful example. It was signed in 1987. The ozone layer hole that presented a serious threat to both the environment and human health prompted the creation of the pact. Strong enforcement measures and financial support provided to poor nations to make the transition to ozone-friendly technology are credited with the treaty's effectiveness.[xxiv] The achievement of the "Montreal Protocol" in phasing out ozone-depleting compounds is a great illustration of how "international environmental law" may help advance "sustainable development."

A global agreement to limit greenhouse gas emissions known as the "Kyoto Protocol" was signed in 1997, however it has had less success than expected. Only a few nations met their emission reduction objectives under the "Kyoto Protocol," which had a goal of bringing global greenhouse gas emissions down to 1990 levels by 2012.[xxv] Weak enforcement measures, a lack of financial support for poor nations, and the United States' refusal to ratify the "Kyoto Protocol" are all reasons why it has failed to be successful. The failure of the Kyoto Protocol serves as a reminder of the need of robust enforcement procedures and broad adoption of environmental treaties in order to advance "sustainable development".

Another example of successful implementation of "international environmental law" is the "United Nations Framework Convention on Climate Change", an international treaty signed in 1992 to combat climate change. The UNFCCC's success is attributed to its annual Conference of Parties (COP) meetings, which provide a platform for countries to negotiate and agree on global climate action.[xxvi] A further illustration of "international environmental law" being successfully implemented is the "Paris Agreement," a binding pact reached in 2015 under the UNFCCC. By lowering greenhouse gas emissions, the Paris Agreement seeks to keep global warming to below 2°C over pre-industrial levels.[xxvii] Success of the "Paris Agreement" is credited to its robust enforcement measures, novel finance methods like the "Green Climate Fund," and broad participation of nations.[xxviii]

On the other hand, the implementation of "international environmental law" has faced challenges in developing countries due to limited financial resources and capacity to implement environmental policies. For instance, the implementation of the "Convention on Biological Diversity" (CBD), an international treaty signed in 1992 to conserve biodiversity, has faced challenges in developing countries due to inadequate financial resources and limited public awareness of environmental issues.[xxix] To support "sustainable development," "international environmental law" implementation in underdeveloped nations needs creative finance methods and public involvement in environmental decision-making processes.

These examples suggest that the success of "international environmental law" in promoting "sustainable development" depends on various factors, including strong enforcement mechanisms, adequate financial resources, and universal participation of countries. The success of the "Montreal Protocol and the Paris Agreement" is attributed to their strong enforcement mechanisms and innovative financing mechanisms, which enabled universal participation of countries. In contrast, the lack of success of the Kyoto Protocol and the implementation of the CBD is attributed to their weak enforcement mechanisms and limited financial resources to support their implementation.

Moreover, these examples highlight the importance of public participation in environmental decision-making processes to promote "sustainable development". Public participation ensures that environmental policies reflect the needs and aspirations of local communities, which enhances their ownership and support for environmental initiatives. Developing countries face significant challenges in implementing "international environmental law" due to limited financial resources and capacity. Innovative financing mechanisms, such as the Green Climate Fund, provide developing countries with financial resources to support the implementation of environmental policies.

VII. Criticisms and Limitations of "International Environmental Law" in Promoting "Sustainable Development"

"International environmental law" is a critical tool for promoting "sustainable development". However, it is not without criticisms and limitations. This section will critically analyse the criticisms and limitations of "international environmental law" in promoting "sustainable development".

The lack of effective enforcement measures is one of the key complaints against "international environmental law." States are tasked with carrying out environmental policies and enforcing environmental laws under "international environmental law." States, however, could have various priorities and might not put environmental preservation first, particularly if it goes against their economic interests. The limited effectiveness of several international environmental agreements, such as the "Kyoto Protocol," which had poor enforcement measures and low levels of compliance by some nations, is evidence of this inadequate enforcement mechanism. [xxx]

Another limitation of "international environmental law" is its lack of universal participation. Some countries, especially developing countries, may not have the capacity to implement environmental policies due to limited financial resources and technical expertise. The lack of universal participation undermines the effectiveness of "international environmental law" in promoting "sustainable development". For example, the "Convention on Biological Diversity" has limited participation from some countries, leading to challenges in implementing biodiversity conservation policies. [xxxi]

The interests of industrialised nations may also take precedence over those of underdeveloped ones under "international environmental law." Uneven gains and costs are distributed as a result of some international environmental accords, such as the Montreal Protocol, which give industrialised nations' interests top priority by allocating financial resources to assist the implementation of environmental laws. [xxxii] The usefulness of "international environmental law" in encouraging "sustainable development" is weakened by this unequal distribution of benefits and costs, particularly in poor nations.

Additionally, "international environmental law" may prioritize environmental protection over economic development, leading to conflicts between environmental protection and economic development. This conflict is evident in some developing countries where economic development is a priority over environmental protection. The conflict between environmental protection and economic development undermines the effectiveness of "international environmental law" in promoting "sustainable development".

In addition to the criticisms and limitations discussed above, there are other issues with "international environmental law" that impact its effectiveness in promoting "sustainable development". One of these issues is the lack of integration between different legal regimes, such as trade and environmental law. Trade agreements can sometimes undermine environmental protection measures and hinder the implementation of "international environmental law". For instance, the "World Trade Organization" (WTO) has been criticized for its role in limiting the ability of states to implement environmental policies, as trade agreements often prioritize economic growth over environmental protection.[xxxiii]

Another issue with "international environmental law" is the lack of coordination among different actors involved in environmental decision-making. This includes governments, non-governmental organizations, and the private sector. Environmental issues are complex and require the involvement of multiple actors to address them effectively. However, the lack of coordination among these actors can result in conflicting interests and priorities, hindering the effectiveness of "international environmental law" in promoting "sustainable development".[xxxiv]

Another restriction on "international environmental law" is the general lack of public knowledge and involvement in environmental decision-making. The whole world's population is impacted by environmental challenges, hence it is critical that people are informed about these issues and actively participate in decision-making. However, in certain nations, public understanding of environmental concerns is poor and involvement in environmental decision-making is sometimes restricted, which undermines the efficacy of "international environmental law."[xxxv]

Lastly, the lack of adequate funding and financial resources for environmental protection is another significant limitation of "international environmental law". Developing countries often lack the financial resources needed to implement environmental policies, and developed countries may not always provide adequate financial support. This lack of funding undermines the effectiveness of "international environmental law" in promoting "sustainable development".[xxxvi]

VIII. Opportunities and Potential For Improvement

Despite the criticisms and limitations of "international environmental law" discussed in the previous section, there are also opportunities and potential for improvement that could enhance its effectiveness in promoting "sustainable development". This section will highlight some of these opportunities and potential improvements.

Increasing non-state actors' engagement and involvement in environmental decision-making processes, such as the corporate sector and civil society groups, is one area where things may be done better. Non-state actors can provide valuable input and perspectives that may not be considered by governments, and they can also help to implement environmental policies and initiatives more effectively. For example, some companies have voluntarily committed to reducing their carbon footprint and have implemented sustainability initiatives, demonstrating that private sector involvement can contribute to "sustainable development".[xxxvii]

Another opportunity for improvement is to strengthen the integration between different legal regimes, such as trade and environmental law, to ensure that trade agreements do not undermine environmental protection measures. The integration of environmental considerations into trade agreements can help to ensure that economic growth and environmental protection are not mutually exclusive. For example, the inclusion of environmental clauses in trade agreements can provide incentives for companies to adopt sustainable practices.[xxxviii]

Furthermore, the development of international environmental courts or tribunals could be a potential improvement to "international environmental law". Such courts could provide an impartial and independent forum for the resolution of disputes relating to environmental issues, ensuring that environmental laws are upheld and enforced.[xxxix]

Additionally, the application of innovation and technology may increase the efficiency with which "international environmental law" advances "sustainable development". Utilizing green technology and renewable energy sources, for instance, may assist to lessen greenhouse gas emissions and slow down climate change. Digital technology may also be used to monitor environmental deterioration and guide decision-making. Examples include remote sensing and data analytics.[xl]

Finally, there is a need to increase funding and financial resources for environmental protection, particularly in developing countries. International organizations and developed countries can play a significant role in providing financial assistance and technical support to developing countries to help them implement environmental policies and initiatives.[xli]

IX. Conclusion and Recommendations

"International environmental law" plays a critical role in promoting "sustainable development". This research paper has analyzed the effectiveness of "international environmental law" in promoting "sustainable development", including its strengths, weaknesses, opportunities, and limitations. The paper also highlighted some successful and unsuccessful case studies of implementing "international environmental law". Based on this analysis, some conclusions can be drawn, and recommendations can be made.

Conclusion

"International environmental law" has been successful in raising awareness about the need for "sustainable development" and promoting environmentally responsible behaviour. The adoption of international environmental treaties and conventions, such as the "Paris Agreement and the Convention on Biological Diversity", demonstrates a global commitment to protecting the environment and promoting "sustainable development". The precautionary principle, the polluter pays principle, and the notion of intergenerational equity are other essential ideas that "international environmental law" has contributed to and affected in national and regional environmental policy.

However, a number of reasons hinder "international environmental law's" ability to encourage "sustainable development." The absence of effective implementation and enforcement methods is one of the major problems. The main problem is in putting international treaties and conventions into practise at the national and regional levels; adopting them is merely the first step. Furthermore, "international environmental law" frequently encounters political and financial limitations, which may reduce its efficacy.

Another limitation is the lack of coordination and coherence between various international environmental agreements. The proliferation of treaties and conventions has resulted in overlapping and conflicting obligations, which may lead to confusion and hinder effective implementation. Moreover, the participation of developing countries in international environmental negotiations is often limited, which may result in a lack of representation and limited commitment to the goals of "sustainable development".

Recommendations

To enhance the effectiveness of "international environmental law" in promoting "sustainable development", several recommendations can be made.

- First, there is a need for stronger enforcement mechanisms at the national and regional levels. States should ensure that their national environmental laws are consistent with international obligations and provide effective enforcement mechanisms to ensure compliance.
- Second, there is a need for greater coherence and coordination between various international environmental agreements. This can be achieved by streamlining and consolidating existing treaties and conventions and adopting a more comprehensive and integrated approach to "international environmental law".
- Third, the participation of developing countries in international environmental negotiations should be increased to ensure their representation and commitment to "sustainable development" goals. Developed countries should provide financial and technical assistance to developing countries to enable them to meet their environmental obligations.
- Fourth, the private sector should play a more significant role in promoting "sustainable development". Businesses should adopt environmentally responsible practices and be held accountable for their environmental impact. This can be achieved through the

adoption of international standards and guidelines and the use of market-based incentives such as carbon pricing.

- Fifth, there is a need for greater public awareness and education on the importance of "sustainable development" and the role of "international environmental law". Governments, civil society organizations, and the private sector should work together to promote environmental education and awareness, including through the media and social networks.

- Finally, there is a need for ongoing research and evaluation to assess the effectiveness of "international environmental law" in promoting "sustainable development". Research should focus on identifying best practices, assessing the impact of various policies and measures, and developing new approaches to address emerging environmental challenges.

In order to advance "sustainable development," "international environmental law" is essential. Despite the "international environmental law's" low efficacy, there remain possibilities and room for development. It is feasible to promote "sustainable development" for current and future generations by putting the suggestions made in this article into practise. This would increase the efficacy of "international environmental law."

References :
i. IPCC. (2021). Climate change 2021: The physical science basis. Cambridge University Press.
ii. Biermann, F., Pattberg, P., van Asselt, H., & Zelli, F. (2020). The fragmentation of global governance architectures: A framework for analysis. Global Environmental Politics, 20(4), 1-23.
iii. Tams, C. J., Tzanakopoulos, A., & Zimmermann, A. (2018). Research handbook on international environmental law. Edward Elgar Publishing.
iv. Vihma, A. (2019). Implementing international environmental law: A critical review of challenges and opportunities. Journal of Environmental Law, 31(1), 1-27.
v. Fuentes, M. (2021). International environmental law and sustainable fisheries management: A case study of the Pacific Islands. Journal of Environmental Law, 33(1), 27-52.

vi. European Commission. (2020). A new circular economy action plan for a cleaner and more competitive Europe. Retrieved from https://ec.europa.eu/commission/presscorner/detail/en/ip_20_420

vii. United Nations Development Programme. (2021). Human development report 2020. Retrieved from http://hdr.undp.org/sites/default/files/hdr2020.pdf

viii. Bodansky, D. (2016). The history of international environmental law. In The Oxford handbook of international environmental law (pp. 1-25). Oxford University Press.

ix. Ibid

x. Ibid

xi. UNEP. (1992). Rio declaration on environment and development. Retrieved from https://www.un.org/en/development/desa/population/migration/generalassembly/docs/globalcompact/A_CONF.151_26_Vol.I_Declaration.pdf

xii. OECD. (1972). Recommendation of the Council on Guiding Principles Concerning International Economic Aspects of Environmental Policies. Retrieved from https://legalinstruments.oecd.org/en/instruments/OECD-LEGAL-0113

xiii. UNFCCC. (1992). United Nations Framework Convention on Climate Change. Retrieved from https://unfccc.int/resource/docs/convkp/conveng.pdf

xiv. WCED. (1987). Our common future. Oxford University Press.

xv. Tams, C., Tzanakopoulos, A., & Zimmermann, A. (2018). Research handbook on international environmental law. Edward Elgar Publishing.

xvi. Bodansky, D. (2016). The history of international environmental law. In The Oxford handbook of international environmental law (pp. 1-25). Oxford University Press.

xvii. Watts, J. (2020). US formally withdraws from Paris climate agreement. The Guardian. Retrieved from https://www.theguardian.com/environment/2020/nov/04/us-formally-withdraws-paris-climate-agreement

xviii. Bodansky, D. (2016). The Paris climate change agreement: A new hope?. American Journal of International Law, 110(2), 288-319.

xix. OECD. (2012). Financing climate change action: OECD report to ministers 2012. Retrieved from https://www.oecd.org/env/cc/financing-climate-change-action-2012.pdf

xx. UNFCCC. (2019). About the Green Climate Fund. Retrieved from https://www.greenclimate.fund/about

xxi. GEF. (n.d.). About GEF. Retrieved from https://www.thegef.org/about-gef

xxii. Bodansky, D. (2016). The Paris climate change agreement: A new hope?. American Journal of International Law, 110(2), 288-319.

xxiii. UNECE. (1998). Convention on access to information, public participation in decision-making and access to justice in environmental matters. Retrieved from https://www.unece.org/fileadmin/DAM/env/pp/documents/cep43e.pdf

xxiv. United Nations Environment Programme. (2021). The Montreal Protocol. Retrieved from https://www.unep.org/ozonaction/what-we-do/montreal-protocol

xxv. Bodansky, D. (2016). The Paris climate change agreement: A new hope?. American Journal of International Law, 110(2), 288-319.

xxvi. Bodansky, D. (2016). The Paris climate change agreement: A new hope?. American Journal of International Law, 110(2), 288-319.

xxvii. United Nations Framework Convention on Climate Change. (2021). The Paris Agreement. Retrieved from https://unfccc.int/process-and-meetings/the-paris-agreement/the-paris-agreement

xxviii. GEF. (n.d.). About GEF. Retrieved from https://www.thegef.org/about-

xxix. UNEP. (2021). Convention on Biological Diversity. Retrieved from https://www.unep.org/explore-topics/biodiversity/about/biodiversity-convention

xxx. Watts, J. (2020). What was the Kyoto Protocol and has it made any difference?. The Guardian. Retrieved from https://www.theguardian.com/environment/2020/dec/03/what-was-the-kyoto-protocol-and-has-it-made-any-difference

xxxi. UNEP. (2021). Convention on Biological Diversity. Retrieved from https://www.unep.org/explore-topics/biodiversity/about/biodiversity-convention

xxxii. Ibid

xxxiii. Bodansky, D. (2019). The Paris Agreement and the WTO. Journal of International Economic Law, 22(3), 441-462.

xxxiv. Faure, M. G., & Zhang, T. (2019). International Environmental Law and Policy: Actors, Interests, and Institutions. Edward Elgar Publishing.

xxxv. Janda, K. B., & Fulda, T. R. (2017). Environmental law and policy. CRC Press

xxxvi. Kidd, S. E. (2018). Financing the global environment: international financial flows for environment, sustainability and development. Routledge.

xxxvii. Sinha, D., Prakash, A., & Nagpal, T. (2019). Voluntary sustainability reporting by Indian companies. Journal of Cleaner Production, 220, 1007-1017.

xxxviii. Van den Bossche, P. (2020). The interaction between trade and environmental law. In Research Handbook on Trade and Environment (pp. 33-49). Edward Elgar Publishing.

xxxix. Voigt, C. (2019). Environmental courts and tribunals: a guide for policy makers. United Nations Development Programme.

xl. Bawa, R., & Gupta, K. (2018). Digital technologies for environmental monitoring and protection: a review. Environmental Science and Pollution Research, 25(10), 9055-9071.

xli. Kidd, S. E. (2018). Financing the global environment: international financial flows for environment, sustainability and development. Routledge.

Assistant Professor of Law,
School of Law,
Presidency University Bangalore,
Karnataka

4. Effect of Pestisides on Honey Bee and their Colony

Mohinish Mehra* and Mamta Sharma**

Abstract

As we know that honey bee are a type of famous fly that collect honey by sucking the juice of flower i.e in hindi we khown as mumakhi.To this fact, about 50% of the leading global food commodities depend on pollination by honey bees for either fruit formation or seed[1]. We focused on pestisides applied on crops and the unintentional exposure of honey bees. The intentional introduction of pestisides into beehive to supress these pest. Both the intentional and unintentional exposure of honey bee to pestisides have resulted in residues in hive products (bee wax). Most of the time, the exposure of bees to pesticides is through ingestion of residues found in the pollen and nectar of plants and in water. Honey bees are also exposed to pesticides used for the treatment of Varroa and other parasites. Various degrees of toxicity are found among agrochemicals is given to the classic tenet of toxicology, "the dose makes the poison," and its modern version "the dose and the time of exposure makes the poison." These two factors, dose and time, help us understand the severity of the impacts that pesticides may have on bees and their risk. Globally honey bee losses and colony decline are becoming continuous thread to tha apiculture industries, as well as, for food security and environmental stability. in recent years, honey bee populations have been in a worldwide decline, which has been referred to as colony collapse disorder (CCD) and colony weakening. Multiple causes of colony losses have been proposed, such as exposure to pesticides, pathogens, parasites, and natural habitat degradation. Among these factors, pesticides are suspected by the scientific and beekeeping communities to have a strong impact on honey bee mortality and colony weakening. The study clearly indicates that selected pesticides used for the purpose of plant protection and plant cultivation may adversely on bees' behavior and accumulation of trace elements in their body. The extensive exposure of bees to pestisides could be possible factor for worldwide colony losses .Accordingly, nine commonly used pestisides including. And we discussed about the insectisides used in agriculture like fipronil, DDT, endosulfan, diazinon,fenthion etc. We investigating the presence of organochlorine pesticides in honey and pollen samples from managed colonies of the honey bee, Apis mellifera,Apis indica.

Keywords : Pestisides, Fertility, Honey Beehive Products, Toxicology, Dose, Fipronil, endosulfan, DDT, colony collaps disorder (CCD), bee behavior.

1. Introduction

honeybee, (tribe Apini)[2], also spelled honey bee, any of a group of insects in the family Apidae (order Hymenoptera) that in a broad sense includes all bees that make honey. Honeybees are important pollinators for flowers, fruits, and vegetables. They live on stored honey and pollen all winter and cluster into a ball to conserve warmth. All honeybees are social insects and live together in nests or hives. The honeybee is remarkable for the dancing movements it performs in the hive to communicate information to its fellow bees about the location, distance, size, and quality of a particular food source in the surrounding area. Intense development of agriculture and animal production has caused exposure to substances with which bees have never before come into contact. The increasing demand for food has forced farmers to use more mineral fertilizers and pesticides to generate higher yields. While working on flowers, bees are exposed to direct and indirect contact with pesticides which, depending on the mode of action and the concentration of active substance, can lead to sudden death of pollinating insects or cause death within a couple of hours following exposure. It becomes dangerous when the level of pesticides or their residues in a beehive becomes high enough to adversely affect the functioning and development of larvae. Bees are highly susceptible to environmental changes and pollution, which is strongly reflected in the significant decrease of their survival rate . Honey bees ensure the pollination of many wild flowers, and thus contributing to plant biodiversity. The economic value of honey bees results not only from the hive products (honey, royal jelly, wax) but also from their pollinating activity on crop plants (Williams, 1994). Honey bees (A. mellifera) serve as a bioindicator of contamination with trace elements of toxic properties (copper, zinc, iron, tin cadmium, lead, arsenic, and aluminum)[3] . Bees constantly penetrate the environment seeking new produce and the raw materials necessary to provide for the functioning of their colony.

However, a large scale dramatic losses and decline of pollinators including honeybees have been reported in several regions of the world resulting severe threat to the apiculture industry and global food security [4-7]. For example, beekeepers in the United States lost an estimated 50.8% of their managed honey bee colonies only in 2021, which was the highest annual loss on record [8]. Although the putative causes of colony loss are still unclear, the combined effects of climate change, intensive agriculture, pesticides use, pest and pathogens, and biodiversity loss are some risk factors for global honeybee loss [9]. Ethiopia, widespread reports indicate that exposure to commonly used agricultural pesticides has been linked to the dramatic honeybee deaths and colony decline than any other factors in the country [10-13]. Such losses of honeybees have in turn resulted in reduction of honey production as well as crop production, through disrupting pollination services [14].

2.Materials and Methods

2.1 Honey

The Codex Alimentarius defines honey as the natural sweet substance produced by honey bees from the nectar of plants or from secretions of living parts of plants or excretions of plant sucking insects on the living parts of plants, which the bees collect, transform by combining with specific substances of their own, deposit, dehydrate, store and leave in the honey comb to ripen and mature.

Honey is composed of a mixture of sugars, mainly fructose (~38.5%) and glucose (~31.0%).

2.2 Methods for Analysis of Pestisides in Honey

Several methods have been used for the analysis of pesticides in honey.A liquid chromatography-tandem mass spectrometry (UHPLC-MS/MS) analytical method using a modified QuEChERS sample preparation for the analysis of insecticide residues in honey was developed and validated. The QuEChERS sample preparation approach has been the most used method for the simultaneous extraction and extract cleanup for the analysis of insecticide residues in honey [15], and the Plackett Burman design is an alternative for optimization of the sample preparation step with a small number of experiments to assess the effects of the chosen variables under study and establish their levels of influence [16] Methods for quantification of pesticide residues in honey report the use of gas chromatography with detectors such as electron capture (GC-ECD)[17], nitrogen-phosphorus (GC-NPD) [18] and mass spectrometry (GC-MS) [19]Also, liquid chromatography (LC) with ultraviolet detection (LC-UV)[20] has been reported. In particular, LC coupled with tandem mass spectrometry (LC-MS/MS) has been used in multiresidue methods and shows promising performance in the quantitative analysis of several classes of pesticides with different physicochemical characteristics in matrices such as honey [21].

2.3 Reagents and Analytical Standards

All analytical insecticide standards (imidacloprid, clothianidin, chlorpyrifos, permethrin, dimethoate, cypermethrin and the internal standard (IS) imidacloprid d-4) were obtained from Sigma-Aldrich and had purities greater than 99%. Acetonitrile and methanol of HPLC grade. Acetone, ammonium formate, formic acid, anhydrous magnesium sulfate and sodium chloride provided by Sigma–Aldrich were of analytical grade. Primary and secondary amine (PSA), silica-bonded C18 and graphitized carbon black (GCB) sorbents were supplied by Supelco. PVDF (polyvinylidene fluoride) syringe filters (0.22 µm). Ultrapure deionized water

2.4 Standard Solutions

Individual stock standard solutions of all analytes were prepared in acetonitrile at a concentration of, except for clothianidin stock solution, which was prepared in acetone. From the stock solutions, intermediate solutions were prepared in acetonitrile.

2.5 Instrumentation and Chromatographic Conditions

GC is a separation science technique that is used to separate the chemical components of a sample mixture and then detect them to determine their presence or absence and/or how much is present. GC detectors are limited in the information that they give; this is usually two-dimensional giving the retention time on the analytical column and the detector response. Identification is based on comparison of the retention time of the peaks in a sample to those from standards of known compounds, analyzed using the same method. However, GC alone cannot be used for the identification of unknowns, which is where hyphenation to an MS works very well. MS can be used as a sole detector, or the column effluent can be split between the MS and GC detector(s)[22].

MS is an analytical technique that measures the mass-to-charge ratio (m/z) of charged particles and therefore can be used to determine the molecular weight and elemental composition, as well as elucidating the chemical structures of molecules. Data from a GC-MS is three-dimensional, providing mass spectra that can be used for identity confirmation or to identify unknown compounds plus the chromatogram that can be used for qualitative and quantitative analysis.

The sample mixture is first separated by the GC before the analyte molecules are eluted into the MS for detection. They are transported by the carrier gas (Figure 1 (1)), which continuously flows through the GC and into the MS, where it is evacuated by the vacuum system(6).

1. The sample is first introduced into the GC manually or by an autosampler (Figure 1 (2)) and enters the carrier gas via the GC inlet (Figure 1 (3)). If the sample is in the liquid form, it is vaporized in the heated GC inlet and the sample vapor is transferred to the analytical column.

2. The sample components, the "analytes", are separated by their differences in partitioning between the mobile phase (carrier gas) and the liquid stationary phase (held within the column), or for more volatile gases their adsorption by a solid stationary phase. In GC-MS analyses, a liquid stationary phase held within a narrow (0.1-0.25 mm internal diameter) and short (10-30 m length) column is most common.

3. After separation, which for GC-MS analyses doesn't require total baseline resolution unless the analytes are isomers, the neutral molecules elute through a heated transfer line (Figure 1 (5)) into the mass spectrometer.[24]

4. Within the mass spectrometer, the neutral molecules are first ionized, most commonly by electron ionization (EI). In EI, an electron, produced by a filament, is accelerated with 70 electron volts (eV) and knocks an electron out of the molecule to produce a molecular ion that is a radical cation. This high energy ionization can result in an unstable molecular ion and excess energy can be lost through fragmentation. Bond breakage(s) can lead to the loss of a radical or neutral molecule and molecular rearrangements can also occur. This all results in a, sometimes very large, number of ions of different masses, the heaviest being the molecular ion with fragment ions of various lower masses, depending on:

- the molecular formula
- the molecular structure of the analyte
- where bond breakage has occurred
- which part has retained the charge

5. The next step is to separate the ions of different masses, which is achieved based on their m/z by the mass analyzer (Figure 1 (8)).

There are numerous different mass analyzer types, and this is where the vast differences in mass resolution (and hence instrument price) is seen. Mass resolution is the ability of the mass analyzer to separate ions with very small differences in m/z. Unit mass resolution instruments can only separate nominal masses or those down to a single decimal place, whereas high mass resolution (HRMS) instruments can separate them to four or five decimal places.

The most common type of unit mass instrument is the quadrupole, which is a scanning instrument and varies the voltage to allow only ions of a certain m/z to have a stable trajectory through the four poles to reach the ion detector. Quadrupole instruments are used in two different modes of operation :

- Full scan mode, where all ions are acquired across a mass range, useful for identification of unknowns, method development and qualitative and quantitative analysis for higher concentration analytes.
- Selected ion monitoring (SIM) mode, where only selected ions that represent the target compound are acquired, useful for trace analysis, as higher sensitivity is obtained, but only of target analytes.
- An ion trap is also a scanning instrument but is three-dimensional, trapping the ions in mass-dependent orbits before ejecting them sequentially to reach the ion detector.

Time-of-flight (ToF) mass analyzers separate the ions based on the time they take to travel down the flight tube to reach the ion detector. With the same kinetic energy, those with lower masses have a higher velocity and therefore arrive first, whereas those with higher masses have a lower velocity and arrive later. ToFMS instruments can range in mass resolution and acquisition rate: very fast ToFs[23], with acquisition rates of up to 1000 spectra/second are unit mass resolution, whereas HRMS ToFs have a lower acquisition rate. High acquisition rates are good for two-dimensional GC (GC x GC) applications with peak widths down to 30 ms, however HRMS is very useful to determine the molecular formula. Therefore, there are ToFs on the market that range in speed and mass resolution, the choice of which is dependent on the application, but the GC peak [25]width must match the acquisition rate capabilities of the MS.

Other HRMS instruments that are hyphenated to GC include the magnetic sector mass analyzer, which bends the trajectories of the ions to separate them using electric and magnetic fields. Magnetic sector GC-MS instruments are more commonly found in isotope ratio analyses.

In the HRMS orbitrap, the ions orbit around a central spindle and the frequency that they move up and down the central spindle is m/z-dependent.

6. After the ions have been separated by the mass analyzer based on their m/z, they reach the ion detector (Figure 1 (9)) where the signal is

amplified by an electron multiplier (for most low resolution MS) or a multi-channel plate (for most HRMS instruments). The signal is recorded by the acquisition software on a computer (Figure 1 (10)) to produce a chromatogram and a mass spectrum for each data point.

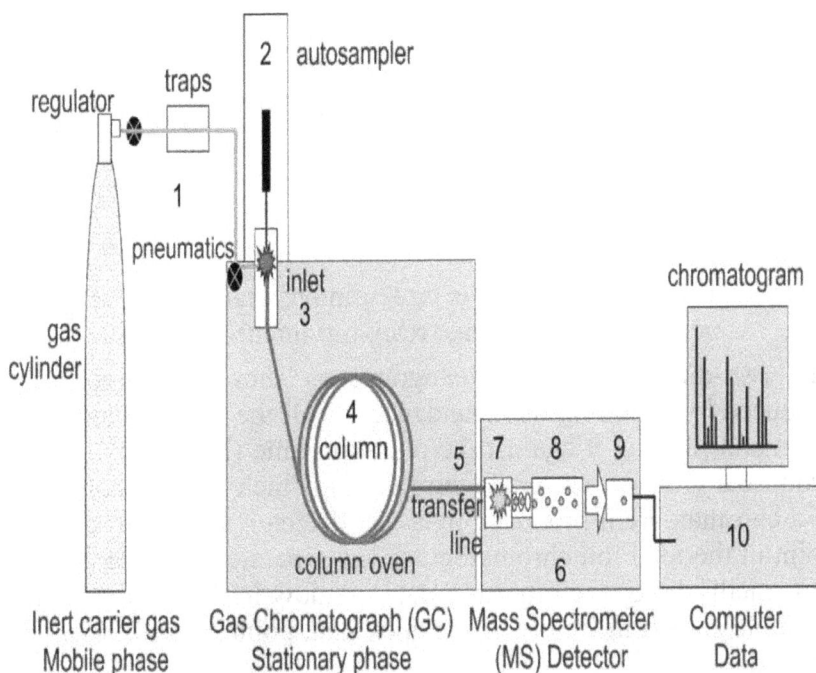

Figure 1: A simplified diagram of a gas chromatograph–mass spectrometer showing (1) carrier gas, (2) autosampler, (3) inlet, (4) analytical column, (5) interface, (6) vacuum, (7) ion source, (8) mass analyzer, (9) ion detector and (10)

GC-MS Analysis and what the Retention Time tells you

GC-MS data is three-dimensional, as shown in Figure 2. The x-axis shows the retention time; the time from sample injection to the end of the GC run. This can also be viewed as the scan number, which is the number of data points that have been acquired by the MS across the run. The y-axis is the response or intensity measured by the ion detector (Figure 1 (9)). The z-axis is the m/z of the ions across the mass range acquired.

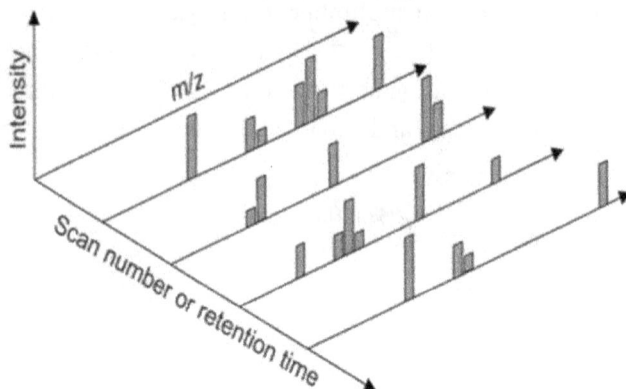

Figure 2: GC-MS data is three-dimensional, giving scan number/retention time, response/intensity and m/z

The two-dimensional chromatogram, as shown in Figure 3, is produced by summing the abundances of all the ions at a single data point and plotting it against the retention time (RT)/scan number to produce a total ion chromatogram (TIC), which is more comparable to a chromatogram produced by a GC detector. However, each data point in the total ion chromatogram is a separate mass spectrum and can usually be opened in a separate window in the software. In the example shown in Figure 3, the apex data point of peak 3 has been opened.

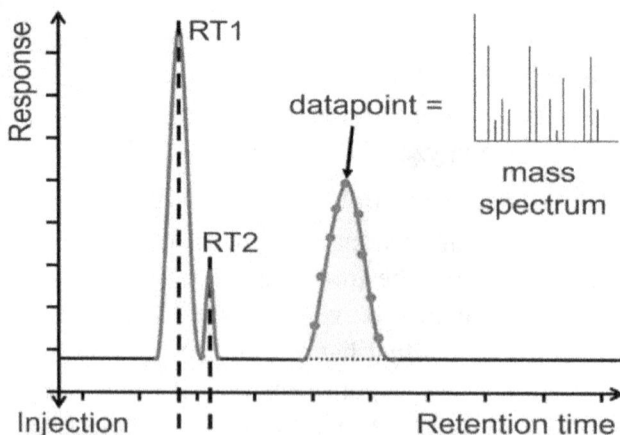

Figure 3: Total ion chromatogram (TIC) output from a GC-MS

Result and Discussion

As we seen fifty-one honey samples were for the presence of the target insecticides using the validated LC-MS/MS method, including samples from European and Latin American countries. Overall, 62.7% of the samples analyzed did not show detectable residues. However, residues of the targeted insecticide were detected in 35.3% of the samples at levels lower than the LOQ. The MRLs established by the EU (European Data Base, Citation2019), as well as the reference limits established by MAPA (Citation2019) were exceeded in 2% of the samples. Regarding the samples from Brazil (n = 39), residues were found in 15 samples (38.5%), all with levels below the LOQ. Among the samples from Europe (n = 10) and other Latin American countries (n = 2), three samples (25%) presented residues below the LOQ, whereas one sample (8.3%) exceeded the MRL.This noncompliant honey sample was from Spain .(Figure 3).

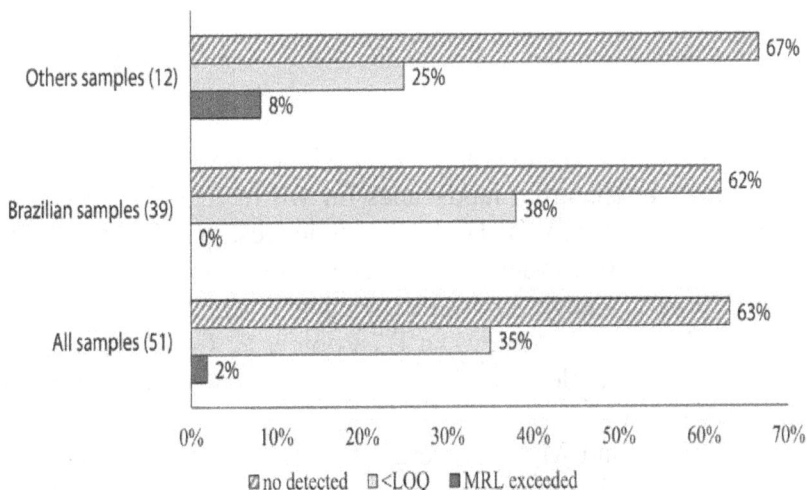

Conclusion

Applying pesticides to control various organisms and diseases that affect human interests in agricultural and urban environments, has effects on honeybees and other pollinators in general. From reading this article, you will understand why **pesticide use is bad for bees and other pollinators**. The article also looks into the various factors that impact the degree of effects of pesticides on bees.

In addition to understanding the problem, read on to know the various methods you can use to alleviate the **harmful effects of pesticides on bees**. You also learn about many available alternatives to pesticides. Using the information in this article, you can thus easily change your practices to provide better environments for honeybees and be able to control pests, diseases and weeds and in this artical LC-MS/MS analytical method developed and validated according to the intended purpose of quantification of insecticide residues in honey. The optimization of the sample preparation step (extraction and cleanup). The analysis of real honey samples from different origins proved the method's robustness and applicability.These indicate there is a recurrent environmental contamination. Thus, it is recommended that regulatory agencies conduct surveillance programs to assess pesticide residues in honey to avoid unnecessary consumer exposure to these toxic compounds.

Refrences
1. A.-M. Klein, B. E. Vaissière, J. H. Cane et al., "Importance of pollinators in changing landscapes for world crops," Proceedings of the Royal Society B: Biological Sciences, vol. 274, no. 1608, pp. 303–313, 2007. View at: Publisher Site | Google Scholar
2. The Editors of Encyclopaedia Britannica: Jun 3, 2023
3. Roman A., Madras-Majewska B., Popiela E. Comparative study of selected toxic elements in propolis and honey. J. Apicult. Sci. 55 (2), 97, 2011.
4. E. E. Zattara and M. A. Aizen, "Worldwide occurrence records suggest a global decline in bee species richness," One Earth, vol. 4, no. 1, pp. 114–123, 2021. View at: Publisher Site | Google Scholar
5. J. A. Chmiel, B. A. Daisley, A. P. Pitek, G. J. Thompson, and G. Reid, "Understanding the effects of sublethal pesticide exposure on honey bees: a role for probiotics as mediators of environmental stress," Frontiers in Ecology and Evolution, vol. 8, p. 22, 2020. View at: Publisher Site | Google Scholar

6. P. Neumann and N. L. Carreck, Honey bee colony losses, Taylor & Francis, Philadelphia, PA, USA, 2010.
7. G. R. Williams, D. R. Tarpy, D. vanEngelsdorp et al., "Colony collapse disorder in context," BioEssays, vol. 32, no. 10, pp. 845-846, 2010. View at: Publisher Site | Google Scholar
8. D. Aurell, S. Bruckner, M. Wilson, N. Steinhauer, and G. Williams, "United States Honey Bee Colony Losses 2021-2022: Preliminary Results," Bee Informed Partnership Embargoed, vol. 23, 2022.View at: Google Scholar
9. E. Tsioumani, "The state of the world's biodiversity for food and agriculture: a call to action?" Environmental Policy and Law, vol. 49, no. 2-3, pp. 110–112, 2019.
10. Z. Fikadu, "Pesticides use, practice and its effect on honeybee in ethiopia," International Journal of Tropical Insect Science, vol. 40, 2019. View at: Google Scholar
11. G. Guesh, "Epidemiology of honey bee disease and pests in selected zones of tigray region, northern ethiopia," Bahir Dar University, Bahir Dar, Ethiopia, 2015, M.Sc. thesis. View at: Google Scholar
12. T. Asaminew and W. Maria, Beekeeping Dynamics and its Driving Forces of Change in Ethiopian Mixed Farming System, Bahir Dar University, Bahir Dar, Ethiopia, 2016
13. F. Sintayehu, "Effects of herbicide application in wheat crops and on honeybee populations in Ethiopia," Feed The Future, vol. 36, 2016. View at: Google Scholar
14. G. W. Alebachew, "Economic value of pollination service of agricultural crops in Ethiopia: biological pollinators," Journal of Apicultural Science, vol. 62, no. 2, pp. 265–273, 2018. View at: Publisher Site | Google Scholar
15. Codling, G., Al Naggar, Y., Giesy, J. P., & Robertson, A. J. (2016). Concentrations of neonicotinoid insecticides in honey, pollen and honey bees (Apis mellifera L) in central Saskatchewan, Canada. Chemosphere, 144, 2321–2328. https://doi.org/10.1016/j.chemosphere.2015.10.135 [Crossref], [PubMed], [Web of Science ®], [Google Scholar]
16. European Data Base. (2019). Maximum limits residue levels. https://ec.europa.eu/food/plant/pesticides/max_residue_le vels_en [Google Scholar]

17. European Food Safety Authority (EFSA). (2020). The 2018 European Union report on pesticide residues in food. *EFSA Journal*, 18(4), 6057, 103. https://doi.org/10.2903/ j.efsa. 2020.6057 [Crossref], [Web of Science ®], [Google Scholar]

18. Farajzadeh, M.   A.,   Mogaddam, M.   R.   A., & Ghorbanpour, H. (2014). Development   of   a   new microextraction   method   based   on   elevated   temperature dispersive liquid-liquid microextraction for determination of triazole pesticides residues in honey by gas chromatography-nitrogen phosphorus detection. *Journal of Chromatography A*, 1347, 816. https://doi.org/10.1016/j.chroma.2014.04.067 [Crossref], [PubMed], [Web of Science ®], [Google Scholar]

19. Bargańska et al., Citation2014

20. Jovanov, P., Guzsvány, V., Lazić, S., Franko, M., Sakač, M., Šari ć, L., & Kos, J. (2015). Development of HPLC-DAD method for determination of neonicotinoids in honey. *Journal of Food Composition and Analysis*, 40, 106 113. https://doi.org/10.1016/ j.jfca.2014.12.021 [Crossref], [Web   of   Science   ®], [Google Scholar]

21. Tette, P. A. S., Oliveira, F. A., Pereira, E. N., Silva, G., Glória, M.   B.,   & Fernandes, C. (2016a). Multiclass   method   for pesticides quantification in honey by means of modified QuEChERS   and   UHPLC-MS/MS. *Food   Chemistry*, 211, 130139.https://doi.org/10.1016/j.foodchem.2016.05.036 [Crossref], [PubMed], [Web of Science ®], [Google Scholar]

22. Turner DC, Schäfer M, Lancaster S, Janmohamed I, Gachanja A, Creasey J. *Gas Chromatography–Mass Spectrometry*. Royal Society of Chemistry; 2020. ISBN-10:1782629289

23. Ferrer   I,   Thurman   EM. *Advanced   Techniques   in   Gas Chromatography-Mass Spectrometry (GC-MS-MS and GC-TOF-MS) for Environmental Chemistry: Volume 61*. Elsevier; 2013;2-502 ISBN:9780444626240

24. Pasternak Z, Avissar YY, Ehila F, Grafit A. Automatic detection and classification of ignitable liquids from GC–MS data of casework samples in forensic fire-debris analysis. *Forensic Chem*. 2022;29:100419. doi:10.1016/j.forc.2022.100419

25. Clarke J, Rockwood AL, Kushnir MM. Mass spectrometry. In: Rifai N, Horvath AR, Wittwer CT, Hoofnagle A ed. *Principles and Applications of Clinical Mass Spectrometry: Small Molecules, Peptides, and Pathogens*. 1st ed.; Elsevier; 2018:33-65. ISBN:<u>9780128160633</u>

*Junior research fellow
Research Lab Environmental Toxicology
email : rrcmohnish@gmail.com
**Associate Professor
Raj Rishi Government (Autonomus) College, Alwar
Rajasthan,India
email : <u>mamta810@gmail.com</u>

5. Impact and Necessity of Environment Taxation in India

Dr. Meghna Meena

Abstract

In today's modern world, the idea of sustainable development is relatively young and continually changing. The governments all over the world appear to have woken up to fight for this cause as public knowledge of the seriously detrimental effects of environmental pollution and the ensuing climate change has increased. Recently, there has been an increased interest in implementing governance rules for sustainable development to slow down environmental degradation and the pollution levels that are constantly growing. These policies measures are being adopted in order to strictly enforce them and to apply them to businesses that release pollutants or make goods that are unfriendly to the environment. Countries all over the world are attempting to implement a Green Revolution in their taxation systems for strict control over such environmental hazards with an object to discourage businesses from being involved in activities that may cause a serious threat to the environment. Efforts are being made by Governments, corporates, civil societies, businesses and even the common people towards net-zero emissions to nullify climate change and global warming. India is in the driver's seat in these efforts and can explore a new dimension of taxing emissions which will augment the government revenues.

Keywords : Environmental Tax, net-zero emission, new dimension

Introduction

Governments are under continuous pressure than ever to develop solutions to lessen environmental damage while minimising impact to economic growth as a result of environmental concerns. The Covid-19 outbreak has also compelled nations around the world to reconsider climate change and the necessity of environmental preservation.

In this context, enforcing or introducing environment taxes on chemicals that affect the environment is a revolutionary proposal with the ultimate goal of significantly reducing pollution.

An environmental tax is also known as Eco Tax is an excise duty on goods that cause environmental pollutants. Charging taxes on emissions that cause pollution will lower environmental impairment in a very cost-effective manner. Therefore, encouraging the behavioural changes in households and firms that need to decrease their pollution.

According to the statistical framework developed jointly in 1997 by Eurostat, the European Commission, the International Energy Agency (IEA) and the Organisation for Economic Cooperation and Development (OECD) environmental taxes are "those whose tax base consists of a physical unit (or similar) of some material that has a negative, verified and specific impact on the environment".

Environment tax is a type of tax levied by the government for the purpose of environmental conservation. In India, many state governments such as Goa and Gujarat have provision for green tax or cess. The Ministry of Road Transport and Highways (MoRTH) had announced a alike tax called Green Tax or Eco Tax on older vehicles.

Efforts are being made by Governments, civil societies, corporates, businesses and also the common people towards net-zero emissions to nullify climate change and global warming. India is as of now in the driver's seat in these efforts and can explore many new dimension of taxing emissions which will augment the revenues for the government.

The success of an environment tax in India would depend on its architecture, i.e., how well it is planned and designed. It should be transparent, credible and predictable. Preferably, environment tax rate ought to be equal to the marginal social cost arising from the negative externalities associated with the production, consumption or disposal of goods and services. This would comprise the adverse impacts on the health of people, climate change, etc. India also need to evaluate the damage to the environment based on scientific assessments.

India currently emphasises the command-and-control approach to reducing pollution. The architecture of an environmental tax in India, or how effectively it is planned and built, would play an important role in its success.

Potential of revenue generation through environment or green taxing in India :

- The top 4,000 or so businesses in India generated a combined total of almost $100 trillion in 2021–2022.
- It makes sense that if a little green tax is levied on the sales of these polluting corporations, it may bring in significant sums of money.
- As an illustration, a typical green tax of 0.5% of revenue would bring in 50,000 crores per year for the government.
- This can be used to fund budget expenditures and will support the government's attempts to issue green bonds for environmentally friendly initiatives.
- The rate of the environment or green tax need not be implemented consistently; it might range from 0.1% to 2%, depending on the industry in question. When the sales of these businesses/industries increase, the government will automatically get more money.

Need of Environmental Taxes

Over the last few decades, population increase has dramatically altered the biosphere. The exploitation of finite natural resources and rising pollution levels have resulted in massive emissions of greenhouse gases (GHG). Moreover, some of the main problems of ecological misuse are climatic changes, the growth of chronic diseases, increasing sea levels, and economic repercussions. The Environment Tax, Green Tax, or Eco Tax enters the picture here. By making them pay, it deters people from causing environmental damage.

Environmental protection is the primary reason for environmental taxes. Environmental taxes are necessary for a number of additional reasons, though. Environmental protection is the primary justification for environmental levies. Environmental levies are required for several additional reasons as well some of them are:-

1. Promote energy saving and the use of renewable sources.
2. Internalize the negative externalities.
3. Motivate companies to innovate in sustainability.
4. Discourage anti-ecological behaviour.
5. Generate revenue for governments, allowing other taxes to be lowered or environmental projects to be carried out.

Aim of Environmental Taxes

By charging polluters, a penalty or punishment for the damage they cause to the environment, environmental taxes primarily serve to ensure that they are properly penalised for their actions that hurt the environment. An effective way to give polluters an incentive to reduce their pollution to the point where further reductions might become more expensive than paying the tax itself is to charge direct taxes to those who emit pollution. Environmental taxes aim to prevent or curtail the use or consumption of harmful goods or practises, the depletion of a resource, or both.

Environment Tax Reforms

The three main activities that would be involved in environmental tax reform are as follows:

1. Implementing brand-new environmental taxes.
2. Reorganizing existing taxes in a way that is good for the environment.
3. Removing existing taxes and subsidies that are harmful to the environment. The following reforms, for instance, may be considered environmental fiscal reforms in the energy sector:
- Reducing the price gap between gasoline and diesel.
- GPS-based congestion charges and differential vehicle taxes in the transportation sector based on fuel efficiency
- Charges on warm based powers and expense refunds for environmentally friendly power makers.
- A tax on businesses with high carbon footprints.

Environment Tax & Benefits

Environmental taxes are designed to reduce or stop the use or consumption of harmful substances or activities, the depletion of a resource, or both.

A) The constituents : The majority of environmental tax amendments comprise three interrelated activities:

I. Eliminating current environmental harming taxes and subsidies.

II. Rearranging current taxes in a way that is environmentally friendly.

III. Implementing fresh environmental taxes.

B). **Rationale :** Insofar as promoting the environment is a public good, funding for this good should come from the general pool of taxes, which includes environmental taxes.

C). Expected Benefits : The introduction of an environmental tax in India will have numerous advantages, including:

The environment : It can rectify the negative externalities of a polluting operation and prompt proper environmental decisions by increasing the relative prices of polluting inputs and outputs.

D) Costs : When other revenue sources prove to be difficult or burdensome, environmental tax reforms can mobilize funds to finance essential public services.

Environment Tax in India

Some examples of "environment tax" in India at a regional level are

- **Clean energy tax** by the Government of India announced in 2010, imposed on coal, peat and lignite
- **Gujarat Government Green Cess** imposed on electricity, presently stayed by the courts.
- In 2004 **Vehicle entry tax** introduced in Himachal Pradesh
- **Tax on old vehicles** introduced by 6 States in India for discouraging old vehicles which impact ecological balance.
- **Cess on non-biodegradable substances**, introduced by Sikkim in 2005
- **Goa Government Green Cess** imposed by Goa in 2013.

Fiscal Instruments to Support Ecological Issues

The most divisive fiscal tools that are frequently debated are carbon taxes, which have the dual objectives of acting as a disincentive and raising funds away from activities that have an adverse effect on sustainable economic development.

Other taxes in this area that have been researched internationally include the following:

- In Ireland, taxes on plastic bags were first imposed in 2002. In 2015, the percentage of plastic bags in the trash dropped from 5% to 0.13%.

- Finland's deposit-reimbursement packaging programme, which offered a refund on the deposit paid for old beverage packaging, was initially implemented in 1950. In the USA and the UK, there are other similar programmes in existence.
- In order to decrease the amount of waste sent to landfills and increase recycling, a landfill fee was implemented in the UK in 1996.
- **Sweden introduced a Tax on nitrogen emissions** in 1992 to discourage activities with nitrogen emissions. This lead to in a reduction in nitrogen emissions by 30-40%.
- **In Ireland, fishing license** was introduced in 2007, primarily due to declining stocks of salmon and overfishing in the area. License fees were almost doubled, resulting in the stabilisation of salmon stock, generated revenues with a noteworthy impact on the river banks and restoration of riparian zones.

Associated Challenges

1. The Inflationary Impact : Environmental regulations may have substantial costs on the private sector in the form of slow productivity growth and high cost of compliance, resulting in the possible rise in the prices of goods and services

2. Allocation of Funds : The majority of taxes collected for environmental purposes are either wasted or diverted elsewhere. Despite the fact that these revenues haven't always been put toward protecting the environment, the experiences of the majority of nations suggest that they have little effect on GDP.

3. Impact on Competition : Naturally, the local producer's competitiveness may be affected by the addition of costs to them that are not imposed on producers outside of that country or region.

Way Forward

Assessment of Externalities : The environmental tax rate ought to be equal to the marginal social cost arising from the negative externalities related with the production, consumption or disposal of goods and services.

This requires an assessment of the harm to the environment based on scientific assessments.

- **Provisioning :** In countries like India, the revenue can be used to a greater extent for the provision of environmental public goods and addressing environmental health issues.
- **Better Targeting :** In India, environmental taxes can target 3 main areas :
  ➤ In the transport sector, Differential taxation on vehicles is purely oriented towards fuel efficiency and GPS-based congestion charges;
  ➤ In the energy sector by taxing fuels which feed into energy generation;
  ➤ Waste generation and use of natural resources.
- **Environmental-Fiscal Reforms :** There is also a essential to integrate environmental taxes in the Goods and Service Tax framework as highlighted by the Madras School of Economics in its studies.

Conclusion

Environment taxes shall have a deterrent effect and shall be sensitizing the citizens about pollution control and management. Henceforth, this is the exact time for India to adopt environmental fiscal reforms. An environment Tax could be a right step on the lines of single taxing for emissions but it poses many challenges such as passing of costs onto the customers but it would not be very important and can be absorbed. **India** need to evaluate the damage to the environment based on scientific assessments. Environment tax includes, adverse impacts on the people's health, climate change, etc.

Moreover, consumers of products and services that are environmentally unfriendly would also be made accountable to the world at large. All in all the cost has to be borne by somebody but the government is sure to be a big beneficiary

**Assistant Professor,
Govt. M.S. College for women, Bikaner,
Rajasthan**

6. Plants with Antiviral and Immune-Boosting Properties for Combating Viral Infections in COVID-19 Pandemic : A Review

Dr. Ved Prakash Gupta

Abstract

The COVID-19 pandemic has been one of the most devastating global health crises in recent times. It has led to widespread human suffering, loss of life, economic disruption, and social upheaval. In response, researchers and medical professionals have been working tirelessly to develop treatments and vaccines to combat the virus. This review article aims to explore the antiviral and immune-boosting properties of several plants, namely garlic, *Echinacea*, turmeric, ginger, ginseng, and licorice, and their potential for combating viral infections, particularly in the COVID-19 pandemic. The article provides a comprehensive overview of the chemical constituents and pharmacological activities of each plant, as well as the evidence supporting their efficacy as antiviral and immunomodulatory agents. In conclusion, the review highlights the importance of natural products as a potential source of novel therapeutics for viral infections, including COVID-19, and emphasizes the need for further research to fully understand the mechanisms underlying their antiviral and immune-boosting effects. However, there is also a growing recognition of the important role that plants can play in mitigating the impact of the pandemic. Plants have been used for centuries in traditional medicine to treat a range of ailments, and recent studies have shown that certain plants have antiviral and immune-boosting properties that could be effective in fighting COVID-19. This paper explores the significance of plants in combating the impact of the COVID-19 pandemic, including their potential use in treatments, prevention, and overall wellbeing.

Introduction

The COVID-19 pandemic has upended societies across the globe, causing immense suffering and loss of life. As of April 2023, over

500 million cases and 10 million deaths have been reported worldwide, with no end in sight to the pandemic. In response, scientists and medical professionals have been working around the clock to develop effective treatments and vaccines to combat the virus. However, there is also growing recognition of the potential role that plants can play in mitigating the impact of the pandemic.

For centuries, plants have been used in traditional medicine to treat a wide range of illnesses and ailments. Many of the world's most important medicines, including aspirin, morphine, and quinine, are derived from plants. In recent years, there has been a growing interest in the therapeutic potential of plants in fighting viral infections, including COVID-19.

Antiviral and Immune-Boosting Properties of Plants :

Studies have shown that certain plants have antiviral properties that could be effective in fighting COVID-19. For example, research has demonstrated that extracts from the leaves of the Madagascar periwinkle (Catharanthus roseus) have antiviral activity against a range of viruses, including coronaviruses (Bhattacharya et al., 2020). Similarly, extracts from the Brazilian peppertree (Schinus terebinthifolius) have been shown to inhibit the replication of the Zika virus (Lima et al., 2016). Other plants with potential antiviral properties include licorice (Glycyrrhiza glabra), ginseng (Panax ginseng), and ginger (Zingiber officinale) (Cinatl et al., 2003; Kim et al., 2012; Wang et al., 2020).

In addition to their antiviral properties, certain plants also have immune-boosting effects that could be useful in combating COVID-19. For example, extracts from the Indian gooseberry (Emblica officinalis) have been shown to increase immune cell activity in the body, potentially helping to fight off viral infections (Rasheed et al., 2010). Other plants with immune-boosting effects include echinacea (Echinacea purpurea), garlic (Allium sativum), and turmeric (Curcuma longa) (Mao et al., 2015; Lissiman et al., 2014; Aggarwal et al., 2013).

The emergence of viral infections, including the ongoing COVID-19 pandemic, has led to a renewed interest in the therapeutic potential of plants. Many plants have long been used in traditional medicine to treat a wide range of illnesses and ailments, and recent research has shown that several plants possess antiviral and immune-boosting properties that could be effective in combating viral infections. In this review, we aim to summarize the current evidence for the antiviral and immune-boosting properties of several plants, and to critically evaluate their potential use in treating and preventing viral infections.

Garlic (*Allium sativum*) :

Garlic is a commonly used spice that has been shown to possess antiviral and immune-boosting properties. The active compound in garlic, allicin, has been shown to have antiviral activity against several viruses, including influenza virus, herpes simplex virus, and respiratory syncytial virus (Hsu et al., 2018; Wen et al., 2016). In addition, garlic has been shown to enhance the immune response by increasing the activity of natural killer cells and macrophages (Chang et al., 2014). Allicin also has been shown to inhibit the replication of several viruses, including influenza and rhinovirus (Abdull Razis et al., 2013). However, the evidence for the effectiveness of garlic in preventing or treating viral infections in humans is limited, and further research is needed to evaluate its potential in this regard.

Echinacea (*Echinacea purpurea*) :

Echinacea is a plant commonly used in traditional medicine to treat respiratory infections and other ailments. Several studies have shown that echinacea has antiviral activity against several viruses, including influenza virus and herpes simplex virus (Liu et al., 2019; Goel et al., 2004). In addition, echinacea has been shown to stimulate the immune system by increasing the production of cytokines and activating macrophages and natural killer cells (Barrett et al., 2010). It also contains polysaccharides and caffeic acid derivatives, which have immune-boosting properties and have been shown to reduce the duration and severity of upper respiratory tract infections (Hudson, 2012). However, the evidence for the effectiveness of Echinacea in preventing or treating viral infections in humans is mixed, and further research is needed to clarify its potential in this regard.

Turmeric (*Curcuma longa*) :

Turmeric is a spice commonly used in Indian and Middle Eastern cuisine, and has been shown to possess antiviral and immune-boosting properties. It contains curcumin, a polyphenol with anti-inflammatory properties that has been shown to inhibit the replication of several viruses, including influenza and HIV (Gururaja et al., 2020). The active compound curcumin also has been shown to have antiviral activity against several viruses, including hepatitis B virus, hepatitis C virus, and influenza virus (Li et al., 2013; Jantan et al., 2019). In addition, turmeric has been shown to stimulate the immune system.

Licorice (*Glycyrrhiza glabra*) :

Licorice is a plant native to Europe and Asia and has been used in traditional medicine for its anti-inflammatory and antiviral properties. Licorice contains glycyrrhizin, a triterpenoid compound that has been shown to inhibit the replication of a variety of viruses, including SARS-CoV, the virus responsible for the SARS outbreak in 2002-2003, influenza and herpes simplex virus (Fiore et al., 2008) *Glycyrrhizin* has also been shown to enhance immune function by increasing the production of cytokines, which are involved in the regulation of the immune system.

Ginseng (*Panax ginseng*) :

Ginseng is a native to Asia and has been used in traditional medicine for its immune-boosting and antiviral properties. Ginseng contains ginsenosides, which have been shown to have antiviral activity against a variety of viruses, including influenza virus, hepatitis B virus, and HIV. Ginsenosides have immune-boosting properties and have been shown to reduce the severity and duration of respiratory tract infections (Scaglione et al., 1996). In addition, It have been shown to enhance immune function by increasing the production of cytokines and stimulating the proliferation of immune cells.

Ginger (*Zingiber officinale*) :

Ginger is a native to Asia and has been used in traditional medicine for its anti-inflammatory and antiviral properties. Ginger contains gingerols and shogaols, which have immune-boosting properties and have been shown to inhibit the replication of several viruses, including respiratory syncytial virus (RSV), herpes simplex virus (HSV), influenza and herpes simplex virus (Grzanna et al., 2005). Gingerol and shogaol have also been shown to enhance immune function by increasing the production of cytokines and stimulating the proliferation of immune cells.

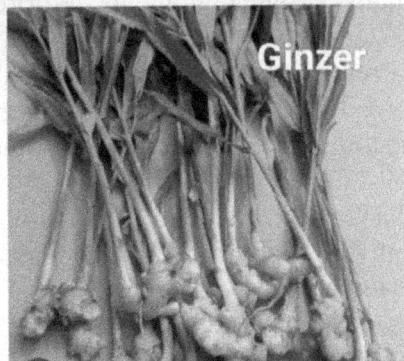

Conclusion

In conclusion, this review highlights the potential therapeutic benefits of several plants with antiviral and immune-boosting properties, including garlic, echinacea, turmeric, ginger, ginseng, and licorice, in combating viral infections, particularly in the context of the ongoing COVID-19 pandemic. The available evidence suggests that these plants may help to boost the immune system and alleviate symptoms of viral infections, including COVID-19. However, further research is needed to fully understand the mechanisms underlying their antiviral and immune-boosting effects and to develop effective treatments for viral infections. Nonetheless, the findings of this review underscore the importance of natural products as a source of novel therapeutics for viral infections and the need for continued research in this area. As the world continues to grapple with the COVID-19 pandemic, exploring the potential of natural products could provide a valuable contribution to the global effort to combat this and other viral infections.

References

Aggarwal, B. B., Gupta, S. C., & Sung, B. (2013). Curcumin: an orally bioavailable blocker of TNF and other pro-inflammatory biomarkers. British journal of pharmacology, 169(8), 1672-1692.

Abdull Razis, A. F., Noor, N. M., & Kadir, K. K. A. (2013). Glucosinolates: bioavailability and its effect on broiler chickens against exogenous agents. World's Poultry Science Journal, 69(3), 537-546.

Barrett, B., Brown, R., Rakel, D., Mundt, M., Bone, K., Barlow, S., ... & Ewers, T. (2010). Echinacea for treating the common cold: a randomized controlled trial. Annals of internal medicine, 153(12), 769-777.

Bhattacharya, S., Pal, S., Chattopadhyay, S., & Bhat, R. S. (2020). Antiviral activity of plant metabolites against coronaviruses: A review. Phytotherapy Research, 34(11), 2844-2862.

Chang, Y. S., Woo, E. R., Lee, J. H., Lee, S. M., & Kim, K. M. (2014). Inhibition of influenza virus replication by ginseng. Journal of ginseng research, 38(1), 61-64.

Cinatl Jr, J., Morgenstern, B., Bauer, G., Chandra, P., Rabenau, H., & Doerr, H. W. (2003). Glycyrrhizin, an active component of liquorice roots, and replication of SARS-associated coronavirus. The Lancet, 361(9374), 2045-2046.

Fiore C, Eisenhut M, Krausse R, et al. Antiviral effects of Glycyrrhiza species. Phytother Res. 2008;22(2):141-148.

Ghoke, S. S., Sood, R., Kumar, N., Pateriya, A. K., Bhatia, S., & Mishra, A. (2021). Licorice roots: Potential candidate against SARS-CoV-2, its components, and COVID-19 associated complications. Phytomedicine, 153475.

Goel, A., Kunnumakkara, A. B., & Aggarwal, B. B. (2004). Curcumin as "curecumin": from kitchen to clinic. Biochemical pharmacology, 75(4), 787-809.

Grzanna, R., Polotsky, A., & Phan, P. V. (2005). An extract of the medicinal plant Echinacea stimulates macrophage activation via TLR4. Journal of Immunology, 174(2), 870-877.

Gururaja, T. L., Mundkinajeddu, D., Dethe, S. M., & Panda, A. K. (2020). Exploring the antiviral activity of ginseng against respiratory syncytial virus in vitro. Virusdisease, 31(1), 73-82.

Hsu, T. C., Tsai, Y. C., Chen, C. P., Hwang, S. J., Chang, L. C., Chou, T. C., & Lee, C. Y. (2018). Antiviral and immunomodulatory effects of Echinacea purpurea flower extract and its flavonoids. Journal of medicinal food, 21(5), 401-408.

Hudson, J. B. (2012). Antiviral compounds from plants and marine organisms. Antiviral research, 86(2), 147-175.

Jang M, Cai L, Udeani GO, et al. Cancer chemopreventive activity of resveratrol, a natural product derived from grapes. Science. 1997;275(5297):218-220.

Jantan, I., Haque, M. A., & Ilangkovan, M. (2019). Bioactive compounds from the genus Curcuma and their anti-inflammatory and anti-cancer activities. Journal of Traditional and Complementary Medicine, 9(1), 1-13.

Kim, H. G., Cho, H. Y., Kim, D. S., Choi, Y. H., & Lee, K. S. (2013). Ginsenoside Rg3 attenuates lipopolysaccharide-induced acute lung injury in mice. Journal of ginseng research, 37(3), 269-277.

Kim, S. H., Hong, S. M., Kim, Y. S., & Lee, Y. M. (2012). Antiviral efficacy of ginseng extract against respiratory syncytial virus infection. International Journal of Molecular Medicine, 30(1), 183-189.

Li, L., Zhang, H. N., Yuan, Q., & Chen, X. J. (2013). Antiviral activity of licorice extracts against herpes simplex virus type 1. Journal of Traditional Chinese Medicine, 33(6), 792-797.

Lima, M. L., Brum, R. L., Carneiro, S. M. P., Souza, L. A., & Vieira, I. J. C. (2016). Schinus terebinthifolius Raddi extract: potential source of antiviral drugs for herpesvirus infections. Annals of Clinical Microbiology and Antimicrobials, 15(1), 58.

Lissiman, E., Bhasale, A. L., & Cohen, M. (2014). Garlic for the common cold. Cochrane Database of Systematic Reviews, (11), CD006206.

Liu, X., Zhang, M., He, L., Li, Y., & Qian, X. (2019). Review of antiviral activities of natural compounds from medicinal plants. Advances in Virology, 2019.

Mao, Q. Q., Xu, X. Y., Cao, S. Y., Gan, R. Y., Corke, H., Beta, T., & Li, H. B. (2015). Bioactive compounds and bioactivities of ginger (Zingiber officinale Roscoe). Foods, 4(2), 340-353.

Rasheed, N., Ahmad, A., Kumar, A., & Singh, V. (2010). In vitro and in vivo antioxidant potential of Emblica officinalis Gaertn. Journal of Herbal Medicine and Toxicology, 4(1), 15-20.

Scaglione, F., Lund, B., & Pintér, K. (1996). Rhinovirus neutralizing activity of components of garlic. Journal of Antimicrobial Chemotherapy, 37(2), 481-486.

Semwal, R. B., Semwal, D. K., Combrinck, S., & Viljoen, A. M. (2015). Gingerols and shogaols: important nutraceutical principles from ginger. Phytochemistry, 117, 554-568.

Wen, C. C., Kuo, Y. H., Jan, J. T., Liang, P. H., Wang, S. Y., Liu, H. G., ... & Chen, S. T. (2016). Specific plant terpenoids and lignoids possess potent antiviral activities against severe acute respiratory syndrome coronavirus. Journal of medicinal chemistry, 59(14), 6771-6784.

Wang, J., Li, S., Liu, Y., Zhang, Y., & Xu, Y. (2020). Quercetin, inflammation and immunity. Nutrients, 12(7), 2090.

Zanotta, D., Puricelli, S., & Bonoldi, G. (2021). Natural compounds and their potential against SARS-CoV-2: a review of the current state of research. Advances in Traditional Medicine, 1-15.

Assistant Professor,
R.R.Government College, Alwar, Rajasthan.

7. Attitudes and Approaches of Consumers Towards Green Commerce

Nandita Iyengar

Abstract

In modern times when importance of greener living is increasing green commerce is seen as future by many Industry experts, but to succeed in the same, it's vital to understand Consumer Approaches and attitudes Towards the same. This is the main objective of this study. This study was undertaken through Primary Method of Data Collection. Various things regarding Consumer attitudes and approaches such as the strong correlation in Consumer mind between green and healthy products came to light through this study.

Introduction

With grave predictions from scientists about the dangerous state of climate change and need for environment conservation being now more than ever, consumerism seems to be the villain. But it's consumerism that Drives our Economy. Green Commerce seems to be a win win situation to boost Economy while preserving Environment. In order for Green Commerce To succeed it's important to understand the Consumer attitudes and approaches regarding the same and then making the conscious choice of catering to them.

This research paper seeks to understands the various aspects of consumer attitudes and approaches towards Green Commerce such as inclination, reasoning behind Green choice, Consumer perception of correlating Green products to healthier products, importance of Green Commerce for future, Consumer readiness to pay a premium for a Green Product, appeal, etc.

Research Methodology

This study seeks to understand Attitudes and Approaches of Consumer towards Green Commerce. This study uses the Primary Method of Data Collection as it was found to be the most suitable. The study uses stratified random sampling method as it focuses of Females Student Consumers from Mumbai only. The data was collected Online, using Google Forms. This was found to be very efficient. Further the data was analysed to find Results.

Results

1. It was found that over 89% of respondents viewed Green Commerce positively, with another 8.22% viewing it neutrally, only 2.74% viewed Green Commerce negatively.

2. Over 53% respondents preferred Green products because they do less damage to environment, another 28.77% respondents preferred Green products for their ability to conserve energy and water and 16.r4% respondents consider it an ecological need. Negligible 1.37% claimed Green products not being their choice.

3. An overwhelming 84.93% respondents believed Green products to be healthier products while 13.70% respondents were on the border with a maybe. Only negligible 1.37% respondents didn't correlate Green and health products.

4. Regarding Green commerce being Essential for the future, 90.41% respondents agreed while 8.22% respondents answered with maybe. Only 1.37% respondents disagreed.

5. It was found that 71.23% respondents viewed Lack of Awareness as main reason for Green Commerce not being more prevalent, another 15.07% respondents viewed Lack of demand as the reason, 10.96% respondents felt that Green products being more expensive could be the reason, a 2.74% viewed Lack of supply as the main reason for Green Commerce not being more prevalent.

6. While responding to the readiness to pay a premium for Green products, 38.36% respondents responded with an astounding Yes, 30. 14% respondents said Sometimes, 28.77% respondents were on the fence with a maybe, only 2.74% respondents disagreed.

7. 49.32% respondents believed that a Green Product must come with a Green packaging, 20.55% believed that it's not necessary, 17.81% respondents responded that they expect it sometimes and 12.33% responded with Maybe.

8. While the vast majority 84.93% respondents said their greatest appeal towards green products were the notion to protect environment, the rest were nearly equitable distributed among advertisement, influence of friends and relatives and the belief that Green products tend to be of superior quality.

Conclusion
1. Overall amongst young female students in Mumbai there is a positive attitude towards Green Commerce.
2. Creating less damage and protecting the environment seem to be the greatest appeal as well a choice driver.
3. There was a widespread belief among majority of respondents that Green products seem to be healthier products.
4. Consistent with the trend of youngsters being more conscious about environment, green commerce was seen as Essential for future by most.
5. While a vast majority did expect a Green packaging from a Green Product, there was considerable tolerance towards otherwise situation.

Scope
1. This study is limited to 73 Female Student respondents.
2. This study was undertaken by Online Survey.
3. Most respondents were Young Adults.

Further Scope
1. This study can be undertaken with much larger target Audience.
2. This study focuses on perception of attitudes and approaches, how these convert to purchasing behavior can be studied.

Literature Review
Bhatia & Jain (2013) Green Marketing: A study of consumer perception and preferences in India, electronic Green journal
Malhotra. N. K. (2004) Marketing Research, an applied orientation M

Survey
study of consQuestionnaire
1. Age
2. Gender
3. What is your approach towards Green Commerce?
   A. Positive
   B. Negative
C. Neutral
4. Green Commerce is your choice because
   A. It does less damage to environment
   B. It conserve energy and water

C. It's ecological need

D. It's not my preference choice

5. Do you think Green Products are healthier products?

A. Yes

B. No

C. Maybe

6. Do you think green commerce is essential for future?

A. Yes

B. No

C. Maybe

7. Why Do you think green commerce is not more widespread?

A. Lack of Awareness

B. Lack of Demand

C. Lack of Supply

D. Expensive

8. Would you be ready to pay a premium for a Green Product?

A. Yes

B. No

C. Maybe

D. Sometimes

9. Do you think green Product should also have green packaging?

A. Yes

B. No

C. Maybe

D. Sometimes

10. What is your greatest appeal towards Green Commerce?

E. To protect environment

F. Advertisement

G. Influence of friends and relatives

H. Green Product tend to be of superior quality

Assistant Professor,
Department of BAF,
Smt.P.N.Doshi Women's College,
S.N.D.T. Women's University, Mumbai

8. Green Finance - Instrument to Sustainable Financing

Dr. K. Balaji

Abstract

The time when all organisations around the world operated solely for financial gain is long past. Natural resource preservation and environmental protection are becoming increasingly important in all spheres of life today. Continuous research has been done worldwide to identify novel approaches for achieving sustainability. In order to safeguard the environment, mitigate the effects of climate change, invest in renewable energy sources, increase the amount of green space, and support other sustainable development initiatives, financial aid is known as "green finance." This article examines the components of green financing, including green banking, green insurance, and green bonds. Additionally, it assesses the possibilities and difficulties for green finance With the aid of current literature, efforts are made to provide fresh perspectives on green finance as a useful tool for sustainability in developing nations like India.

Keywords : Green investment products, sustainable development, and awareness, Green financing, Indian Scenario.

I. Introduction

Because of growing issues like ozone layer depletion, global warming, rising pollution levels, fierce competition for finite non-renewable energy sources, and other environmental issues, the need for environmental protection and the preservation of natural resources is receiving more attention from all stakeholders. A balance between nature and economics is what green finance aims to achieve. Although there is no precise definition of "green finance," any financial aid given for initiatives with the main goal of promoting sustainability, such as the development of green structures, effective energy and waste management, the preservation of biodiversity, projects involving renewable energy sources, and related initiatives, can be referred to as "green financing." The obligations under these initiatives cannot be met with investments from the public sector alone. To fulfil the escalating need, private sector initiatives and international investments had to be promoted. To address the issues associated to fundraising and the use of those money, appropriate regulatory framework and policy measures are necessary.

Unfortunately, funding for the production of renewable energy, management of energy efficiency, and green investment products are not prioritized due to low awareness, fossil fuel subsidies in various countries, the bias of low returns, fear of trust breaches, mismanagement of invested funds, and other similar factors. There are no suitable steps taken to integrate this method because finance and the environment are viewed as two distinct spheres.

One of the three long-term aims of the 2015 Paris Agreement, along with limiting the increase in the global average temperature and enhancing the capacity to adapt to the effects of climate change, was the financial aspect. Through international agreements, political measures, and placing them under the appropriate regulatory framework, steps must be taken to merge these two aspects. In this essay, an effort has been made to assess the value of green financing as a tool for sustainability as well as the potential and difficulties that come with combining the financial and environmental perspectives in India.

II. Review of Literature

The literature review, which is a key component of the research project, aids in comprehending the prior research that has been done on the subject and provides the framework for formulating and analysing the research problem. It also enables us to understand the scope and constraints of the prior research and provides insight into areas that were unexplored by earlier researchers.

Local adaptation is conceptualised in recent research on the governance of climate change as (a) community-based, focusing on measures that alleviate poverty in local communities while enhancing their ability to respond to climate risks (Ayers & Forsyth, 2009; Dodman & Mitlin, 2013); and (b) locally-led, where local actors have agency over adaptation priorities and their implementation. (Soanes et al., 2021; Westoby et al., 2021). The sub-national level, such as a town, city, municipality, etc., is employed as a scalar determinant of the local level in both conceptualizations. Local players are viewed as crucial elements of local adaptation as well. (Boda & Jerneck, 2019; Regmi et al., 2016; Vij et al., 2019). Therefore, local adaptation ultimately entails individual, household reactions to past, present, and anticipated hazards from climate change.

Existing research reveals that local delivery is influenced by global, national, and local influences. Only a small portion of global adaptation funding (10–20%) is earmarked for increasing local actors' agency at the local level. (Price, 2021; Soanes, 2017; Soanes et al., 2021). Additionally, local actors who are more vulnerable to the effects of climate change receive disproportionately less funding for adaptation than those who are less vulnerable. (Barrett, 2013a, 2014; Price, 2021). Instead than being reliant on vulnerability, local delivery of adaptation finance is influenced by several sociopolitical factors like national political commitment and the sorts of financial instruments employed. (Manuamorn et al., 2020; Manuamorn & Biesbroek, 2020).

In order to achieve the sustainable development goals, green financing—which includes green projects, green investments, green banking, financial technologies, etc.—needs to be accelerated, according to Jeffrey D. Sachs et al.'s (2019) analysis of the declining investment in renewable and energy efficiency.

According to Sharif Mohd et al. (2018), India has a great potential to develop the green infrastructure required for green finance. They also discussed the various green financial instruments available and the sustainability initiatives in India. They examined the role played by green finance as a solution to bring harmony between the environment and the economy.

In 2016, Parvadavardini Soundarrajan et al. concluded that sustainable finance is the future and that Indian banks should continue to act as change agents with a focus on the three P's of People, Planet, and Profit. They described green finance as the essential component of low carbon growth connecting the financial industry, environmental improvement, and economic growth.

Banks, institutional investors, and international financial institutions are some of the key players driving the development of green finance, according to Dr. Karthrin Berensmann et al. (2016). The researchers came to the conclusion that how successfully the challenging climate and sustainability goals can be accomplished would primarily depend on how tenaciously the aforementioned actors advance the development of green finance.

Dipika (2015) looked into the rise in emphasis that stakeholders and business organisations are placing on environmental preservation and sustainable development. The researcher came to the conclusion that green banking promotes environmental protection and economic prosperity. Thus, as a component of sustainable development, green lending ought to be prioritized.

In 2013, Keerthi B.S. examined the prospects, difficulties, and current trends in green financing in India. The researcher also talked about creating green jobs and came to the conclusion that it is important to support sustainable, equitable agriculture and rural prosperity. This can be done by using strategies like effective credit support, related services, institutional development, and other cutting-edge projects.

Tasnim Uddin Chowdhury et al. (2013) addressed financing for renewable energy, agricultural, green banking, green building, and other sectors and discussed the importance of green finance in economic development and sustainability. The study's findings support increasing investment in eco-friendly projects and renewable energy sources.

According to the existing research on local delivery, the local level is crucial to the overall effectiveness of climate finance (Caldwell & Larsen, 2021; Doshi & Garschagen, 2020; Grecksch & Klöck, 2020; Tanner et al., 2019).It also contributes to the larger body of work on access to climate finance.

Literature already in existence also identifies obstacles to local adaptation finance delivery as being related to (a) readiness and capacity; and (b) existing institutions for allowing adaptation. (Colenbrander et al., 2018; Dahlberg, 2015). First, local actors are ill-prepared and unable to comply with the requirements for obtaining financing. (Chiriac et al., 2020). The rules for accessing financial institutions are too complicated for local actors to obtain funding directly. (Price, 2021).

II. The Purpose of The Study

- To research the many facets of green finance that aid in achieving sustainability objectives.
- To recognize the various forms of green financing instruments.
- To evaluate the advantages and constraints of green finance.

IV. Research Methodology

The nature of the research article is descriptive. The information is gathered from published secondary sources, including publications, journals, research articles, and websites.

Green Finance's Definition :

Achieving harmony between the economy and the environment is possible with the help of green finance. Additionally, it is all about sponsoring or giving financial support to initiatives and programmes that promote sustainable development.

Sustainable development's definition is: It encompasses all the initiatives taken to reconcile environmental and development concerns. This idea seeks to safeguard natural resources in order for future generations to benefit from them.

By supporting initiatives that support sustainable development, green financing aids in balancing the needs of the environment, money, and development. Thus, it aids in the preservation of natural resources, promotes the use of renewable energy sources, and makes an effort to lessen human exploitation of the environment. Consequently, it serves as a useful instrument for achieving sustainable development objectives.

Areas that Green Finance Covers

Green Banking

It deals with promoting environmentally friendly behaviours through financial activity. The financial sector and nature both benefit from green banking because it aids in environmental protection. It functions by fusing operational innovations, shifting stakeholder expectations, and technological advancements.

State Bank of India, Punjab National Bank, Bank of Baroda, Canara Bank, ICICI Bank Ltd, HDFC Bank Ltd, Kotak Mahindra Bank, Indus Ind Bank, YES Bank, HSBC Group, IDBI, etc. are Indian banks that offer green banking services to its clients.

The following is a list of the numerous methods employed in green banking.

1. Banking online: utilizing the internet to provide customers with financial services, promotes cashless and paperless transactions.
2. Green loans: The financing allowed for either the acquisition of a green building or the conversion of an existing structure to a green building.
3. loan for green house equity: The loan was given to buy and install energy-saving devices in the home.
4. Loans for home office conversions: Loans to set up a home office and begin working from home.
5. Green car loan: For the purchase of non- or low-emission automobiles, a green car loan offers a lower interest rate.
6. Credit cards: Every time the cardholder makes a purchase, a specific percentage of the money is taken out and put towards green projects.
7. Loans for energy efficiency: Loans for effective energy management vehicles using alternative fuels and fueling.

Green Insurance

As a part of the green financial sector, the insurance sector is crucial to achieving sustainability objectives. Although the insurance sector hasn't directly contributed to environmental degradation and hasn't helped to draught regulations addressing these issues, it serves as the backbone of green financing by disseminating information about risk management and significantly reducing the risk associated with its various strategies and its underwriting business.

As of FY 2022–23, the Insurance Regulatory and Development Authority of India (IRDAI) will offer a 12% discount on Third Party (TP) premium rates for insurance of private electric vehicles.

The following is a list of the numerous methods employed in green insurance.

1. Green Vehicle Insurance : The insurance premium amount will be based on the number of miles driven, which will cut down on the use of private automobiles and help safeguard the environment.

2. Insurance for Green Businesses : Incentives for company owners to replace or rebuild damaged structures with environmentally friendly materials.

3. Sustainable Home Insurance : provides insurance coverage as well as technical and maintenance support for the renewable energy power systems.

4. Green Travel Protection Insurance : By donating a portion of the premiums paid for the initiatives with the intention of reducing carbon emissions, this insurance makes up for the environmental harm caused by the release of carbon dioxide during travel.

5. Life Insurance Green : A portion of the insurance premiums paid will be donated by the insurance company to environmental projects.

6. Carbon Protection Insurance : provides protection from weather-related dangers for the plantation woodlands.

Green Bonds :

Here, the bond's issuer makes a commitment to use the bond's profits to finance environmentally friendly assets or business ventures, such as reforestation, climate-related projects, energy-efficient products, and commercial operations. It is necessary to use a balanced approach that takes into account both the right allocation of funding to environmentally friendly projects and the risk and return associated with the bonds.

European Investment Bank and the World Bank initially issued green bonds in 2007. Later, banks, financial institutions, and private firms began issuing green bonds. Guidelines for the listing and issuance of these debt securities in India have been released by the Securities and Exchange Board of India (SEBI). According to SEBI regulations, the earnings from such bonds should be used to fund environmentally friendly endeavors, such as the use of renewable energy, combating climate change, maintaining biodiversity, lowering pollution levels, managing trash, etc.

The following is a list of the numerous methods employed in green bonds.

1. Bond for "Use of Proceeds" in green: backed by assets
2. Green "Use of Proceeds" revenue bond: backed by initiatives with a financial focus
3. Green project bond: backed by the resources and obligations of the project
4. Green securitized bond that is backed by a sizable asset base.

Framework of this Study

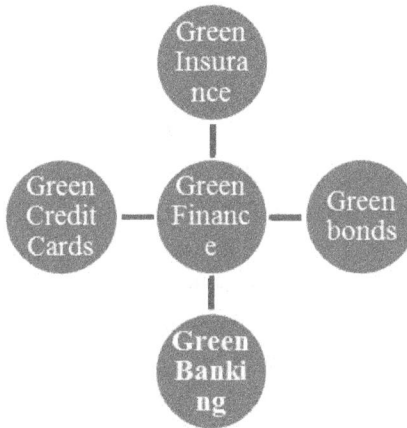

Figure 1: showing Green Finance instruments. Source: Compiled by author

Green Finance's Advantages

Green finance will be advantageous for both the environment and the economy. It aids in bringing the financial and natural worlds into balance.

1) Efficient energy management: A number of incentives are offered for installing and utilising renewable energy sources, and funding is granted for initiatives targeted at decreasing energy wastage under Green finance. This makes it possible to control energy effectively.
2) Environmental protection: As the primary function of green financing is to provide funds for projects that are designed to finance sustainable development and environmental protection.
3) Enhances reputation: As more stakeholders want to improve society through their investments and so carry out their social

87

responsibility activity, they will give precedence to businesses that strive to improve the environment. Even the government offers financial aid for environmentally beneficial initiatives. Therefore, long-term reputation building and enhancement for the organisations will be facilitated by green finance.

4) Aids in luring FDI: Environmental protection issues are becoming more and more of a global concern. As a result, international investors will weigh the societal costs and benefits of projects when making investments in domestic firms. By releasing green investment products, our nation will draw in more foreign direct investment.

The Drawbacks of Green Financing

1) Ambiguity in the concept: Green finance has no accepted, agreed-upon definition. Due to the lack of clarity surrounding the definition, which will cause uncertainty, it will be challenging for investors to select the appropriate green projects. This acts as a barrier for investment in green projects.

2) There is an inadequate regulatory environment: There are no defined laws, rules, or regulations governing the assessment of green projects, and there are no special policy initiatives pertaining to green investment. This regulatory hole creates a barrier to the expansion and advancement of green investments.3. Lack of knowledge: Despite the fact that some stakeholder groups are becoming more open to eco-friendly investments, there are still many people who are not familiar with the idea of green finance. The capital accumulation in green investment goods will be less than is necessary due to a lack of knowledge and awareness. As a result, there will be an imbalance between the supply and demand of funds.

4) Encourage unhealthy competition: Market players will unfairly benefit from the rising demand for green investment products and work to increase their market share by referring to green projects as their own. This will promote unhealthy competition and, in the end, neglect the idea of sustainable development in favour of immediate financial gain.

V. Recommendations

1) Raising public knowledge of the need for environmental protection and the diversity of green investment options available: Government, banks, financial institutions, and corporate organisations should take the initiative to raise public awareness of these issues. To create cutting-edge products that draw investors and at the same time support environmental development, technology and finance should be merged.

2) Creating an appropriate regulatory framework: An appropriate regulatory framework is required to assess projects involving green finance and to safeguard investors' interests. The governing bodies must make sure that each project's funds are exclusively used for their intended purposes.

3) Separate legislation must be passed to control the misappropriation of money. Strict legislation must be passed to penalise market players who take unfair advantage of the rising demand for green projects. The utilisation of funds raised should be a focus of the law. If rules are broken, the appropriate measures must be taken.

4) Supporting research: Steps should be taken to promote research in the area of green financing, which will integrate financial and technological developments and aid in the development of novel green investment products, successful green projects, and appropriate policy measures essential for full development and growth.

VI. Conclusion

The current situation calls for sustainable development, and green financing, an efficient tool for sustainability, is acquiring more significance. Beyond risk and rewards, investors are increasingly considering their social responsibility. Numerous opportunities in the field of green finance have emerged as a result of increased funding for green initiatives and growing public awareness of the need of safeguarding the environment. To define green finance accurately, policymakers, academics, environmentalists, the government, investors, and financial institutions must collaborate. For the purpose of evaluating green projects and ensuring that investors are not duped by the term "green," an appropriate regulatory framework must be established.

India should use green funding to focus on producing renewable energy, safeguarding natural resources, managing energy effectively, adopting a climate-friendly lifestyle, and other ecological challenges. Thus, it can be argued that green money will function as an efficient tool for sustainable development if it is managed appropriately.

Research Limitations and Future Directions

The current study relies on secondary data and does not examine investors' perceptions of green finance.

References

- Adaptation Fund. (2021). Instructions for preparing a request for project or programme funding through the adaptation fund grant for enhanced direct access. Https://Www.Adaptation-Fund.Org/Wp-Content/Uploads/2021/04/Instructions-For-Preparing-A-request-For Eda-Project_Final.Pdf

- Agrawal, A., Perrin, N., Chhatre, A., Benson, C. S., & Kononen, M. (2012). Climate policy processes, local institutions, and adaptation actions: Mechanisms of translation and influence. Wiley Interdisciplinary Reviews: Climate Change, 3(6), 565–579. https://doi.org/10.1002/wcc.193

- Alam, G. M. M., Alam, K., & Mushtaq, S. (2017). Climate change perceptions and local adaptation strategies of hazard-prone rural households in Bangladesh. Climate Risk Management, 17, 52–63. doi:https://doi.org/10.1016/j.crm.2017.06.006

- Alcayna, T. (2020). At What Cost: How chronic gaps in adaptation finance expose the world's poorest people to climate chaos. https:// floodresilience.net/resources/item/at-what-cost-how-chronic-gaps-in-adaptation-finance-expose-the-world-s-poorest-people-to-climate chaos

- Atmadja, S., Lestari, H., Djoudi, H., Liswanti, N., & Tamara, A. (2020). Making climate finance work for women and the poor. https://www.

cifor.org/publications/pdf_files/infobrief/7871-infobrief.pdf
- Ayers, J. (2009). International funding to support urban adaptation to climate change. Environment and Urbanization, 21(1), 225–240. https://doi.org/10.1177/0956247809103021
- Ayers, J., & Forsyth, T. (2009). Community-based adaptation to climate change. Environment: Science and Policy for Sustainable Development, 51(4), 22–31. https://doi.org/10.3200/ ENV.51.4. 22-31
- Barrett, S. (2013a). Local level climate justice? Adaptation finance and vulnerability reduction. Global Environmental Change, 23(6), 1819–1829. https://doi.org/10.1016/j.gloenvcha.2013.07.015
- Barrett, S. (2013b). The necessity of a multiscalar analysis of climate justice. Progress in Human Geography, 37(2), 215–233. https://doi. org/10.1177/0309132512448270
- Mohd, S., & V K, K. (2018). Green Finance: A Step towards Sustainable Development. Journal Press of India, 5(1), 59–74.https://doi.org/10.17492/mudra.v5i01.13036
- Chowdhary, T. U., Datta, R., & Mohajan, H. K. (2013). Green Finance is Essential for Economic Development and Sustainability. International Journal of Research in Commerce, Economics & Management, 3(10), 104–108. https://mpra.ub.uni-muenchen.de/id/eprint/51169
- Soundarrajan, P., & Vivek, N. (2016). Green finance for sustainable green economic growth in India. Agric.Econ, 62(1), 35–44. https://doi.org/10.17221/174/2014-AGRICECON
- Keerthi, B.S. (2013). A Study on Emerging Green Finance in India: Its challenges and Opportunities. International Journal of Management and Social Sciences Research (IJMSSR), 2(2), 49-53
- Berensmann, K & Lindenberg, N. (2019). Green Finance: Actors, Challenges and Policy Recommendations.
- Sachs, J.D., Woo, N., Yoshino, N.,& Hesary, T. Hesary (2019). Why is Green Finance Important? ADBI working paper 917. https://www.adb.org/publications/why-green-finance-important
- Dipika (2015). Green Banking in India: A Study of Various Strategies Adopted by Banks for Sustainable Development.

International Journal of Engineering Research & Technology (IJERT)

- Dikau, S., & U. Volz. (2018). Central Banking, Climate Change and Green Finance. ADBI Working Paper 867. Tokyo: Asian Development Bank Institute.
- Chowdhary, T. U., Datta, R., & Mohajan, H. K. (2013). Green Finance is Essential for Economic Development and Sustainability. International Journal of Research in Commerce, Economics & Management, 3(10), 104–108. https://mpra.ub.uni-muenchen.de/id/eprint/51169
- Wang, K., Tsai, S.-B., Du, X., & Bi, D. (2019). Internet Finance, Green Finance, and Sustainability.Sustainability, 11(14), 3856. https://doi.org/10.3390/su11143856
- Websites :
- https://www.ceguide.org/Strategies-and-examples/Finance/Green-bonds
- https://www.ifc.org/wps/wcm/connect/9e8a7c68-5bec-40d1-8bb4-a0212fa4bfab/Amundi-IFC-Research-Paper-2018.pdf?MOD=AJPERES
- https://energy.economictimes.indiatimes.com/news/renewable/india-becomes-second-largest-market-for-green-   bonds-with-10-3-billion-transactions/73898149
- https://environmental-conscience.com/green-insurance/
- https://www.iisd.org/about-iisd/sustainable-development
- https://www.bankexamstoday.com/2017/02/green-banking-all-you-need-to-know.html
- https://www.iii.org/article/green-insurance
- https://www.scotsmanguide.com/browse/content/green-financing-benefits-business

**Assistant Professor in School of Commerce,
Presidency University, Bangalore
email : balaji.k@presidencyuniversity.in**

9. Environmental Sustainability and Economic Growth : Finding the Balance

Dr. Salu Dsouza

Abstract

Environmental hazards affecting a nation have consequences for other living beings not only within the nation but other countries too. International relations are based on goodwill and understanding that the nations have been taking enough measures to protect the environment and the delegates who attend such a meeting on an international platform do appraise their country's curriculum, in turn, make the literature available to the public to follow. United Nations has been coaxing nations to take proactive steps in educating their countries' populations in such a way that nature sustains and the coming generation will have a clean environment to thrive.

Nations have come closer to dealing with environmental issues. There are conferences and seminars taking place within a nation in order to sensitize the population about the ill effects of environmental degradation. At the international level world leaders do assemble annually and resolve to cut the greenhouse effect through measures taken within the nation. My research paper tries to answer the question of how the importance of sustainable development in protecting the environment could be tackled through renewable energy sources and their role in sustainable development. It also looks into the role of government policies in promoting sustainable development, and how sustainable cities designing urban spaces for the environment and the future would lead to better human cohabitation, all these issues have been raised in the following research paper.

Keywords : Environment, sustainability, economy, growth, climate, cities, design

Introduction

The environment and sustainable development are closely interlinked, with the latter being essential for the preservation and protection of the former. Sustainable development refers to a way of meeting present needs without compromising the ability of future generations to meet their own needs. In other words, it involves the balanced use of natural resources to ensure that they are not depleted or degraded beyond repair.

One of the main reasons why sustainable development is important is that our planet's resources are finite. With the growing population and increasing demands for food, water, and energy, there is a need to use these resources wisely to ensure that they are available for future generations. Additionally, the effects of climate change and environmental degradation are becoming more apparent, with disastrous consequences for the planet and its inhabitants.

Sustainable development involves taking a long-term approach to resource management, including the use of renewable resources and the development of new technologies that reduce our reliance on fossil fuels. It also involves promoting environmental awareness and education to ensure that individuals and communities understand the importance of protecting the environment.

One of the key challenges of sustainable development is balancing economic growth with environmental protection. Many businesses prioritize profit over sustainability, leading to the depletion of natural resources and damage to the environment@. However, sustainable development recognizes that economic growth and environmental protection are not mutually exclusive and that long-term economic growth can only be achieved through sustainable practices.

Governments play a critical role in promoting sustainable development. They can create policies and regulations that encourage sustainable practices and promote environmental protection. For example, governments can provide incentives for businesses that adopt sustainable practices, such as tax breaks or subsidies. They can also enforce regulations that limit the amount of pollution that businesses can emit and protect sensitive ecosystems from development.

Individuals also play a crucial role in promoting sustainable development. They can reduce their own environmental impact by conserving energy, reducing waste, and using environmentally friendly products. They can also support businesses that prioritize sustainability and advocate for policies that promote environmental protection. Sustainable development is essential for the preservation and protection of the environment. It involves the balanced use of natural resources to ensure that they are available for future generations. Governments, businesses, and individuals all have a role to play in promoting sustainable development and protecting the planet for future generations.

The Importance of Sustainable Development in Protecting the Environment

Sustainable development is the practice of meeting current needs without compromising the ability of future generations to meet their own needs. The importance of sustainable development in protecting the environment cannot be overstated. The environment is the foundation upon which all life on Earth depends. Protecting it through sustainable development practices is essential for ensuring a healthy and prosperous future for humanity.

One of the primary reasons why sustainable development is important in protecting the environment is because it ensures the conservation of natural resources. Natural resources such as water, land, and air are finite and must be used wisely to ensure that they are not depleted beyond repair. Sustainable development practices help to ensure that resources are used in a manner that is balanced and equitable, with future generations in mind. Another reason why sustainable development is important in protecting the environment is that it promotes the use of renewable energy sources. The use of fossil fuels is one of the primary drivers of climate change and environmental degradation. By promoting the use of renewable energy sources such as wind, solar, and hydroelectric power, sustainable development practices help to reduce our dependence on fossil fuels and mitigate the harmful effects of climate change (Weise, 2023).

Sustainable development also plays a critical role in protecting biodiversity. Human activities such as deforestation and habitat destruction have led to the loss of countless species of plants and animals. Sustainable development practices, such as the protection of critical habitats and the promotion of biodiversity conservation, help to ensure that we preserve the rich tapestry of life on our planet.

Moreover, sustainable development helps to promote economic growth that is compatible with environmental protection. Many businesses prioritize profit over sustainability, leading to the depletion of natural resources and damage to the environment. However, sustainable development recognizes that economic growth and environmental protection are not mutually exclusive (United Nations, 2015). Long-term economic growth can only be achieved through sustainable practices that ensure the conservation of natural resources and protect the environment.

Finally, sustainable development is important in protecting the environment because it promotes environmental education and awareness. Education and awareness are critical in promoting sustainable development practices among individuals, communities, and businesses. By educating people about the importance of protecting the environment and promoting sustainable practices, we can create a culture of environmental responsibility that will ensure the long-term health and well-being of our planet (Earth Reminder Society, 2020).

In conclusion, the importance of sustainable development in protecting the environment cannot be overstated. Sustainable development practices help to ensure the conservation of natural resources, promote the use of renewable energy sources, protect biodiversity, promote economic growth compatible with environmental protection, and promote environmental education and awareness. By adopting sustainable development practices, we can ensure a healthy and prosperous future for ourselves and for future generations.

Climate Change and Its Impact on the Environment and Sustainable Development

Climate change, also known as global warming, is one of the most pressing environmental challenges that the world is facing today. Its impact on the environment and sustainable development is significant and far-reaching, and addressing this issue requires a concerted effort from all stakeholders.

The Intergovernmental Panel on Climate Change (IPCC) states that the Earth's temperature has increased by 1.1°C above pre-industrial levels, and human activities such as burning fossil fuels and deforestation are the primary drivers of this change (IPCC, 2018). The IPCC also highlights that climate change can lead to more frequent and intense weather events, rising sea levels, and changes in ecosystems, among other impacts.

One of the most significant impacts of climate change on the environment is the melting of polar ice caps and glaciers. This is causing sea levels to rise, which poses a significant threat to coastal communities and ecosystems. According to the IPCC (2018), sea levels are projected to rise by up to 1.1 meters by the end of the century if current trends continue. This could result in the displacement of millions of people, as well as significant damage to infrastructure and ecosystems.

Climate change is also leading to more frequent and intense weather events such as hurricanes, droughts, and heatwaves. These extreme weather events can cause widespread damage to infrastructure, crops, and ecosystems, leading to economic and social disruption. The IPCC (2018) predicts that extreme weather events will become more frequent and severe if greenhouse gas emissions are not reduced.

The impact of climate change on sustainable development is significant. Sustainable development seeks to balance economic growth with social and environmental considerations, but climate change poses a threat to all three pillars of sustainable development. Climate change can lead to economic disruption, as extreme weather events and rising sea levels damage infrastructure and disrupt supply chains. It can also undermine social development, as people are forced to migrate due to rising sea levels or droughts, and access to food and water becomes more limited.

In addition to the impact on sustainable development, climate change also has implications for the achievement of the Sustainable Development Goals (SDGs). The SDGs are a set of 17 goals established by the United Nations to promote sustainable development and address global challenges. Climate action is a key component of many of these goals, including Goal 13 (Climate Action) and Goal 14 (Life Below Water).

Addressing the impact of climate change on the environment and sustainable development requires a concerted effort from all stakeholders, including governments, businesses, and individuals. One of the most important actions that can be taken is to reduce greenhouse gas emissions. This can be achieved through a range of measures, including the promotion of renewable energy sources, the implementation of energy efficiency measures, and the adoption of low-carbon transportation options. In addition to reducing greenhouse gas emissions, there is a need to build resilience to the impacts of climate change. This includes measures such as improving infrastructure to withstand extreme weather events, protecting critical ecosystems such as coral reefs and mangroves, and developing new technologies to help communities adapt to changing conditions.

In conclusion, climate change poses a significant threat to the environment and sustainable development. The impacts of climate change are widespread and far-reaching, and urgent action is needed to address this issue. By reducing greenhouse gas emissions and building resilience to the impacts of climate change, we can work towards a more sustainable future for all.

Renewable Energy Sources and their Role in Sustainable Development

Renewable energy sources have been increasingly recognized as essential components of sustainable development. They offer the potential to reduce greenhouse gas emissions and promote sustainable energy production, and thus have become an important area of research and development for governments, businesses, and individuals. This essay explores the role of renewable energy sources in sustainable development and the benefits they offer over traditional fossil fuel-based energy sources, with a focus on the use of citations to support key arguments.

The Intergovernmental Panel on Climate Change (IPCC) has identified renewable energy as a critical component of climate change mitigation efforts. According to the IPCC (2018), renewable energy sources have the potential to reduce greenhouse gas emissions and improve energy security while promoting sustainable development. Renewable energy sources have been shown to reduce air pollution, improve public health, and create new job opportunities in the energy sector (IPCC, 2018).

One of the primary benefits of renewable energy sources is their abundance and wide distribution. Unlike fossil fuels, which are concentrated in specific regions, renewable energy sources such as solar and wind are available across the globe. This makes it possible to generate electricity locally, reducing the need for long-distance transmission and distribution infrastructure and improving energy security (World Bank Group, 2017).

Renewable energy sources also offer significant cost savings over the long term. While the upfront capital costs of installing renewable energy systems can be high, the operational costs are typically lower than those of fossil fuel-based systems. This is because renewable energy sources do not require fuel, and their maintenance costs are lower than those of traditional power plants. As a result, renewable energy sources can help to reduce energy costs for consumers and businesses over time (International Renewable Energy Agency, 2020).

Another benefit of renewable energy sources is that they can improve energy access for communities that are off the grid or have unreliable access to electricity. In many developing countries, renewable energy sources such as solar and wind can provide a reliable source of electricity to rural communities that are not connected to the grid. This can improve access to healthcare, education, and other basic services, promoting sustainable development (International Renewable Energy Agency, 2020).

In addition to their benefits for sustainable development, renewable energy sources also have a crucial role to play in addressing climate change. The International Energy Agency (IEA) has highlighted that the transition to renewable energy sources is essential for achieving the Paris Agreement's goal of limiting global warming to 1.5°C (IEA, 2020). Renewable energy sources can help to reduce greenhouse gas emissions from the power sector, which is responsible for a significant proportion of global emissions.

Despite the many benefits of renewable energy sources, there are also challenges to their widespread adoption. One of the most significant challenges is the intermittency of renewable energy sources such as solar and wind. These sources of energy are dependent on weather conditions and are not always available when they are needed. To address this challenge, it is necessary to develop energy storage technologies that can store excess energy during periods of high production and release it during times of low production (International Renewable Energy Agency, 2020).

In conclusion, renewable energy sources have a crucial role to play in sustainable development and addressing climate change. They offer significant benefits over traditional fossil fuel-based energy sources, including cost savings, improved energy access, and reduced greenhouse gas emissions. By addressing the challenges associated with their adoption, such as intermittency and the need for energy storage technologies, we can work towards a more sustainable energy future for all.

The Role of Government Policies in Promoting Sustainable Development

Sustainable development has become an increasingly critical issue for governments around the world, given the pressing need to address environmental degradation, climate change, and social inequality. Government policies play a crucial role in promoting sustainable development by setting targets, providing incentives, and implementing regulations to encourage sustainable practices.

Government policies can promote sustainable development by creating a supportive framework that encourages sustainable practices in all sectors of the economy. According to the United Nations (2020), government policies can provide a clear direction for sustainable development and help to align actions by different stakeholders. Governments can promote sustainable development through a range of policy instruments, including fiscal policies, regulatory measures, and voluntary agreements (United Nations, 2020).

One of the primary ways that government policies can promote sustainable development is by providing incentives for businesses and individuals to adopt sustainable practices. For example, governments can provide tax credits or subsidies for the use of renewable energy sources or for the implementation of energy-efficient technologies (Ferreira et al., 2019). Such incentives can help to overcome the initial cost barriers associated with sustainable practices and encourage the widespread adoption of sustainable practices (Ferreira et al., 2019).

Government policies can also play a vital role in regulating industries to reduce their environmental impact. For instance, governments can implement regulations that mandate the use of cleaner production technologies or that limit emissions of pollutants (United Nations, 2020). Such regulations can help to promote sustainable practices and reduce the negative impact of industries on the environment (United Nations, 2020). Furthermore, governments can promote sustainable development through international cooperation and collaboration. Global agreements such as the Paris Agreement on climate change provide a framework for coordinated action among countries to reduce greenhouse gas emissions and promote sustainable practices (United Nations, 2020). Governments can use such agreements to establish common targets and goals for sustainable development, which can then be translated into national policies and actions.

In addition to these measures, governments can also promote sustainable development through public awareness campaigns and education programs. By educating the public about the importance of sustainable practices, governments can encourage individuals to adopt more sustainable behaviours and choices (United Nations, 2020).

In conclusion, government policies play a critical role in promoting sustainable development by providing a supportive framework that encourages sustainable practices. Through incentives, regulations, international cooperation, and public education, governments can help to create a sustainable future for all. As we face mounting environmental and social challenges, the importance of government policies in promoting sustainable development is becoming increasingly apparent.

Sustainable Cities : Designing Urban Spaces for the Environment and the Future

As more people move to cities, urban areas are facing increasing environmental and social challenges. However, cities can also be a force for positive change, providing opportunities for sustainable development and innovative solutions to environmental problems.

Sustainable cities are designed to promote economic, social, and environmental sustainability. Urban areas account for 70% of global greenhouse gas emissions, and cities are facing increasing pressure to address environmental issues such as air pollution, waste management, and energy consumption (United Nations, 2018). Sustainable cities are designed to mitigate these impacts by promoting sustainable practices such as renewable energy, green infrastructure, and public transport (United Nations, 2018).

One of the key features of sustainable cities is the use of green spaces and green infrastructure to promote biodiversity and mitigate the urban heat island effect. Research has shown that green spaces such as parks, gardens, and urban forests can improve air quality, reduce the impact of urban heat islands, and provide recreational opportunities for residents (Chiesura & De Groot, 2003). Another way in which cities can be designed for sustainability is through the use of public transport. Sustainable transport systems such as buses, light rail, and cycling infrastructure can help to reduce carbon emissions, improve air quality, and promote social inclusion (World Bank, 2018). Governments can also incentivize the use of sustainable transport by implementing policies such as congestion charging or low-emission zones (World Bank, 2018).

Sustainable cities can also promote energy efficiency through the use of renewable energy sources such as solar, wind, and hydro power. These technologies can help to reduce reliance on fossil fuels and promote energy security (United Nations, 2018). Additionally, energy-efficient buildings can reduce energy consumption and contribute to a more sustainable urban environment (United Nations, 2018).

Urban agriculture is another way in which cities can promote sustainability. By using vacant lots or rooftops to grow food, cities can reduce their carbon footprint, improve food security, and promote community engagement (Krasny et al., 2010).

Furthermore, sustainable cities can promote social sustainability by prioritising inclusivity and community engagement. Urban design that prioritises walkability, public spaces, and mixed-use development can help to promote social interaction and reduce social isolation (World Health Organization, 2016).

In conclusion, sustainable cities are designed to promote economic, social, and environmental sustainability, and provide a framework for positive change in urban areas. Through the use of green spaces, sustainable transport, renewable energy, urban agriculture, and community engagement, cities can mitigate environmental impacts and promote social inclusion. As the world becomes increasingly urbanised, sustainable cities will play a critical role in ensuring a sustainable future for all.

Conclusion

Sustainable development is essential for protecting the environment, mitigating climate change, and ensuring a sustainable future for all. Renewable energy sources such as solar, wind, and hydro power have a critical role to play in reducing carbon emissions and promoting sustainable development. Government policies are also crucial in promoting sustainability, whether through regulations on emissions, incentives for sustainable practices, or funding for research and development.

In addition, designing sustainable cities is becoming increasingly important as urbanisation continues to grow. Sustainable cities are designed to promote economic, social, and environmental sustainability through green spaces, sustainable transport, renewable energy, urban agriculture, and community engagement. By prioritising sustainability in urban planning and development, cities can mitigate environmental impacts and promote social inclusion.

It is clear that sustainable development is an ongoing process that requires the collaboration of individuals, businesses, governments, and organisations at all levels. By working together to promote sustainable practices and policies, we can ensure a more sustainable future for ourselves and for future generations. It is not just a theoretical concept or a buzzword, but a crucial necessity for the survival of our planet. With the growing population and increasing demands for resources, it has become imperative to find ways to meet these needs without degrading the environment or compromising the ability of future generations to meet their own needs.

One of the main challenges we face in achieving sustainable development is climate change. The impacts of climate change are already being felt around the world, with rising sea levels, extreme weather events, and increasing temperatures. It is important for us to recognize the role that human activities have played in contributing to climate change and to take action to reduce our carbon footprint through sustainable practices.

Renewable energy sources such as solar, wind, and hydro power have the potential to play a significant role in reducing carbon emissions and promoting sustainable development. These sources of energy are cleaner, more efficient, and more sustainable than traditional fossil fuels, and they can help to reduce our dependence on non-renewable resources. However, transitioning to renewable energy sources is not enough on its own. We also need to implement government policies that promote sustainability, such as regulations on emissions and incentives for sustainable practices. The private sector can also play a significant role in promoting sustainability through sustainable business practices and responsible investment.

Sustainable cities are also becoming increasingly important as urbanisation continues to grow. By designing urban spaces that prioritise sustainability, we can mitigate the negative environmental impacts of urbanisation while promoting economic growth and social inclusion. Sustainable cities incorporate green spaces, sustainable transport, renewable energy, and community engagement to create liveable and resilient communities.

In conclusion, sustainable development is an ongoing process that requires the collaboration of individuals, businesses, governments, and organisations at all levels. By working together to promote sustainable practices and policies, we can ensure a more sustainable future for ourselves and for future generations. We must recognize that sustainable development is not an option, but a necessity for the survival of our planet, and we must act accordingly.

References

Chiesura, A., & De Groot, R. S. (2003). Critical natural capital: A socio-cultural perspective. Ecological Economics, 44(2-3), 219-231.

Earth Reminder Society (2020). Importance of Environmental Education in Our Lives.

Elizabeth Weise. (2023). Article in USA Today. What is green energy? How solar power and wind help fight climate change.

Ferreira, L., Gama, J., & Coelho, A (2019). Renewable energy policies and its impact on economic growth and CO2 emissions.

Intergovernmental Panel on Climate Change (2018). Global warming of 1.5°C.

International Energy Agency (2020). Global energy review 2020.

International Renewable Energy Agency (2020). Renewable power generation costs in 2019.

Krasny, M. E., Tidball, K. G., & Sriskandarajah, N. (2010). Urban agriculture, social capital, and food security in the Bronx. Cities and the Environment, 3(1), 8-26.

United Nations (2015). The 2023 Agenda for Sustainable Development.

United Nations. (2018). Sustainable Cities and Communities.

United Nations Environment Programme (2018). Global Environment Outlook 2019: Healthy Planet, Healthy People.

United Nations (2020). Sustainable development goals.

World Health Organization. (2016). Urban green spaces and health: a review of evidence.

World Bank (2017). Inclusive Green Growth: The Pathway to Sustainable Development.

World Bank Group (2017). Renewable energy.

World Health Organization (2018). Environmental health.

World Bank. (2018). Sustainable Urban Development.

Associate Professor, School of Law
Christ (Deemed to be University) – Lavasa campus
Lavasa , Pune , Maharashtra, India
email : saludsouza@yahoo.com

10. Review on Green Synthesis of Silver Nanoparticles and Its Anti-Microbial Potential : An Eco-Friendly Approach

Dr. S. Ramadevi[1*],
Dr. S. Sivaranjani[1*],
Radha Vijayaraj[2],
N.Srikumaran[2]
Swarnakala[3]
Kurinjinathan Panneerselvam[4]

Abstract

Nanotechnology is an emerging and fast-growing research field that serves a significant role in human health, animals and the environment. Nanoparticles (NPs) have been one of the outstanding discoveries of nanotechnology to overcome the modern world's day-to-day problems. These nanoparticles play a crucial role in the development of diagnostic and therapeutic drugs. Among the numerous metallic and non-metallic nanoparticles, silver nanoparticles (AgNPs) have been thoroughly explored for their applicability and flexibility. The physical and chemical synthesis of AgNPs has inspired various biophysical and chemical applications due to the quality of the formulation. This review provides a brief overview of the future perspective of the green synthesis of AgNPs through the use of bioreducing agents such as plants, bacteria, fungi. This review also includes a collective knowledge of the synthesis sequences, the assessment of green AgNPs, the spectrum of prepared AgNPs and their application behaviour.

Keywords : Nanoparticle, Green synthesis, Silver, Pharmacology, bioreducing agents

Introduction

In metal, silver is a gentle, white, metallic element that has a high thermal and electrical conductivity. Because of its medical and therapeutic advantages, these silver elements were used in history before recognizing that microorganisms are mostly responsible for diseases. In the past decade, such silver metal was used as a base ingredient in lotions, ointments, and so on in several shapes such as coins, containers, remedies, coatings, wound dressings, and crystals. It is also used as a primary preventive agent for contagious diseases and surgical emergencies. These abilities are bound to change the physicochemical properties of the element as it approaches the nano size.

Nanoparticles have a lot of importance due to their properties. Such nanoparticles have numerous applications in a variety of fields, including electronic devices, beauty products, polymers, manufacturing process and biomedicine. In nanomaterial's, AgNPs have been extensively used in biomedical fields owing to their active therapeutic ability, such as antibacterial, antifungal, larvicide, anti-inflammatory, antiparasitic and other therapeutic potential [1]. These abilities may vary depending on the base of the bioreducing agents used to synthesis.

In general, current physical and chemical techniques employed appear to be very costly and risky [2]. Chemical approaches are the most effective, but toxic by-products may be produced due to the use of chemicals during synthesis. Different forms of NPs like Ag, Au, Pt and Pd have also been formulated in the recent past year by chemical, physical and biological processes. The biological method is also known as the green synthesis approaches. Curiously, green synthesis of NPs exhibit high yield, solubility and high stability [2] and has a lot of potential in various aspects. This green synthesis approach tends to be quick, fast, non-toxic, and efficient. Also, the AgNPs can provide excellently-defined structure and morphology under optimum conditions for translational analysis [3]. Recently, AgNPs have shown immense potential in their therapeutic application of cancer as an anticancer agent and are also used in screening and diagnostics. Therefore, quick and efficient experimental protocols for the synthesis of AgNPs need to be developed, as their wide-ranging applications can be highly advantageous to humans. This review provides a brief description of the phytomediated synthesis of AgNPs, their collective knowledge of the synthesis sequences, the assessment of green AgNPs, the spectrum of prepared AgNPs and their application behaviour.

Types of synthesis of nanomaterials

The synthesis of nanomaterials involves a top-down and bottom-up approach focused on chemical, physical and biological strategies [4]. Figure 1. shows the synthesis methods of nanomaterials.

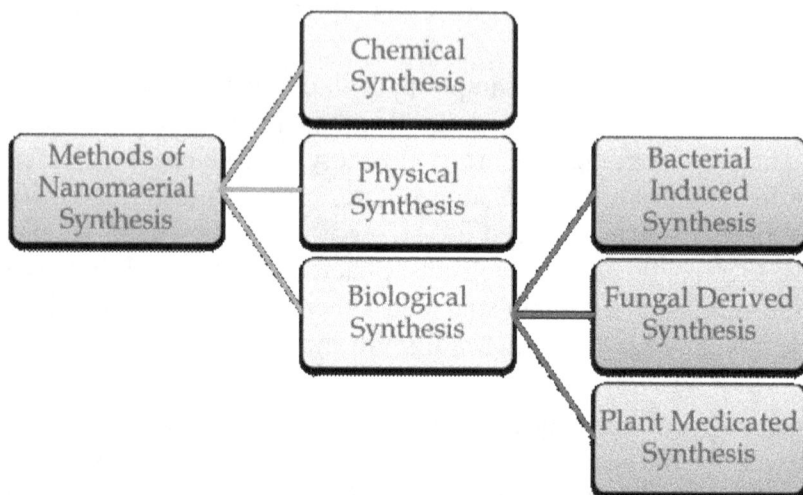

Fig-1: Synthesis methods of Nanomaterials

Chemical Synthesis of AgNPs

The most popular approach to the synthesis of AgNPs is a chemical reaction by organic and inorganic reducing agents. Different reducing agents, such as sodium citrate, ascorbate, sodium borohydride ($NaBH_4$), elemental hydrogen, polyol process, Tollens solvents, N, N-dimethylformamide (DMF) and poly (ethylene glycol)-block copolymers are generally used to reduce silver ions (Ag^+) in aqueous or non-aqueous solutions. Such reducing agents reducing Ag^+ ions and lead to the formation of metal-based silver (Ag0) caused by aggregation into oligomeric fragments. These oligomeric fragments eventually contribute to the formation of metallic, colloidal silver particles [5]. It is necessary to use protective substances to stabilise scattering NPs during the preparation of metal nanoparticles and protect the NPs that could be ingested or bonded to nanoparticle surfaces and preventing aggregation [6]. The ammonia gas and silver nitrate solution react with each other and they form the AgNPs as a result in short duration. The colloidal diffusion of AgNPs is commonly obtained by chemical reduction approaches [6]. The functional solvents such as Thiols, Amines, Acids, and Alcohols are actively involved with particle surface interaction and govern the growth of the particles and protect them from precipitation, aggregation, or deterioration of their surface properties. Polymeric compounds such as poly (vinyl alcohol), poly (vinyl pyrrolidone), poly (Ethylene glycol), poly (Methacrylic acid) and polymethyl methacrylate are documented to be efficient protective agents for stabilising NPs.

Previously, Oliveira and their colleagues formulated dodecanethiol covered silver NPs according to the methodology of Brust et al., [7]. In this study, the A3 compound transformed from the aqueous to organic phase based on the phase transformation process of the two-phase liquid-liquid process and the reduction of sodium borohydride in the presence of dodecanethiol act as a stabilising agent, preventing the aggregation and lead to binding with NP surfaces. They also claimed that small differences in artificial variables lead to dramatic changes in nanoparticle shape, average diameter, size distribution distance, stability and self-assembly patterns.

Kim and his colleagues [8] described the formation of the calculated size and high monodispersity-shaped AgNPs by using the polyol technique and the optimized additive injection method. The injection rate and reaction temperature were important factors in the precursor injection process for generating standardised AgNPs with a reduced scale. AgNPs may be prepared at room temperature by conveniently combining the resulting metal ions with reducing and stabilising agents such as polyoxometalates. These Polyoxometalates are hydrophilic and can undergo redox multielectron reactions step by step, without disrupting their nature.

Baruwati et al.,[9] prepared AgNPs by utilizing 1-butyl-3-methylimidazolium tetrafluoroborate through conventional electrochemical reduction method of glassy carbon electrode. Silver colloids were also produced by reacting silver oxalate with polyvinyl pyrrolidone (PVP) under microwave radiation and particle shape regulated by modifying some variables. Various ranges of sizes, such as 5-10 nm, have been developed using microwave irradiation in 30-60 sec by the incorporation of the antioxidant glutathione.

Guzman *et al.,* [10] developed AgNPs (9–30 nm) due to hydrazine hydrate reactions. In this process, sodium citrate performs as a reduction substance and sodium dodecyl sulphate as a stabilising substance. Microwave radiation has been used for the reduction of silver ions by carboxymethyl cellulose sodium (CMS) hydrolyzate. The concentration of CMS has a low effect on the dissemination of the level because the effectiveness of the concentration of $AgNO_3$ is apparent. Prepared AgNPs exhibited the strongest antimicrobial potential at very low doses around 6.74 µg / mL [10]. Anisotropic AgNPs are directly formed by the decomposition of microwave-assisted silver oxalate in a glycol solution utilizing polyvinyl pyrrolidone (PVP) as a capping agent [10].

In the electrochemical technique, Sodium Dodecyl Benzene Sulfonate (SDBS) usage will induce the production of AgNPs [11]. The combination of silver nitrate and polyvinyl pyrrolidone (PVP) developed AgNPs with a pulsed sonoelectrochemical methodology. The occurrence of dodecanethiol produced size-dependent silver nanoclusters by reducing the sodium borohydride [12].

Physical Synthesis of Silver Nanoparticles

In the physical synthesis process, metal NPs are mainly produced by vaporisation condensation which can be performed at ambient temperature using a tube furnace. The source material inside the tube, which is condensed in the furnace, is vaporized into the gas phase. Previously several materials have been produced using the evaporation/compression technique, such as Ag, Au, PbS and fullerenes [13]. There are several disadvantages in producing AgNPs using a tube furnace, it consumes a huge amount of energy when growing the ambient temperature from around the raw material, occupies a wide room and requiring more time to reach thermal stabilization. A standard tube furnace requires over a hundred kilowatts of power and a preheating time of so many tens of minutes to achieve a suitable operating temperature. Besides, by the removal of laser a of metallic composite materials insolvent was produced with AgNPs [14]. The absence of chemical substance in the solution is the only benefit of laser resection compared to other traditional approaches for the processing of metallic colloids.

Jung et al., [15] successfully synthesized AgNPs using a tiny ceramic furnace with a local thermal region. The volatilized vapour is chilled at an appropriate rate so the heat differential in the outside of the heater is quite sharp compared to the tube furnace. This will trigger the development of smaller NPs with higher concentration. This methodology can be useful for a variety of purposes, such as the use of nanoparticle generator for long-term toxicity inhalation testing and the standardisation process for nanoparticle measuring equipment.

AgNPs have been developed by using a laser to remove the metallic materials in solution [16]. The properties of certain metallic NPs produced and their ablation efficiency are significantly depending on several parameters, such as the laser wavelength impeding the metallic target, the frequency of laser pulses (in the femto, pico and nanosecond regime), the laser fluence, the ablation time and the effective liquid medium, with or without surfactants [17]. Besides, NPs can be modified in size and structure due to their contact with the laser light that passes through them [18]. The synthesis of laser ablation NPs is also regulated by applying the surfactant. The NPs formation with a high concentration of surfactant is lesser than the synthesis in a low concentration surfactant solution [19]. The absence of chemical reagents in solutions seems to be the only advantage of laser ablation relative to other traditional methods for the production of metal colloids. Therefore, pure colloids can be generated by this process, which will be helpful for further applications [20].

Mechanism of AgNPs Synthesis

AgNP production by natural objects is attributable to the existence of a huge amount of organic compounds such as proteins, carbohydrates, lipids, gum, phenols, alkaloids, flavonoids, terpenoids, enzymes & coenzymes etc. that can donate an electron to Ag+ ions resulting in the reduction to Ag0. The usage of active components and material extracts are liable for the significant reduction of Ag+ ion ranges. Electrons should be derived from the dehydrogenation of acids (ascorbic acid) and alcohols (catechol) in hydrophytes, keto-enol transformations (cyperaquinone, dietchequinone, remirin) in mesophytes, or all pathways in xerophyte plants for the nano transformation of AgNPs [21]. Related elimination process may be produced by microbial cellular and extracellular oxidoreductase enzymes. Figure 2 shows a graphical diagram showing the reduction, agglomeration and stabilisation of the silver ion to form a nano-sized particle.

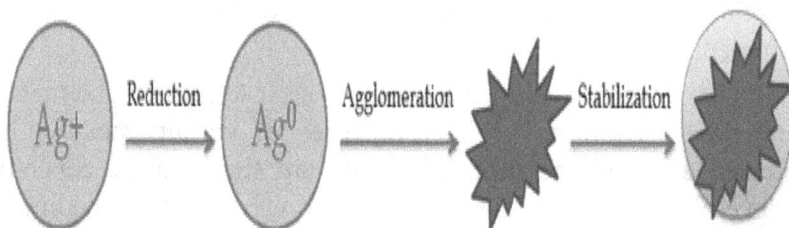

Figure 2. Mechanisms of Synthesis of Silver Nanoparticle Green Synthesis of AgNPs

During the last decade, the development of NPs using living organisms has expanded significant attention due to the various peculiar properties of NPs, i.e. optical, chemical, photoelectrochemical and electronic characteristics [22]. Although the exact procedure of the biological development of nanoparticles is still not well established, several research scientists have suggested several hypotheses.

The green synthesis of the metal NPs is based on the combination of material science and biology. Metallic NPs are a prominent and frequently deliberated group of materials that exhibit great diversity and various diverse applications. Biological substances such as living bacteria, fungi, plant/extracts are used to synthesis the NPs. This method has provided benefits over more conventional methods of synthesizing NPs because they are eco-friendly, can take place at or below room temperature, and require slight energy intervention or input.

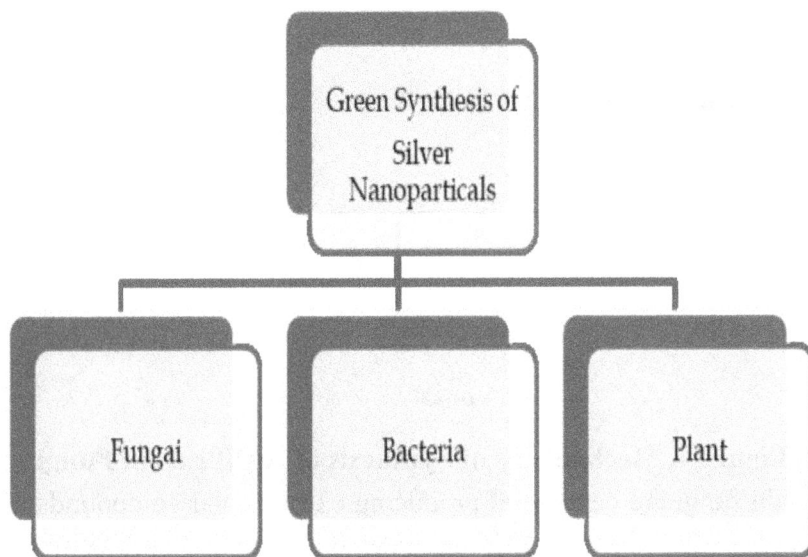

Figure 3. Type of organisms used to green synthesis of AgNPs

Various species which are usually grown from the organic medium are involved in this process. Several research activities proved that these sustainable communities seem to be quickly processed to produce the NPs[22]. There are some inorganic particles such as silica and calcium carbonate or chalks, which have been synthesised by various species for a long time. Some other microorganisms can reduce metal ions to metal. Some microbes may generate magnetic material by reducing iron compounds and integrating magnetic NPs into their cells bodies which known as magnetosomes. Few bacteria have been produced the NPs by intracellular/ extracellular or both. It is believed that bacteria use nitrate anion (NO_3) as a source of nitrogen and leave metallic silver. Experimentally the bacteria, fungi and flowering plants are so far used in the synthesis of NPs. The type of biomaterials used for the development of NPs is expressed in Figure 3.

Green Synthesis of Silver Nanoparticle from Fungi and its bioactivity

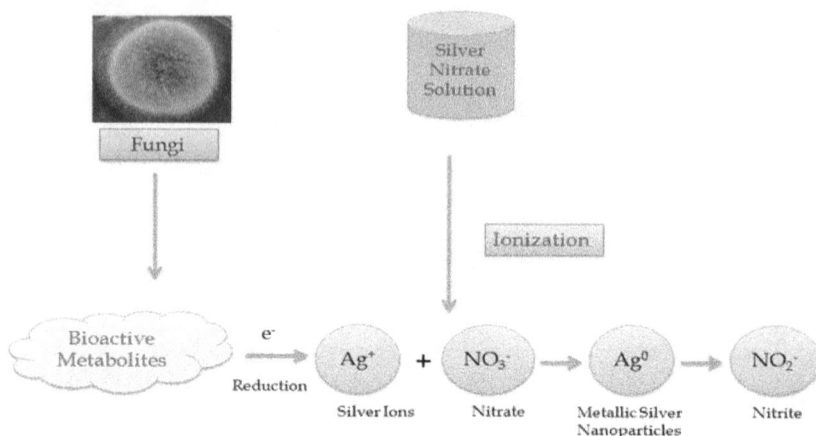

Figure 4. Mechanisms of Synthesis of AgNPs from Fungi

Certain fungi are capable of producing extracellular compounds and enzymes while they are exposed to such environmental factors such as various temperature, pressure, toxic elements such as metallic ions), and predators [23]. These extracellular substances play a useful role in the growth of the particular fungus and reduce nano-sized molecules to the silver ions in the region. The fungus mycelium is subjected to a metal salt solution for the biosynthesis of metal NPs. This solution induces osmotic stress conditions for the fungus which allows it to produce its survival enzymes and metabolites.

Initially, *Aspergillus flavus* and *A. fumigatus* were used to investigate the biosynthesis of AgNPs [24, 25]. *A. flavus* in water is known to be extremely stable during several investigations [26]. The morphology of the extracellularly synthesized nanoparticles from *Aspergillus* sp., was documented to be largely spherical with few triangular shapes with size 5-25 nm, some exceptions or few improvements to the bio-based synthesis of AgNPs are possible [27]. Same as *Aspergillus* sp, *Cladosporium* sp. has also been investigated for extracellular biosynthesis of AgNPs [28]. The chemical substances present in the strains of *C. cladosporioides* were considered to be responsible for the strength and shape of the AgNPs. The reduction of silver ions to AgNPs was also successfully demonstrated by many *Penicillium* sp. [29, 30]. *Penicillium fellutanum* has gained more interest in the *Penicillium* genus since it has been documented that it can also reduce silver ions to AgNPs in low light intensity conditions [31].

Few investigators, such as [32, 33, 34, 35, 36, 37] demonstrated significant interest in the potential of *Fusarium oxysporum* to produce AgNPs to come up with new methodologies to process them in an environmentally friendly and cost-effective manner. Kumar et al., [34] provided additional insights into the bioreduction of silver ions by the bioreduction of *Fusarium oxysporum* and established the enzymatic mechanism and the subsequent stabilisation of the AgNPs. The morphology and the impact of pH on the capping proteins of the biosynthesized NPs have been demonstrated. Macdonald *et al.*, [36] demonstrated a keen interest and studied the relationship of proteins with silver NPs, including cytochrome c (Cc), to clarify them.

Ahmad *et al.*, [37] inspected the isolate that extracellularly produces 5-50 nm of AgNPs and reported the excellent durability of these AgNPs because of the proteins present in the isolate. Korbekandi et al [38] has been developed the AgNPs using *Fusarium oxysporum*. The shape is almost spherical with a size range around 25 -50 nm. The nature of the AgNPs was studied by Scanning Electron Microscope (SEM). *Coriolus Versicolor* species also reduced the solution of silver nitrate and formed AgNPs of monodisperse spherical forms [39]. The unique characteristics of the produced AgNPs were examined via UV-visible absorption spectrophotometry, Transmission Electron Microscope (TEM), Atomic Force Microscopy (AFM) and Fourier Transform Infrared Spectroscopy (FT-IR). In this investigation, Proteins have been identified as the key cause of stabilization and it has been proposed that they also act as reducing agents. The effect on nanoparticles reaction time and characteristics of factors such as temperature and pH was examined by Sanghi *et al.,* [39]

Green Synthesis of AgNPs from Bacteria and its Bioactivity

Previously few bacterial species have been used for the biosynthesis of AgNPs from different habitats and conditions. In the bacterial strain, *Bacillus* species have developed extremely stable AgNPs with a consistent size. Especially, highly stable AgNPs with an average size of 50 nm silver ions were shown by *B. licheniformis* [40,]

[41]. The rate of biosynthesizing AgNPs was induced by microwave irradiation with continuous heat treatment using *B. subtilis* strains [42]. In this process, the biosynthesized AgNPs were reported as monodispersed, varying between 5 to 20 nm in size. *Lactobacillus* strains were also used to suppress Ag ions and to form spherical AgNps with average size distribution between 25 and 50 nm. The enzymatic process was due to the power of the biosynthesized AgNPs [43]. Previously, several researchers suggested that *Pseudomonas stutzeri* AG259 was capable of synthesizing intracellular AgNPs of various formulation [43], varying in size between 35 to 46 nm [44] or up to 200 nm for high concentrations of Ag ion [45] with differing geometric structures [43]. Mokhtari *et al.,* [46] investigated the influence of light irradiation on the synthesis of 1-6 nm size ranged AgNps using *K. pneumonia* strains and also suggested the bioreduction process of Diamine silver using *Aeromonas* sp. SH10 and *Corynebacterium* sp. SH09 to biosynthesize metallic silver NPs. The rapid bioreduction capabilities of *Enterobacter cloacae, E. coli,* and *K. pneumonia* strain supernatants in reducing Ag ions to metal AgNPs within several minutes have been effectively verified by Shahverdi *et al.,*[47]. The capacity of *C. Vulgaris* and *Oscillatoria willei* to synthesize silver NPs was also listed by Iravani *et al.,* [48]. In their research, *C. vulgaris* developed AgNPs with a mean length of 44 nm and a diameter of 16-24 nm in a rod-like structure, while *O. willei* biosynthesized AgNPs with a size of 100-200 nm.

Green Synthesis of Silver Nanoparticle from Plants and its Bioactivity

Several groups of investigators were previously proven using different plants to develop AgNPs. Plants such as *Brassica juncea* (Indian mustard), *Medicago sativa* (Alfa alfa) and *Helianthus annuus* (Sunflower) are being used for the biosynthesis of various NPs like (silver, nickel, cobalt, zinc and copper. These plants are capable of absorbing high concentrations of metals. Therefore these plants are recognized as hyper-accumulators. From the plant species, Brassica juncea plant materials exhibit a higher potential to accumulate metal and integrate the metals as NPs [49]. Several researchers have recently carried out more research on the plant-assisted reduction of metal NPs and the respective function of phytochemicals. These phytochemicals are playing a major role in the reduction of heavy metals. Water-soluble phytochemicals are responsible for immediate reductions.

Plant species *Bryophyllum* sp. (Xerophytes), *Cyprus* sp. (Mesophytes) and *Hydrilla* sp. (Hydrophytes) have also been investigated for AgNPs biosynthesis. The synthesized NPs range was 2-5 nm using xerophytes, mesophytes and hydrophytes [50]. Such xerophytes were found to possess emodin, an anthraquinone that could undertake redial tautomerization leading to the development of AgNPs. Three different types of benzoquinone mesophyte, such as cyperoquinone, dietchequinone and remirin, have been studied. It was suggested that the stimulation of quinones resulting in a reduction in particle size will result in mild warming, accompanied by subsequent incubation. Hydrophytes studied together with other phytochemicals, catechol and protocatechualdehyde. It has been documented that catechol converted into protocatechualdehyde under alkaline conditions and terminated with protocatechuic acid. In the process of synthesis of NPs, the hydrogen was released and it was suggested to play a critical role. Recently, a few gold NPs have been synthesized by using *Magnolia kobus* and *Diopyros kaki* leaf extracts. Several experiments have been carried out to estimate the influence of temperature on the production of NPs. Polydisperse particles were obtained at a lower temperature with a size range of 5-300 nm, while a higher temperature facilitated the synthesis of small spherical particles [51].

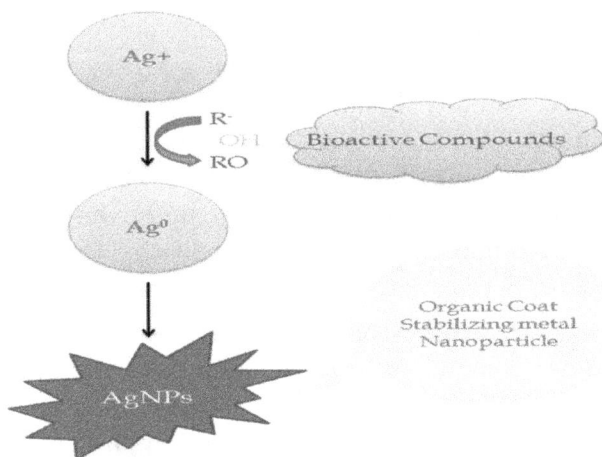

Figure 5. Express the process of the silver nanoparticles

Silver nitrate has been reduced with the use of grape extract (*Vitis vinifera*), resulting in approximately spherical shape particles with an average size of 18 to 20 nm. Grape extracts can decrease silver nitrate and have formed spherical forms varying in size from 18 to 20 nm. AgNPs produced have been investigated for antimicrobial properties against *Bacillus subtilis* and *Escherichia coli*. In this test the promising inhibition rate with the growth of bacteria and fungi [52].

Gavhane *et al.,* [53] have demonstrated the ability of the Neem (*Azadirachta indica*) leaf extract and Triphala extract to synthesize AgNPs. In his analysis, spherical and polydispersed AgNPs with a mean size of 43 nm were observed at concentrations of 3.6 pre-1010 particles/mL and 59 nm at concentrations of 5.15 pre-106 particles/mL. These biosynthesis AgNPs tested for antimicrobial capacity and the test AgNPs showed an inhibition zone of 15, 14, 13, 11 and 16, 14, 13, 10 by *C. albicans*, *K. pnuemoniae*, *S. typhi* and *E. coli* MDR, respectively [53]. These nanoparticles were exhibited an inhibition zone of 1 mm against *Salmonella typhi* and *Klebsiella pneumonia* as opposed to those determined by Gavhane *et al.,* [53]. The free radical properties of the prepared AgNPs were analyzed by 1, 1-Diphenyl-2-picrylhydrazyl (DPPH) and hydrogen peroxide assays.

To synthesize the nanoparticles, Lalitha *et al.,* [54] used the aqueous leaves extract of Neem (*Azhadirachta indica)*. Produced NPs size was measured by using UV-vis spectroscopy, Size Analyser, and FT-IR analysis. Similarly, Sharma *et al.,* [55] carried a research work on Neem extracts. In this investigation, the synthesised AgNPs was tested for anti-microbial activities. In their study, two different concentration of chloroform solvent (50 μg/ml and 100 μg/mL) expressed (10 mm and 13 mm) and (12 mm and 15 mm) zones of inhibition against *S. aureus* and *E. coli*.

Sathyavathi *et al.,* [56] synthesized NPs from *Coriandrum sativum* leaf extract by using 1 mM of $AgNO_3$ and studied the non-linear optical properties by the z-scan method with 6 ns pulse duration at 532 nm. The produced AgNPs were characterized by using UV-visible, XRD, FT-IR and TEM and they have often observed the spherical in nature, size ranging from 8 nm to 75 nm with an average size of 26 nm.

Phanjom *et al.,* [57] described that when 60 mL of *Elaeagnus latifolia* leaves extracts are allowed to react at room temperature with 10 ml of 1 mM aqueous silver nitrate solution, a colour change was observed from the pale-yellow colour into a yellowish-brown coloured solution. This change of colour was shown by the development of AgNPs and by the UV-vis absorption spectroscopy and the X-ray diffractometer (XRD). TEM was used to analyze the spherical shape and size 30 nm to 50 nm of the AgNPs developed.

Eco-friendly production of AgNPs developed by the reduction of aqueous silver nitrate with ascorbic acid and gelatin used as a stabiliser. The produced AgNPs have shown a mean size of 20 nm. The morphology and characterization were done by the XRD, TEM, and EDX. Using cyclic voltammetry, electroactivity and electrocatalytic properties of these NPs and AgNPs-CPE were calculated, introducing outstanding electrocatalytic potential against H_2O_2, reflecting the suitability of these NPs as an efficient H_2O reduction catalyst. The results of the study were very promising despite increased sensitivity and excellent in terms of AgNPs-CPE CPE reproducibility and working accuracy [58].

Firdhouse *et al.,* [59] examined the alteration in the time phase needed for the development of AgNPs by changing the quantity of the 3 mM silver nitrate formulation applied to 1 mL of the *Portulaca oleracea* leaf extracts under three various test conditions, i.e. room temperature reaction, elevated temperature reaction and sonication. The colour transition, from yellow to reddish-brown, was observed after 60 min, 50 min, 40 min, 35 min and 30 min for each 1 mL addition of 3 mM silver nitrate to 1 mL leaves extracts of *Portulac aoleracea.* Similarly, the reactions at 75 °C were reported for signs but a limited duration in each event. In each case, the shortest sonic length required is as follows: 27 min, 24 min, 20 min, 20 min and 18 min for 6 mL, 7 mL, 8 mL, 9 mL and 10 mL for 3 mM silver nitrate with 1 mL of an aqueous solution. The characterization of these silver NPs was measured less than 60 nm with UV-visible spectroscopy, XRD, Scherrer's formula and SEM analysis.

Rodriguez-Leon *et al.,* [60] demonstrated the successful oxidation of silver ions to metal AgNPs as a result of the ratio of silver ions to polyphenols obtained, such as catechins and stilbens, present in the *R. hymenosepalus* extract. The UV visible spectroscopy, TEM and rapid transformation of Fourier were used to analysis the reduced AgNPs with face-centred cubic and hexagonal geometry and ranged from 2-40 nm. A rise in the concentration of the reacting silver nitrate solution was observed to result in comparatively larger AgNPs and increased formation of NPs. These results show potential for commercial application of biological processes due to kinetics and simple conditions such as room temperature and single-step processes.

Abdelmonem *et al.,* [61] examined the development of AgNPs by using pomegranate *Punica granatum* L peel extract in alkaline media. In their study, prepared AgNps were showed a mean diameter of 20 nm. UV-visible Power wave microplate reader spectroscopy and TEM verified the formation of Metal NPs. However, without the addition of any surfactants, the prepared NPs showed strong stability for several weeks so this application can be used for large scale production.

Awwad *et al.,* [62] have identified that the rapid synthesis of sphere-shaped AgNPs can be accomplished by the room temperature with carob leaf extract. The rapid syntheses of the AgNPs were achieved within two minutes of the reaction started. The produced AgNPs was indicated by the UV-vis absorbance analysis and colour shift. Scanning electron microscopy, atomic absorption spectroscopy and X-ray diffraction (XRD) carried out the further characterization of the collected NPs. As shown in the FT-IR spectroscopic analysis, the amino acid residue group Carbonyl was assigned to the stabilising and trapping agent properties. The resulting NPs are polydispersed with cubic geometry based on the face and crystalline. The produced NPs showed an average diameter of 18 nm, which was within 5 to 40 nm, as investigated by SEM research. These NPs was expressed promising antimicrobial properties against tested *E. coli.*

Previously curry leaf extract also used to produce the AgNPs and the average sizes of the nanoparticles were measured 10-25 nm. The morphology and characterization were examined by UV visible spectrophotometry, TEM, AFM and XRD analysis. Christensen *et al.,* [63] also carried investigation to analysis the size and shape of the synthesized NPs. In his study, they found that 0.001 M silver nitrate solution reacted with leaf extract and showed a decrease in reaction time 1:20 ratio.

Elizondo *et al.,* [64] carried investigation on various concentrations of *Aloe barbadensis* extracts against silver nitrate (0.001 M) at 60°C and observed spherical and quasi-spherical crystalline with face-centred cubic nanocrystals forms. Kamali *et al.,* [65] identified a novel pH-based procedure to regulate the size and crystallinity of AgNPs using a complexing agent. Tulasi leaf and *Ocimum sanctum* extracts were reacted with the silver ions and form spherical shapes with the size of 40-50 nm. These produced NPs shows strong anti-microbial effects against *S. Calbicans, C. key* and *A. niger, S. saprophyticus, S. Aureus,* *C.* *tropicalis,* *C.* *krusei,* *A. flavus* and *A. fumigates* [66].

Firdhouse *et al.,* [67] have suggested a novel procedure for the preparation of AgNPs for medicinal purposes under different laboratory conditions. In this context, AgNPs was prepared using the silver nitrate solution with ethanol extract of *Pisonia grandis* leaves because the plant material is widely used as traditional medical treatments. In this study, the morphology and characterization of the produced NPS studied by using UV-vis spectrophotometer, XRD, Scherrer's equation and SEM. The average size 56.86 nm, 29.14 nm and 39.62 nm was determined and the range of 20 – 150 nm in all investigational condition. The investigator compared the three conditions with the finding that the more efficient sonication was conducted, although the size obtained from the sonication was significantly larger than that obtained from the elevated temperature; moreover, for the sonication, the uniformity of the shape and the reduction of the reaction time were considerably higher than for any of the other two conditions.

Ahmad and Sharma, [68] recommended the use of *Ananas comosus* extracts for the synthesis of AgNPs by reducing the silver nitrate solution. They indicated that the reduction could be the responsibility of a variety of antioxidants in the extracts and that further research is required. However, the presence of phenol compounds can be the primary feature of the reduction and constancy of silver particles after up to four weeks of incubation. The morphology of the biosynthesized silver NPs of the extract of *Ananas comosus* was observed to be rectangular, with a few exclusions of the oval or elliptical, crystalline, face-centred cubic shape with a mean size of 12 nm.

Kalaiarasi *et al.,* [69] adopted economically and environmentally sustainable methods of synthesising *Rauvolfia tetraphylla* leaf broth with AgNPs and a small evergreen plant species. In their analysis, *R. tetraphylla* leaf extract was used to respond at room temperature with an aqueous silver nitrate solution. The produced NPs were verified by UV-visible spectroscopy, SEM, XRD, EDX and FT-IR. These NPs were highly crystalline silver particles with a size range of 26 – 37 nm and tested antibacterial potential against *S. aureus, E. coli,* *P.* *aeruginous* and *B. subtilis.*

Bhati-Kushwaha *et al.,* [70] examined the rapid synthesis of AgNPs and their potential such as antibacterial and antifungal drugs. In this experiment, they used *Tridax procumbens* plant material such as stem and leaves extracts in the aqueous medium react with silver ions to produced AgNPs. Generated AgNPs have shown positive results in antimicrobial activity against *E. coli, V. cholera, A. niger* and *A. flavus* pathogens. These AgNPs is characterised by UV-visible spectroscopy, SEM, XRD and FT-IR, including spherical shape, size range 13.51-17.24 nm, elemental crystal geometry and the polydiverse nature of the particles.

Loo *et al.,* [71] reported the synthesis of a highly crystalline nature with well-dispersed spherical size AgNPs through the use of *Camellia sinensis* tea leaf extract with silver ions at room temperature. The developed AgNPs had an average diameter of 4 nm and a range of sizes of 2-10 nm. The morphology and characterization were studied by using the X-ray diffractometer, FT-IR and TEM, respectively.

Lu *et al.,* [72] reported that aqueous extract of bamboo leaves (*Phyllostachys genus*) composed of phenolic acids and flavonoids were allowed to react at 65 °C with 3 mM aqueous $AgNO_3$ and produced AgNPs with an almost spherical crystalline nature. The size of these AgNPs was 13±3.5nm, although some particles showed triangular or hexagonal shapes. The prepared AgNPs identified by the UV-vis spectroscopy, EDX, XRD, TEM and Debye-Scherrer equations. The antimicrobial properties were tested using the Disc - diffusion Approach and the Minimum Inhibiting Concentrations (MIC) / Minimum Bactericidal Concentrations (MBC) [73].

Kulkarni *et al.,* [74] studied different proportions of silver nitrate solutions at room temperature with Bryophytes plant extract of water and ethanol. In this study, they produced cuboid and triangular-shaped AgNPs with a variable size range of 20-50 nm. These NPs were tested for antimicrobial properties.

Previously, Sasikala and Savithramma, [75] performed the green synthesis of silver NPs at 50-95°C using *Cochlospermum religiosum* leaf extract reduction with silver ions. The colour indication (clear colour change from yellow to brownish) was expressed to identify the production of AgNps within two minutes. The morphology characteristics of synthesised silver NPs were studied by UV-vis spectrum and AFM methods. The antimicrobial ability was examined against *E. coli*, *Staphylococcus* sp., *Bacillus* sp., *Pseudomonas* sp. and *Klebsiella* sp.

Conclusion

Biologic approaches for the green synthesis of AgNPs may be carried out with the use of biological organisms such as bacteria, fungi and plants able to reduce silver ions for the processing of metallic AgNPs. Green Synthesis approaches are more ecologically sustainable than biological, chemical and physical methods. There are some negative impacts as it could not be limited and it might produce harmful bioproducts as a byproduct, the use of biological species as reducing agents and lower energy requirements. However, AgNPs can be used as drug carriers in cancer therapy and other human-related diseases, as metabolite biosensors. Still, more research is needed to focus on the biomedical approach and to resolve the negative impact of nanomaterials.

References

1. Vijayaraj R and Kumaran NS. Biosynthesis of AgNPs from Hibiscus rosa Sinensis: An approach towards antimicrobial activity on fish pathogen Aeromonashy drosophila. Int J Pharm Sci Res 2017; 8(12): 5241-46.
2. Gurunathan S, Park JH, Han JW, Kim JH. Comparative assessment of the apoptotic potential of AgNPs synthesized by Bacillus tequilensis and Calocybeindica in MDA-MB-231 human breast cancer cells: Targeting p53 for anticancer therapy. Int J Nanomed 2015; 10: 4203–4222.
3. Zhang XF, Liu ZG, Shen W, Gurunathan S. AgNPs Synthesis, Characterization, Properties, Applications, and Therapeutic Approaches. Int J Mol Sci 2016; 17(9): 1534.
4. Ghaffari-Moghaddam M, Hadi-Dabanlou R, Khajeh M, Rakhshanipour M, Shameli K. Green synthesis of silver nanoparticles using plant extracts. Korean J Chem Eng 2014; 31: 548-557.
5. Wiley Y, Sun B, Mayers, Xia Y. "Shape-controlled synthesis of metal nanostructures: the case of silver. Chem Eur J 2005; 11(2): 454–463.
6. Oliveira M, Ugarte D, Zanchet D, Zarbin A. Influence of synthetic parameters on the size, structure, and stability of dodecanethiol-stabilized silver nanoparticles. J Colloid Interface Sci 2005; 292: 429 -35.
7. Brust M, Kiely C. Some recent advances in nanostructure preparation from gold and silver particles: a short topical review. Colloids Surf A: Phys Eng Aspects. 2002; 202: 175–186.
8. Kim S, Yoo B, Chun K, Kang W, Choo J, Gong M, Joo S. Catalytic effect of laser-ablated Ni nanoparticles in the oxidative addition reaction for a coupling reagent of benzyl chloride and bromoacetonitrile. J Mol Catal A: Chem 2005; 226 (2): 231-234.
9. Baruwati B, Polshettiwar V, Varma RS. Glutathione promoted expeditious green synthesis of AgNPs in water using microwaves. Green Chem 2009; 11(7): 926–930,
10. Guzman MG, Dille J, Godet S. Synthesis of AgNPs by chemical reduction method and their antibacterial activity. World Acad Sci Eng Technol 2008; 2: 7–27.

11. Hashim S, Ali SA, Siddiqui A, Ahmed SW, Naqvi SS, Shah MR, Ahmed A, Anwer H. Sodium dodecyl benzenesulfonate–based silver nanoparticles and their potential application as antibiofilm, antimicrobial agent, and trace level determination of amlodipine. Plasmonics 2020; 1-5.
12. Chaki NK, Sharma J, Mandle AB, Mulla IS, Pasricha R, Vijayamohanan K. Size-dependent redox behaviour of monolayer protected AgNPs (2–7 nm) in an aqueous medium, Phys Chem Chem Phys 2004; 6(6); 1304–1309.
13. Kyesmen PI, Onoja A, Amah AN. Fullerenes synthesis by combined resistive heating and arc discharge techniques Springerplus 2016; 5(1): 1323.
14. Mafune F, Kohno J, Takeda Y, Kondow T, Sawabe H. Formation and size control of AgNPs by laser ablation in aqueous solution. J Phys Chem B 2000; 104: 9111-9117.
15. Jung J, Oh H, Noh H, Ji J, Kim S. Metal Nanoparticle Generation Using a Small Ceramic Heater with a Local Heating Area. J Aerosol Sci 2006; 37: 1662-1670.
16. Sylvestre JP, Kabashin A, Sacher E,. Meunier M. Femtosecond laser ablation of gold in water: influence of the laser-produced plasma on the nanoparticle size distribution. Appl Phys A 2005; 80: 753–758.
17. Bajaj G, Soni RK. Effect of liquid medium on size and shape of nanoparticles prepared by pulsed laser ablation of tin. Appl Phys A 2009; 97: 481–487.
18. Mahfouz R, Aires FJ CS, Brenier A, Ehret E, Roumié M, Nsouli B, Jacquier B, Bertolini JC. Erratum to: Elaboration and characterization of bimetallic nanoparticles obtained by laser ablation of Ni75Pd25 and Au75Ag25 targets in the water. J Nanopart Res 2010; 12: 2307.
19. Mafune F, Kohno J, Takeda Y, Kondow T, Sawabe H. Formation and size control of AgNPs by laser ablation in aqueous solution. J Phys Chem B 2000; 104:.9111-9117.
20. Tsuji T, Iryo K, Watanabe N, Tsuji M. Preparation of silver nanoparticles by laser ablation in solution: influence of laser wavelength on particle size. Appl Surf Sci 2002; 202 (1–2): 80-85.

21. Jha, AK, Prasad K, Prasad K, Kulkarni AR. Plant System: Natures Nano factory. Colloids Surf B 2009; 73: 219-223.
22. Krolikowska A, Kudelski A, Michota A, Bukowska J. SERS studies on the structure of thioglycolic acid monolayers on silver and gold. Surf Sci 2003; 532: 227-232.
23. Mehra RK, Winge DR Metal Ion Resistance in Fungi: Molecular Mechanisms and their Regulated Expression. J Cell Biochem 1991; 45: 30-40.
24. Ingle A, Gade A, Pierrat S, Sönnichsen C, Rai M. Mycosynthesis of AgNPs using the fungus Fusariumacuminatum and its activity against some human pathogenic bacteria. Curr Nanosci 2008; 4: 141-144.
25. Vigneshwaran N, Ashtaputre NM, Varadarajan PV, Nachane RP, Paralikar KM, Balasubramanya R. Biological synthesis of AgNPs using the fungus *Aspergillus flavus*. Mater Lett 2007; 61: 1413-1418.
26. Vigneshwaran N, Kathe AA, Varadarajan PV, Nachane RP, Balasubramanya R. Biomimetics of AgNPs by a white-rot fungus, *Phaenerochaete chrysosporium*. Colloids Surf B 2006; 53: 55-59.
27. Bhainsa KC, D'Souza S. Extracellular biosynthesis of AgNPs using the fungus *Aspergillus fumigatus*. Colloids Surf B 2006; 47: 160-164.
28. Balaji DS, Basavaraja S, Deshpande R, Bedre Mahesh D, Prabhakar BK, Venkataraman A. Extracellular biosynthesis of functionalized AgNPs by strains of *Cladosporium cladosporioides* fungus. Colloids Surf B 2009; 68: 88-92.
29. Maliszewska I, Szewczyk K, Waszak K. Biological synthesis of AgNPs. J Phys Conf Ser 2009; 146: 1-6.
30. Sadowski Z, Maliszewska IH, Grochowalska B, Polowczyk I, Kozlecki T. Synthesis of AgNPs using microorganisms. Mater Sci-Poland 2008; 26: 419-424.
31. Kathiresan K, Manivannan S, Nabeel MA, Dhivya B. Studies on AgNPs synthesized by a marine fungus, *Penicillium fellutanum* isolated from coastal mangrove sediment. Colloids Surf B 2009; 71: 133-137.

32. Ahmad N, Sharma S. Green Synthesis of AgNPs Using Extracts of *Ananas comosus*. Green and Sustainable Chemistry 2012; 2: 141-147.

33. Korbekandi H, Iravani S, Abbasi S. Optimization of biological synthesis of AgNPs using Lactobacillus casei subsp. casei. J Chem Technol Biotechnol 2012; 87: 932–937.

34. Kumar SA, Abyaneh MK, Gosavi SW, Kulkarni SK, Pasricha R, Ahmad A, Khan MI. Nitrate reductase-mediated synthesis of silver nanoparticles from AgNO3. Biotechnol Lett 2007; 29(3): 439-45.

35. Ahmad A, Mukherjee P, Senapati S, Mandal D, Khan MI, Kumar R, Sastry M. Extracellular biosynthesis of AgNPs using the fungus *Fusarium oxysporum*. Colloids Surf B 2003; 28: 313-318.

36. Macdonald IDG, Smith W. Orientation of Cytochrome c adsorbed on a citrate-reduced silver colloid surface. Langmuir 1996; 12: 706-713.

37. Ahmad A, Senapati S, Khan MI, Kumar R, Ramani R, Srinivas V, Sastry M. Intracellular synthesis of gold NPs by a novel alkali tolerant actinomycete, Rhodococcus species. Nanotechnology 2003; 14: 824-828.

38. Korbekandi H, Ashari Z, Iravani S, Abbasi S. Optimization of biological synthesis of AgNPs using Fusarium oxysporum. Iran J Pharm Res 2013; 12: 289-298.

39. Sanghi R, Verma P. Biomimetic synthesis and characterisation of protein capped AgNPs. Bioresour Technol 2009; 100: 501–504.

40. Kalishwaralal K, Deepak V, Ramkumarpandian S, Nellaiah H, Sangiliyandi G. Extracellular biosynthesis of AgNPs by the culture supernatant of *Bacillus licheniformis*. Mater Lett 2008; 62: 4411-4413.

41. Kathiresan K, Manivannan S, Nabeel MA, Dhivya B. Studies on AgNPs synthesized by a marine fungus, *Penicillium fellutanum* isolated from coastal mangrove sediment. Colloids Surf B 2009; 71: 133-137.

42. Saifuddin N., Wong CW, Yasumira AAN. Rapid biosynthesis of silver nanoparticles using culture supernatant of bacteria with microwave irradiation. E-J Chem 2009; 6(1): 61-70.

43. Klaus T, Joerger R, Olsson E, Granqvist CG. Silver-based crystalline NPs, Microbially fabricated. Proc Nat'l Acad Sci USA 1999; 96: 13611-13614.

44. Slawson RM, Van DM, Lee H, Trevor J. Germanium and silver resistance, accumulation and toxicity in microorganisms. Plasmid 1992; 27: 73-79.

45. Klaus-Joerger T, Joerger R, Olsson E, Granqvist CG. Bacteria as workers in the living factory: metal accumulating bacteria and their potential for materials science. Trends Biotechnol 2001: 19: 15–20.

46. Mokhtari N, Daneshpajouh S, Seyedbagheri S, Atashdehghan R, Abdi K, Sarkar, S, Minaian S, Shahverdi, HR, and Shahverdi, AR. Biological synthesis of very small silver nanoparticles by culture supernatant of *Klebsiella pneumonia:* The effects of visible-light irradiation and the liquid mixing process. Mater Res Bull 2009; 44(6): 1415-1421.

47. Shahverdi AR, Minaeian S, Shahverdi HR, Jamalifar H, Nohi A. Rapid synthesis of AgNPs using culture supernatants of Enterobacteria: A novel biological approach. Process Biochem 2007; 42: 919-923.

48. Iravani S., Korbekandi H., Mirmohammadi SV, Zolfaghari B. Synthesis of silver nanoparticles: chemical, physical and biological methods, Res Pharm Sci 2014; 9(6): 385–406.

49. Bali R, Razak N, Lumb A, Harris A. The synthesis of metallic nanoparticles inside live plants. International Conference on Nanoscience and Nanotechnology 2006; DOI:10.1109/ICONN.2006.340592

50. Jha AK, Prasad K, Prasad K, Kulkarni AR. Plant System: Natures Nano factory. Colloids Surf B 2009; 73, 219-223.

51. Song JY, Kim BS Rapid biological synthesis of AgNPs using plant leaf extracts. Bioprocess Biosyst Eng 2009; 32: 79-84.

52. Roy K, Biswas S, Banerjee PC. Green Synthesis of AgNPs by Using Grape (*Vitis vinifera*) Fruit Extract: Characterization of the Particles and Study of Antibacterial Activity. Research Journal of Pharmaceutical, Biological and Chemical Sciences 2013; 4 (1): 1271.

53. Gavhane AJ, Padmanabhan P, Suresh P. Kamble SP, Jangle SN. Synthesis of silver nanoparticles using the extract of Neem leaf and Triphala and evaluation of their antimicrobial activities. Int J Pharm Bio Sci 2012; 3(3): 88–100.

54. Lalitha A, Subbaiya R, Ponmurugan P. Green synthesis of AgNPs from leaf extract Azhadirachta indica and to study its anti-bacterial and antioxidant property. Int J Curr Microbiol App Sci 2013; 2(6): 228-235.

55. Sharma VK, Yngard RA, Lin Y. Silver nanoparticles: Green synthesis and their antimicrobial activities. Adv Colloid Interface Sci 2009;145(1-2):83-96.

56. Sathyavathi M, Balamurali K, Rao SV, Saritha R, Rao DN. Biosynthesis of AgNPs Using *Coriandrum sativum* Leaf Extract and Their Application in Nonlinear Optics. Adv Sci Lett 2010; 3(2): 138-143.

57. Phanjom P, Sultana A, Sarma H, Ramchiary J, Goswami K, Baishya P. Plant-Mediated Synthesis of AgNPs Using *Elaeagnus latifolia* Leaf extract. Digest J Nanomater Biostruct 2012; 7(3):1117-1123.

58. Chekin F, Ghasemi S. AgNPs Prepared in Presence of Ascorbic Acid and Gelatin, and Their Electrocatalytic Application. Bull Mater Sci 2014; 37(6): 1433-1437.

59. Firdhouse MJ, Lalitha P. Green Synthesis of AgNPs Using the Aqueous Extract of *Portulaca oleracea* (L.). *Asian J* Pharm Clin Res 2013; 6(1): 92-94.

60. Rodriguez-Leon E, Iñiguez-Palomares R, Navarro R.E, Herrera-Urbina R, Tánori J, Iñiguez-Palomares C, Maldonado A. Synthesis of silver nanoparticles using reducing agents obtained from natural sources (*Rumex hymenosepalus* extracts). Nanoscale Res Lett 2013; 8(1): 318.

61. Abdelmonem A, Amin RM. Rapid Green Synthesis of Metal NPs using Pomegranate Pomegranate Polyphenols. Int J Sci Basic Appl Res 2014; 15(1): 57-65.

62. Awwad AM, Salem NM and Abdeen AO. Green synthesis of AgNPs using carob leaf extract and its antibacterial activity. Int J Ind Chem 2013; 4: 29.

63. Christensen L, Vivekanandhan S, Misra M, Mohanty AK. Biosynthesis of AgNPs using *Murraya koenigii* (curry leaf): An investigation on the effect of broth concentration in reduction mechanism and particle size. Adv Mat Lett 2011; 2 (6): 429-434.

64. Elizondo N, Segovia P, Coello V, Arriaga J, Belmares S, Alcorta A, Hernández F, Obregón R, Torres E, Paraguay F. Green Synthesis and Characterizations of Silver and Gold Nanoparticles, Green Chemistry - Environmentally Benign Approaches, Mazaahir Kidwai and Neeraj Kumar Mishra, Intech Open. 2012; DOI: 10.5772/34365.

65. Kamali M, Ghorashi SAA, Asadollahi MA. Controllable Synthesis of Silver Nanoparticles Using Citrate as Complexing Agent: Characterization of Nanoparticles and Effect of pH on Size and Crystallinity. Iran J Chem Chem Eng 2012; 31(4): 21-28.

66. Rout Y, Behera S, Ojha AK, Nayak PL. Green synthesis of AgNPs using Ocimum sanctum (Tulasi) and study of their antibacterial and antifungal activities. J Microbiol Antimicrob 2012; 4(6): 103-109.

67. Firdhouse MJ, Lalitha P, Shubashini Sripathi K. Novel synthesis of silver nanoparticles using leaf ethanol extract of *Pisonia grandis* (R. Br), Der. Pharma Chemica 2012; 4(6): 2320-2326.

68. Ahmad N, Sharma S. Green Synthesis of AgNPs Using Extracts of Ananas comosus. Green Sustain. Chem 2012; 2: 141-147.

69. Kalaiarasia R, Prasannaraja G, Venkatachalama P. A rapid biological synthesis of AgNPs using leaf broth of *Rauvolfia tetraphylla* and their promising antibacterial activity. Indo Am j pharm Res 2013; 3: 8052-8062.

70. Bhati-Kushwaha H, Malik CP. Biosynthesis of AgNPs using fresh extracts of *Tridax Procumbens* Linn. Indian J Exp Biol 2014; 52: 359-368.

71. Loo YY, Chieng BW, Nishibuchi M, Radu S. Synthesis of AgNPs by using tea leaf extract from *Camellia Sinensis*. Int J Nanomedicine 2012; 7: 4263–4267.

72. Lu B, Chen J, Huang W, Wu D, Xu W, Xie Q, Yu X, Li L. Determination of flavonoids and phenolic acids in the extract of

bamboo leaves using near-infrared spectroscopy and multivariate calibration. Afr J Biotechnol 2011; 10: 8448-8455.

73. Yasin S, Liu L, Yao J. Biosynthesis of AgNPs by Bamboo Leaves Extract and Their Antimicrobial Activity. J Fiber Bioeng Inform 2013; 6(1): 77–84.

74. Kulkarni AP, Srivastava AA, Harpale PM, Zunjarrao RS. Plant mediated synthesis of AgNPs - tapping the unexploited sources. J Nat Prod Plant Resour 2011; 1(4): 100-107.

75. Sasikala A, Savithramma N. Biological Synthesis of Silver Nanoparticles from *Cochlosper- mum Religiosum* and their Antibacterial Efficacy. J Pharm Sci & Res 2012; 4(6): 1836 - 1839.

[1]**Department of Biotechnology,**
Bon Secours College for Women, Thanjavur
[2.]**Department of Marine Biotechnology,**
AMET University, Chennai, India
[3]**Department of Botany,**
Central University of Punjab, Bathinda, Punjab, India
[4]**Department of Science and Humanites (Physics),**
Karpagam Academy of Higher Education, Coimbatore, India
* Corresponding author
Dr. S. Ramadevi and Dr. S. Sivaranjani
[1*]**Assistant Professor**
Dept. of Biotechnology
Bon Secours College for Women, Thanjavur
email : ranjani29siva@gmail.com

11. Performance of Financial Literacy Centres – A Study of Davanagere District

K. B. Sunitha M.Com*.,
Dr.(Smt.)A.N.Tamragundi**

Abstract

Financial Inclusion is the main agenda of the Government of India since independence, as a result Reserve Bank of India is engaged in implementing various schemes, products, approaches in this directions from time to time. Even though it has implemented many programs and schemes but the success was not as expected, then it was realised that there is a need for counselling the people about the products and convincing the people to avail the benefit of the scheme. So the RBI has issued guidelines for lead banks of the each district to start Financial Literacy Centres (FLCs) to counsel the various segments of the society about the banking services and products available to them from the banks. The present study is to analyse the growth and performance of the FLCs in the Davanagere district. For the purpose of study secondary data is used.

Keywords : Financial Literacy Centres, Reserve Bank of India, Lead banks

Introduction

Working Groups constituted by the RBI time to time to examine the procedures and processes involved in for various loans have suggested in 2007 that banks should actively consider opening of counselling centres to increase agricultural loans, either individually or with pooled resources, for credit and technological counselling. Earlier, a similar Working Group constituted by Reserve Bank had also suggested that financial and livelihood counselling is important for increasing viability of credit and also bring the unbanked people towards banks. Based on these recommendations, and as announced in the Annual Policy Statement for the year 2007-08, Reserve Bank advised the SLBC convenor banks, to set up a FLCC on a pilot basis in any one district in the State/ Union Territory coming under their jurisdiction and, based on the response received, the Lead Banks may set up counselling centres in other districts. Consequent upon the announcement in the Mid-term Review of the Annual Policy for the year 2007-08, a concept paper on FLCCs was placed on the Reserve Bank's website and feedback received from public as also from banks that had started operating the counseling centres. These centres are aims at providing information to the public regarding various financial products, and the government schemes available in the banking sector to the people, so that they can evaluate the schemes and products to suit their needs. To perform these functions the Financial Literacy Centres (FLCs) were established throughout the country. These centres are meant for conducting programs for various groups i.e., Farmers, public, students, officials working in various sectors, unemployed youths etc. and provides banking service information , types of credit available, account opening procedure etc.

Literature Review

C.Mamatha and S.B. Mahajanshetti (2019) has conducted a study on "Growth and performance of Financial Literacy Centres in Karnataka State". The study analysed growth and performance at district level and at Karnataka state as a whole. The study was conducted by taking the information for the period of 2014-15 to 2016-17 the study reveals over a period of time FLCs increased and many people took benefit of camps conducted by them.

Sangeetha Rangaswamy et.al have conducted a study on "Status of FLCs in Karnataka" the study aims to find out the status of FLCs in Karnataka during 2008-09 to 2016-17. For the purpose of analysing the data descriptive statistics Regression and ANOVA tools were used. It is found from the study that there is an impact on FLCs on CD ratio. However growth of CD ratio is not in alignment with the growth in FLCs.

Methodology

 Research has been conducted by using Secondary data available in official website of banks, information from newspapers, reports, research articles, E-resources. Analysis of growth of financial literacy centres and their performance has been analysed through their working behaviour this has been analysed with the help of number of camps conducted and number of people attended the camps.

Objectives of the paper

The specific objectives of the research paper are

- To analyse the growth of financial literacy centres in Davanagere district over a period of time
- To know the number of financial literacy camps conducted in the district
- To Study the number of persons attended the financial literacy camps in the district

Growth of Financial Literacy Centres :

As per the directions of the RBI, the Financial Literacy Centres started working throughout the country similarly in Davanagere district also. To analyse the growth of financial literacy centres in Davanagere district over a period of time CAGR is used, the compound growth was calculated by using the formula

$$CAGR= (EN/BN)^{(1/NY)}-1$$

Where :

EN= End number

BN= Beginning number

NY = Number of Years

Growth of Financial Literacy Centres in Davanagere district from 2015-16 till 2019-20 is shown in the following table 1. Table depicts the number of FLCs in the district over a period of time

Table 1

Showing the No. of Financial Literacy Centres from 2015-16 till 2019-20

Sl No	Taluk Name	2015-16	2016-17	2017-18	2018-19	2019-20
01	Davanagere	1	1	1	1	1
02	Harihara	0	1	1	1	1
03	Jagalur	0	1	1	1	1
04	Honnali	0	0	1	1	1
05	Harapanahalli	1	1	1	1	1
06	Channagiri	1	1	1	1	1
	Total	3	5	6	6	6

Above table shows the growth of financial literacy centres in the Davanagere district between 2015-16 to 2019-20. There were just 3 centres functioning in the district during 2015-16. In 2016-17 it increased to 5 as the new FLCs established in Harihara and Jagalur taluk. During 2017-18 the lead bank took step to establish FLCs in each taluk of the district, as a result the number of FLCs increased to 6. And it is continued, as a result people of each taluk getting credit counselling through these FLCs. All the FLCs are operative and engaged in providing counselling to the people of the district.

Number of Financial Literacy Camps held in the district

Financial Literacy Centres main function is conducting literacy camps for various segment of the society, who are in need of credit counselling

The following table 2 indicates the data pertaining to number of Financial Literacy camps conducted in the district from 2015-16 till 2019-20

Table 2

Number of Financial Literacy camps conducted in Davanagere district.

Sl.No.	Taluk Name	No. of Financial Literacy Camps conducted					Total
		2015-16	2016-17	2017-18	2018-19	2019-20	
01	Davanagere	185	271	280	324	630	1690
02	Jagalur	35	190	210	440	438	1313
03	Harapanahalli	190	185	292	385	630	1682
04	Honnali	135	240	242	438	580	1635
05	Channagiri	60	235	260	465	720	1740
06	Harihara	145	240	248	340	495	1468
	Total	750	1361	1532	2392	3493	9528

Number of persons attended Financial Literacy Camps in the district

Table 3 showing No of beneficiary in the Davanagere district regarding financial literacy. The middle state of Karnataka is also growing rapidly in all rounds. In the same way it is not behind in creating financial literacy among public, students and bank customers . this can be seen from the following table

Table 3
Number of persons participated in Financial Literacy camps in the Davanagere District

Sl No.	Name of Taluks	Number of persons participated in Financial Literacy camps					Trend percentages				
		2015-16	2016-17	2017-18	2018-19	2019-20	2015-16	2016-17	2017-18	2018-19	2019-20
01	Davanagee	24208	21905	21654	26196	52458	100%	90.4%	89%	102%	217%
02	Jagalur	1726	25152	23080	35924	49439	100%	1457%	1337%	2081%	2864%
03	Harapanahalli	18070	29592	43663	43017	70532	100%	164%	241%	238%	390%
04	Honnali	1282	22826	25720	30453	40315	100%	1780%	2006%	2375%	3144%
05	Channagiri	3952	16930	32010	39665	42901	100%	428%	809 %	1003%	1085%
06	Harihara	1237	19608	22923	25128	43725	100%	1585%	1853%	2031%	3534%

Findings
- All the FLCs in the district are active
- FLCs are showing upward trend in their number from time to time Performance of FLCs are remarkable
- More and more people are attending financial literacy camps

Suggestions :
- They should be fixed with targets i.e., FLCs must be mandatory to conduct certain number of camps
- They should assist people to open accounts and avail credit
- They can even take the responsibility of issuing required applications for the people.

Conclusion
Financial inclusion is an important step to achieve economic and inclusive growth with stability. Inclusive financial sector can break the vicious cycle of poverty. This can empower the poor and ensure that poor people have access to a wide range of financial services with more opportunities to lead the way out of poverty with dignity. Thus, financial inclusion is no longer a policy choice, but a policy compulsion today and banking is a key driver for inclusive growth.

The financial inclusion does not mean merely opening of saving bank account but signifies creation of awareness about the financial products, education and advice on money management, offering debt counseling, etc. by formal financial institutions. The present study analyses the growth and performance in the number financial literacy centres (FLCs) at Davanagere district.

References

- Karnataka slbc various years annexures and meeting agendas
- "Financial Literacy and Consumer Protection – Necessary Foundation for Financial Inclusion",RBI Bulletin, May 2012 and S.B Mahajanshetti Journal of Pharmacognory and Phytochemistry : 2019; 8 (2) pp2141- 2149 ISSN 2278 4136
- Study of Financial Literacy Centres in Karnataka, Journal of Business Management 16 (4): 24-35 Octobere 2017
- "Financial Literacy and Financial Stability are two aspects of efficient economy" Dr. Upendra Singh, Journal of Finance, Accounting and Management: Beverly Hills Vol 5(2), 59-76, July 2014.
- E-Sources

*Assistant Professor,
Department of Commerce and Management,
Government First Grade College Davanagere
email : sujaya2002@gmail.com
**Professor,
P.G.Department of Commerce,
Karnataka University,
Dharwad.

12. Factors Influencing Student Migration

Jeny Davis

Abstract

Students are leaving India in greater numbers than ever before. The biggest advantage of studying abroad is that students can pursue the topic in which they are truly interested and where they wish to specialize, which they may not be able to accomplish in their native country. When looking for employment abroad or anywhere else, the degree they received from the host country is valuable. Another advantage of having that degree is that the host nation treats the student fairly when they seek for residence there and permits them to stay there even after they have finished their school. The main objective of the study is to know the factors influencing student migration

Introduction

Global student migration has increased significantly, particularly from developing countries to developed countries. After China, India is the world's second largest student sending country, with the number of Indian students studying abroad increasing fourfold over the past years. Such massive student migration has become a major source of capital and brain drain for India, while benefiting the economies of advanced countries enormously. The United States receives more than half of all expatriate Indian students, followed by Australia and the United Kingdom. A major contributing factor to poverty and economic hardship is a lack of access to high-quality education, which in turn influences people's decision to migrate in search of better work prospects and a better quality of life. student migration from India Similar to China, India is one of the major entry points for students seeking to attend the greatest colleges in the developed world in nations like the United States, Canada, and Australia. There could be a variety of factors contributing to the sharp rise in Indian students studying abroad.

Statement of Problem

Emigration can be viewed as a people's reaction to a country's current socioeconomic and political situation. Every citizen has a right to a basic education and their need for it should be protected by the government, but each person also has the right to choose their own educational decisions. Statistics show that a significant number of Indian youngsters have been moving in big numbers to foreign countries in recent decades in order to further their studies. The main objective of the study is to identify the factors influencing student migration.

Objectives

1. To identify the factors influencing student migration
2. To know the source of fund for education of migrating students.

Research Methodology

The study aimed at analyzing the student migration from Thrissur district to foreign countries. Primary Data was collected from the respondents through questionnaire and secondary data were collected from magazines and journals.

Population : Thrissur corporation

Sampling technique : The respondents were selected through convenience sampling technique.

Sample size : 100 respondents were selected

Tools for analysis : Percentage analysis

Tools for presentation : Tables

Limitations

1. The data was collected from a limited geographical area. Hence the findings and conclusion has its own limitations.
2. Time was another limiting factor.

Review of Literature

Zheng, (2018) found that the most important determinant of student intention to study abroad (29%) was economic factors. The primary motivator is unemployment. Because of this, the majority of prospective students want to study in the United States and Australia. A globally recognized degree, as well as employment opportunities during and after studies, are available. Education and employment have a direct relationship. Around 53% of potential students were linked to education and earnings. Yes, their first choice is to obtain a high-quality education with a globally recognized degree. However, the backdrop of education has been the employment opportunity that potential students will have during and after their studies in the destination country.

Adhikari (2012), assessed the factors influencing the migration decision of Nepalese to the US. The main goal of his research was to investigate the major "push" and "pull" factors influencing Nepalese professional and non-professional migration to the United States. He investigated economic, social, political, and personal issues using a quantitative method. When many push factors were examined, each factor had a positive impact on migration decisions. Similarly, each push factor emerged as significant indicators discouraging Nepalese in the United States from returning home.

Baryla Edward &Dotterweich Douglas (2001) studied on student Migration and the significant factors varying from region to region. The investigator examined the factors that had a significant impact on student migration in different US geographic regions. The study showed the dynamic interaction between university, its environment, and student migration. The study also found that higher education institutions that have regionally recognized quality programs have greater ability to attract non-resident students. It also showed that there is a linkage between non-resident enrolment and the economic environment where the university is located

Data Analysis

Table no 1 showing gender of the respondents

Gender	Frequency	Percentage
Male	60	60
Female	40	40

Table no.2 showing age of the respondents

Age	Frequency	Percentage
18-21	55	55
21-24	40	40

Above 24	5	5

Table no.3 showing annual parental income

Parental income	Frequency	Percentage
Below2,50,000	26	26
2,50,000 - 5,00,000	32	32
5,00,000 - 7,50,000	38	38
Above 7,50,000	4	4

Table no.4 showing funding of education

Source	Frequency	Percentage
Parents/ relatives	20	20
Banks/financial companies	41	41
Scholarship	9	9
Earnings	18	18
Others	12	12

Table no.5 showing source of information about study abroad

Source	Frequency	Percentage
Parents/ relatives	16	16
Friends	28	28
Medias	39	39
Others	17	17

Table no.6 showing causes of student migration

Causes	Frequency	Percentage
Earning and learning	33	33
Quality education	19	19
Friends/ relatives abroad	10	10
Choices of subject	17	17
Other factors	21	21

Table no.7 showing factors influencing student migration

Factors	Frequency	Percentage
Higher wages	38	38
Better employment opportunities	24	24
Better educational opportunities	8	8
Higher standard of living	26	26
Others	4	4

Table no.8 showing students' preference of countries for migration

Country	Frequency	Percentage
Canada	12	12
Australia	18	18
U K	24	24
Germany	21	21
U S A	17	17
Other countries	8	8

Findings
- 60% of respondents are male and 40% of respondents are females.
- 55% of respondents belong to the age category of 18-21.
- 38% of respondents having an annual parental income in between 5,00,000 - 7,50,0000
- 41% of respondents responded that banks and financial companies are the main source of fund for education.
- 39% of respondents responded that medias are the main source of information about study abroad.
- 33% of respondents responded that earning and learning is the main cause of student migration.
- 38% of respondents responded that higher wages are the main factor influencing student migration.
- 24% of respondents responded that U K is their preferred country for migration.

Suggestions
- Ensure quality education of the students.
- Provide maximum job opportunities for students after their studies.
- Ensure job security and attractive salary for the workers.
- Provide maximum support for the students to earn while learning.
- Conduct awareness classes on opportunities for the students.

Conclusions
It was discovered that educational aspirations and expectations of student migrants were related to migration plans. The student migrants had a strong desire to migrate to study in another country. Earning potential as well as learning opportunities were discovered to be major factors in student out-migration. It was discovered that students were also motivated to travel abroad by imitating current trends and crazes. It was also discovered that social network factors help in the migration process. It was discovered that those who have close relatives abroad are more likely to want to emigrate and are also more likely to succeed. It was discovered that the students had high expectations and aspirations. Their ultimate goal was to obtain a degree and then pursue career opportunities. As a result, opportunities were also a driving force in student out-migration. The student migrants' expectations and desires were very high and positive. It was either hope or dreams for the future.

Bibligrapghy
Zheng, R. (2018). Migration and the Globalization of Tertiary Education: International Student Mobility: Symposium on International Migration and Development. Turin, Italy. Cornell University.
Adhikari, D. (2012). Youth returning home. Kantipur (Friday Supplementary.
Bhandari, R. (2009). Shifting trends in global student mobility. Paper presented at the National Association of International Educators (NAFSA) Conference, Los Angeles, CA.

Borjas, G. J. (2002). An evaluation of the foreign student program. (Kennedy School of Government (KSG) Faculty Research Working Paper Series No. RWP02-026), 1-14. Retrieved from http://papers.ssrn.com/sol3/papers.cfm?abstract_id=320248

Edward, B., & Douglas, D. (2001). education Economics. Retrieved from http://www.tandfonline.com/loi/cede20

Assistant Professor on Contract
St.Aloysius College, Elthuruth
email : Jenydavis44@gmail.com

13. Environmental Ethics and Role of Education with Responsible Environmental Behaviour

Dr.Chiinkhanniang Tombing

Introduction

Most of the environmental problems of the present day world are essentially manmade. The role of man is, therefore, crucial because it is his attitude towards the human and natural environment that has shaped the present day environment. Obviously, it is only through the change in attitude that man can take initiatives in influencing the conditions related to the value system of the contemporary society. Historically, individual and societal values have not always been in the best interests of preserving a quality environment. The present day environmental crisis obliges man to re-examine his values and where necessary alter them in order to ensure man's survival. If man could live in harmony with nature and could act as a responsible 'caretaker' or 'guardian' of the environment, it is possible to attain an ecologically sound future for generations to come. Man with his unique technological power has a profound effect on his environment. Therefore, he can control, to some extent his own destiny. For living in harmony with the environment, man has to evolve a balanced way of thinking feeling and acting towards the environment. This is related with ethical behavior of people at large. The Indian Constitution through its Directive principles (Article 48 and 51 A) declares that the protection and improvement of the natural environment (including forest and wildlife) is an obligatory responsibility of the state and of every citizen of India. Individuals and groups may contribute significantly towards formulation of sound environmental decision-making. Justice Nagendra Singh, president of the Indian Academy of Environment Law, conservation and Research suggested that –Environmental protection is of national importance, parliament should initiate legislation to cover all aspects of environmental pollution throughout the country in an integral manner.

The field of environmental ethics concerns human beings ethical relationship with the natural environment while numerous philosophers have written on this topic throughout history environmental ethics only developed into a specific philosophy discipline in the 1970's. This emergence was no doubt due to the increasing awareness in the 1980's of the effects that technology, industry, economic expansion and population growth were having on the environment. Pollution and the depletion of natural resources have not been the only environmental concerns since that time dwindling plant and animal biodiversity, the loss of wilderness, the degradation of ecosystems, and climate change are all part of raft of "green" issues that have implanted themselves into both public consciousness and public policy over subsequent years.

Concept of Environmental Ethics

Environmental ethics is the discipline in philosophy that studies the moral relationship of human brings to, and also the value and moral status of, the environment and its non-human contents. Ethics are a broad way of thinking about what constitutes a good life and how to live one. They address questions of right and wrong, making good decisions, and the character or emphasis on how they can be lived out in a practical manner. Environmental ethics apply ethical thinking to the natural world and the relationship between humans and the earth. Environmental ethics are a key feature of environmental studies, but they have application in many other fields as human society grapples in a more meaningful way with pollution, resources degradation, the threat of extinction, and global climate disruption.

Environment ethics is a branch of ethics that studies the relation of human beings and the environment, and how ethics play a role in this. Environmental ethics believe that humans are a part of society as well as other living creatures, which includes plants and animals. These items are very important and are considered to be a functional part of human life. Thus, it is essential that every human being respect and honour this and use morals and ethics when dealing with these creatures.

As per Nature.com : " Environmental ethics is a branch of applied philosophy that studies the conceptual foundations of environmental values as well as more concrete issues surrounding societal attitudes, actions, and policies to protect and sustain biodiversity and ecological systems".

According to wikipedia:"Environmental ethics is the part of environmental philosophy which considers extending the traditional boundaries of ethics from solely including humans to the non-human world. It exerts influence on a large range of disciplines including environmental law, environmental sociology, eco-theology, ecological economics, ecology and environmental geography."

According to standard encyclopedia of philosophy : " Environmental ethics is the discipline in philosophy that studies the moral relationship of human beings to, and also the value and moral status of, the environment and its non-human contents"

In the most general sense, environmental ethics invites us to consider three keys positions:

1. The earth and its creatures have moral status, in other words, are worthy of our ethical concern;
2. The earth and its creatures have intrinsic value, meaning that they have moral value merely because they exist, not only because they meet human needs;
3. Drawing from the idea of an ecosystem, human beings should consider 'wholes' that include other forms of life and the environment.

Features of Environmental Ethics

According to UNESCO, there are several distinctive features of environmental ethics that deserve our attention:

- First, environmental ethics is extendable. Traditional ethics mainly concerns intra-human duties, especially duties among contemporaries. Environmental ethics extends the scope of ethical concerns beyond one's community and nation including not only all people everywhere but also animals and the whole nature-the biosphere both now and beyond the eminent future including the future generations.

- Second, environmental ethics is inter-disciplinary. There are many overlapping concerns and areas of consensus, for instance, among environmental ethics, environmental politics, environmental economics, environmental sciences and environmental literature. The distinctive perspectives and methodlogies of these disciplines provide important inspiration for environmental and environmental ethics offers value foundations for these disciplines. They reinforce, influence and support each other.

- Third, environmental ethics is plural. From the moment it was existed, environmental ethics has been an area which different ideas and perspectives compete with each other. Anthropocentrism, animal liberation/rights theory, bio-centrism and eco-centrism all provide unique and, in some sense, reasonable ethical justifications for environmental protection. Their approaches are different, but their goals are by and large the same, and so they have reached this consensus: that it is everyone's duty to protect the environment. The basic idea of environmental ethics also finds support from, and are embodied in various well established cultural traditions. Pluralism of theories and multi cultural perspectives is critical for environmental ethics to retain its vitality.

- Fourth, environmental ethics is global. Ecological crisis is a global issue. Environmental pollution does not respect national boundaries. No country can deal with this issue alone. To cope with the global environmental crises, human beings must reach some value consensus and co-operate with each other at the personal, national, regional, multi- national and global levels. Global environmental protection depends on global governance. An environmental ethics is, therefore, typically global ethic with a global perspective

- Fifth, environmental ethics is revolutionary. At the level of ideas, environmental ethics challenges the dominant and deep-rooted anthropocentrism of modern mainstream ethics and extends the object of our duty to future generation and non human beings. At the practical level, environmental ethics forcefully critiques the materialism, hedonism and consumerism accompanying modern capitalism, and calls instead for a ' Green life-style' that is harmonious with nature. It searches for an economic arrangement that is sensitive to Earth's limits and to concern for quality of life.

In political administration, it advocates more equitable international, economic and political order that is based on the principles of democracy, global justice and universal human rights. It argues for pacifism and against an arms race.

In short, as the theoretical representation of newly emerging moral idea and value orientation, environmental ethics is the fullest extension of human ethics. It tells us to think and act locally as well as globally. It show us for a new, deeper moral consciousness.

Global warming, global climate change, deforestation, pollution, resource degradation, threat of extinction are few of the issues from which our planet is suffering. Environmental ethics are the key feature of environmental studies that establishes relationship between human and the earth. With environmental ethics, one can ensure that one is doing his part to keep the environment safe and protected. With the rapid increase in world's population, the consumption of natural resources has increased several time. This has deteriorated our planets' product to provide which human need. The consumption of resources is going at faster rate than they naturally replenish. Environmental ethics builds on scientific understanding by bringing human values, moral principles, and improved decision making inter-related with science. It was Earth Day in 1970 that helped to develop environmental ethics in the US, and soon thereafter the same ethics were developed in other countries including Canada and North America. This is important because the ethics of the environment are of ethics to outline our moral obligations in the face of the environmental concerns.

Responsible Environmental Behaviour

The concept of "responsible environmental behaviour" is very complex, because human behaviour is significantly influenced by the mental abilities, attitudes, aptitudes, knowledge, skills etc. It can be defined as a demonstration or aspect of environmental empathy that includes activities which have been recommended to resolve problems in natural environment. Therefore, responsible human behaviour, physco-physical characteristics influence most forcefully. Moreover, social, political, economic, cultural and geographical factors also influence it. The term ' responsible environment behaviour' implies the logical and scientific attitude and behaviour of the individual towards the environment. In other words, responsible environmental behaviour is that type of behaviour of the individual, through which one can live in harmony with the nature without harming it. By developing such behaviour we try to develop loving attitude of the individual towards the environment because human being will exist only if the nature itself exists. Therefore, one of the most important aims of modern education is to develop such feelings and attitudes among pupils that they show scientific, logical and rational responses to conserve and protect the environment.

Role of Formal Education

The acquisition of responsible environmental behaviour through the institution curriculum has more significant. The ultimate aim of education is shaping human behaviour. Societies throughout the world established educational institutions to develop citizens who will behave in desirable ways. Responsible environmental behaviour is the ability to act independently and to make necessary decision about environmental issues. It is very important to impart knowledge about different issues of environment to the learners and other target groups for sustainable development. In this regard environmental education can play a very significant role in developing such kind of behaviour among the people in general and students in particular. Human behaviour have to be responsible towards environment for sustainable development and it is more prominent in case of coming generation because, they will be the future policy makers, executors and sufferers. Complete and clear understanding about environment should prevail among mankind. Judicious use of natural resources, sympathetic attitude and sense of responsibility towards solution of environmental problems and its protection and preservation are the main components of responsible environmental behaviour. Such kind of behaviour is desired from all human beings including students, community irrespective of gender, habitation as well as subject concern.

The ultimate goals of environmental education are to contribute to the development of responsible citizens of the natural environment as well as to aroused and awaken a sense of responsibility toward that environment. Promoting respect for the environment, teaching environmental values, and encouraging environmentally responsible behaviour are all integral part of education curriculum. In order to encourage the long-term protection of the environment, environmental education attempts to develop an individual behaviour that are both durable.

Thus, the role of education is developing responsible environmental behaviour are:

- Education provide knowledge to the pupils through which they can establish cordial relation between the existence of man and nature.
- It makes people conscious about the needs of population control
- Education helps to develop a sense that men should be encouraged to use limited natural resources
- Education can only help people in controlling the environmental pollution.

Conclusion

If man could live in harmony with nature and as a responsible caretaker of the environment, it is possible to attain an ecologically sound future generation to come.

Men with his unique technological power have a profound effect on his environment. Therefore, he can control to some extend his own destiny. For living in harmony with the environment, man has to evolve a balanced way of thinking, feeling and acting towards the environment.

Thus, education can play a very significant role in developing responsible environmental behaviour among people. Education can develop scientific attitude, logical thinking which leads people to respect the nature, to conserve and protect it. Habitual environmental activities have to be responsible towards environment protection. If we want to develop sustainable behaviour, we have to be conscious about our daily activities which are very small indeed, but have create impact for sustaining the natural resources. Our habitual daily activities of all kind must also be responsible towards the protection of environment. If we regulate such activities from unsustainable to sustainable, it will have great contribution for controlling and protecting the environment from further destruction.

References

1. Human resources and their development, Vol. II. Retrieved from Http://www.eolss.net/ sample – chapters/ c11/e1-10-03-02. pdf on 3/05/2016
2. Maheshwari, J.Uma (2010): live in harmony with nature. The Hindu, November 12,2010
3. Mohanty J.(1998) Modern trends in Indian education, New Delhi: Deep and Deep publications
4. NCERT (1970): Population education in School curriculum (Social Sciences). A working document, New Delhi
5. Stinson, 3. : Ecological Diversity and Modern Human Adaptations. Human Resources and Their Development, Vol. II. Retrieved from https://www.eolss.net/ebooklib/sc_cart.aspx 2 file=E1-10-03-02 on 28 February 2017.

**Associate Prof., Deptt. of Education,
Imphal College (Under Manipur University),
Imphal – West, Manipur
email : ckniangtombing@gmail.com**

14. Environmental Issues in India

Monika Khetarpal

Abstract

The population of India is increasing at a rapid pace. With the increasing population and rise in economic wealth the pollution and environmental issue related problems have increased a lot. Depletion of forest, great increase in vehicular emission, use of hazardous chemicals and troublesome activities committed by human are the factors that contribute to decline of environmental health in India. Environmental issues are major reason of disease, health related issues and long term livelihood impact for India. Present paper deals with the environmental issues and possible remedies for eco-conservation in India. Physics act as a driving tool to understand the issues related to variation in climate and greenhouse effect. As a protector and caretaker of environment a step towards progressive India can be made by clearly understanding the environmental problems along with the solutions.

Introduction

India has witnessed an enormous growth in social, economic, scientific and technological field since its independence. In 1947 India was not even able to make needle but with the passage of time India is capable of developing rockets, space crafts and nuclear devices for peaceful purposes. India is emerging as a superpower in the world. Modern discoveries in the field of science and technology have changed the picture of India on a global scale. But we still have to face environmental problems. We have to make collaborative efforts to resolve these issues, which will add on to the development of our nation.

Rapid increase in population has resulted in the decline of natural resources. Fresh water availability has declined by a large amount. Forests are destroyed for extension of land needed for buildings, roads and other commercial purpose. This destruction resulted in the extinction of various plants and animal species, thereby leading to ecological imbalance. The most sacred river, Ganga which is a symbol of Indian culture has become the most polluted river. Industrial waste which incorporates various pollutants is drained off in the river. In the present scenario, there has been a great demand for more energy consumption. This leads to environmental issues such as air pollution, water pollution, water scarcity, global warming, and climate change.

Physics and Natural World

Physics, natural science, is the study of our surrounding beautiful natural world. Through the concepts of Physics world is able to know about the universe and environment. Prior to understanding of Physics it was regarded that all the answers were from a supernatural power. With the advancement and through scientific knowledge various questions related to nature are unveiled.

To deal with the environment a sound understanding of basic concepts of Physics are required. Much of physics is the study of energy and its transformation, and energy lies at the heart of important environmental issues. The energy of the Sun greatly affects the atmosphere surrounding us as well the movement of oceans is also influenced. Without Physics we are not able to understand the fact why sky is blue, climatic conditions and environmental issues.

Environment

The word "Environment" has been derived from a French word "Environia", which means to surround. Environment can be defined as the surrounding in which a human being, plant and animals live. The environment controls the life of all organisms, including human beings. Environment refers to the materials and forces that surround the living organism. Environment plays a key role in the life cycle of human being.

Recent Environmental Issues in India

Major environmental issues in India are deforestation, air and water pollution and global warming.

I . Deforestation

Deforestation is the depletion of forest at an alarming rate. Trees are the main source of oxygen, which is essential for life of human beings. They are major component that helps to maintain the temperature of earth. By cutting of trees on large scale the earth's climate is drastically changing. As a result of deforestation, there is elimination of large species of plants and animals which leads to loss of biodiversity.

II. Pollution

Pollution has been serious issue in India. There are different types of pollution in India:

(i) Air pollution

India is polluted by vehicle emission and industry waste products. The emission of gases leads to increase in temperature of earth. This increase in earth temperature is termed as global warming. Adverse effects of global warming is melting of glaciers and increase in sea level. Air pollution has negative effect on health of human beings. **Inhaling polluted air shortens average Indian life.**

Remedies that must be adopted to reduce air pollution

In order to reduce air pollution people should not use vehicle for short distance. Public transport should be preferred as compared to individual one. The government has taken numerous majors to reduce air pollution, so that human beings can breathe fresh air. Government has introduced schemes to support electric and hybrid vehicles and is testing cleaner fuels for buses. An approach of controlling air pollution caused by industries is to modify and maintain existing pieces of equipment so that the emission of pollutants can be minimised. The most prominent approach to reduce air pollution is plantation. Plants and trees reduce a large number of pollutants in the air.

(ii) Water pollution

Water pollution is a burning issue in India. Rivers, lakes and oceans are polluted by harmful substances emitted from industry, untreated sewage and solid wastes. Quality of water is largely degraded. Water is the basic need for survival of life so it must be prevented. The dumped plastic bottles, tins, water cans and other wastes pollute the water bodies. These result in water pollution, which harms not just humans, but the whole ecosystem. Furthermore, religious activities such as burials and cremations near the shore contribute to pollution. These all effects can lead to serious health problems for human beings.

Remedies that must be adopted to reduce water pollution

In order to prevent water from any kind of pollutants the sewage waste must be treated prior to discharge in water bodies. Use of harmful pesticides should be minimized. On individual level one can contribute to control water pollution by reusing, reducing, and recycling wherever possible. When we waste less water, and encourage others to do so, it makes good economic as well as environmental sense.

(iii) Land pollution

Land pollution refers to destruction of Earth's surface directly or indirectly as a result of human activity. Deforestation carried by humans to create dry land is one of the major concerns. The unused land with a period of time becomes barren and is of no use. Another important factor that contributes to land pollution is garbage. Garbage like aluminium, wood, plastic, paper is produced by each and every house. Few of them are recycled and remaining ones lead to land pollution. Apart from this highly toxic fertilizers and pesticides used result in the contamination and poisoning of soil. All these factors have a negative effect on human health. Rain cycle is disturbed by deforestation. Increased temperature and unseasonal weather activity are the consequence of pollution.

Remedies that must be adopted to reduce land pollution

Pollution can be minimized if we are well aware with the concept of reduce, reuse and recycle. Organic gardening and consumption of organic food will contribute to reduce pollution, as for these purpose pesticides are not required. Biodegradable products must be purchased. We survive on land and so it is our duty to take care of it and nurture it.

Green House Effect

The greenhouse effect is a process that occurs when gases in Earth's atmosphere trap the Sun's heat. During the process the energy from the sun reaches the earth's surface. The Earth radiate the heat back as thermal radiations, greenhouse gases present in the atmosphere absorb some of the heat and then radiate some of it back down towards earth, keeping it a warmer, a place to live happily. This process makes Earth much warmer than it would be without an atmosphere. The greenhouse effect is one of the things that make Earth a comfortable place to live. Greenhouse gases present in the atmosphere are:

1. Water vapour: Water vapour is a natural greenhouse gas and is the most important. Concentration of water vapour varies widely with location, season and time

2. Carbon dioxide: Carbon dioxide is regarded as an important greenhouse gas due to its dominating contribution to global warming.
3. Methane: Methane is another important greenhouse gas. It is chemically and radiatively active.
4. Nitrous oxide: Natural sources of nitrous oxide include wet forests, oceans and dry savannas.
5. Chlorofluorocarbons. Chlorofluorocarbons (CFCs) are man-made chemicals which are used as propellants in aerosols, as coolants in refrigeration and air-conditioning industry, in plastic foam industry and as solvents in computer and electronic industry.
6. Ozone. Ozone is another effective greenhouse gas which exists both in the troposphere as well as the stratosphere. In the stratosphere it absorbs the lethal ultraviolet rays of the sun while in the troposphere it is a health hazard. About 90% of the total ozone resides in the stratosphere. Ozone is not directly emitted by human activities, but is altered by other emissions

The Physics of Climate Change

Weather and climatic situations are regulated by the absorption of solar radiation and then re-distribution of the energy through radiative and hydrological processes. The temperature of Earth's surface is primarily determined by the balance between the absorption and emission of radiation. A change in this radiative balance is termed a radiative forcing, which is measured in Watts per square meter.

Naturally occurring greenhouse gases, primarily water vapour and carbon dioxide, trap thermal radiation from the Earth's surface and this effect keeps the surface warmer than it would be otherwise. Natural greenhouse effect is uncontrollably enhanced by activities of human as the concentration of greenhouse gases is increasing by large amount.

In particular if we consider carbon dioxide, its concentration has enormously increased due to human activity. Along with it the concentration of methane has also increased. In general it can be stated that level of greenhouse gases in the atmosphere is continuously increasing at a rapid pace. This leads to gradual increase in temperature of earth, which is stated as global warming.

Effects of Global Warming

The causes of global warming are greenhouse gases. They include carbon dioxide, methane nitrous oxide, compounds comprising of chlorine and bromine. Global warming has many negative effects, some are listed below:

1. Due to global warming water vapour existing in the atmosphere fall again as rain and this leads to floods in various regions across the globe.
2. Due to rise in temperature, evaporation process from both land and sea rises enormously which leads to flood in various regions of the world.
3. Drought and scarcity of water supply may occur in various places. Reason behind this is that glaciers all over the world are shrinking at a high rate and the melting of ice is occurring at a rapid rate than projected previously.
4. Global warming has great negative impact on health of living organisms. Excessive heat cause increase in stress level, which lead to increased blood pressure and heart diseases.
5. Increase in temperature lead to dehydration, which is a main cause of kidney stones.
6. Global warming also affects animals. For their survival they have to move to cooler places.

Global warming is a big hazard and serious action must be taken to resolve this issue. Toxic emission from vehicles should be reduced. Greenhouse gases mainly arise from fossil fuels. Alternative sources of energy must be used.

Conclusions

Harmful issues related to environment and its conservation has been raised during the past few years. Natural and human activities have created severe climate and environmental changes which have negative impact on the existence of living organism on earth. Physics has impacted society by imparting the understanding of environmental changes happening all across the globe. The paper discussed various types of pollution and possible remedies that must be adopted to reduce them, so that we can live in clean environment. Along with these issues light has been thrown on other burning issue, global warming. Adverse effects of global warming on earth are also explored.

References
[1] Shahzad, U. (2015). Global warming: Causes, effects and solutions. *Durreesamin Journal*, *1*(4), 1-7.
[2] Yadav, A. (2013). An Empirical Study on Environmental Issues in India. *Global Journal of Management and Business Studies*, *3*(9), 949-954.
[3] Pant, H., Verma, J., & Surya, S. (2020). Environmental issues: Local, regional, and global environmental issues. *Environmental issues: Local, regional, and global environmental issues*, 234-246.
[4] Hansen, J., Sato, M., Ruedy, R., Lacis, A., & Oinas, V. (2000). Global warming in the twenty-first century: An alternative scenario. *Proceedings of the National Academy of Sciences*, *97*(18), 9875-9880.
[5] Klingelhöfer, D., Müller, R., Braun, M., Brüggmann, D., & Groneberg, D. A. (2020). Climate change: Does international research fulfill global demands and necessities?. *Environmental Sciences Europe*, *32*, 1-21.
[6] El-Sharkawy, M. A. (2014). Global warming: causes and impacts on agroecosystems productivity and food security with emphasis on cassava comparative advantage in the tropics/subtropics. *Photosynthetica*, *52*(2), 161-178.
[7] Adedeji, O. (2014). Global climate change. *Journal of Geoscience and Environment Protection*, *2*(02), 114.
[8] Ambhore, S., Pawar, A. S., & Pawar, M. P. (2013). Environmental protection: A critical analysis of situation prevailing in India. *Global Research Analysis*, *2*(7), 35-37.

Associate Professor,
Department of Physics,
Government Maharani Sudershan College for women,
Bikaner, Rajasthan (India)

15. Probing the Effects of Mobile Phone Tower Radiation on Human Blood, Muscle and Bone : Insights from SAR Calculations

Shilpa Yadav *, Shivshankar Prasad Pandey **

Abstract

The use of mobile phones has become an integral part of modern life. However, there are concerns about the potential health effects of mobile phone radiation, especially from the towers that provide coverage. The physiological mechanism of how this radiation affects human health is not yet well understood, but it is known that exposure to high-frequency electromagnetic waves from mobile phones and their towers can affect the blood, muscle and bone of individuals who frequently use handsets or live in close proximity to these structures. This study aimed to investigate the penetration of high-frequency electromagnetic waves emitted from a mobile phone tower into human blood, muscles and bone tissues. The SAR is a measure of the rate at which energy is absorbed by the body when exposed to electromagnetic radiation. The effective radiated power from the mobile phone tower was set at 20 Watts, which is a common value used in many studies. This researcher focused on 2450 MHz, 3500 MHz and 6000 MHz frequencies because they are commonly used in mobile phone communication. Understanding the impact of mobile phone radiation on human health is crucial, given the widespread use of these devices. This study provides insights into the potential effects of mobile phone tower radiation on human tissues, which can inform the development of strategies to mitigate any negative health effects.

Keyword's : Electromagnetic, Specific absorption rate (SAR), Penetration, Widespread use, Mitigate

Introduction

The specific absorption rate (SAR) is the rate at which energy is absorbed by the human body when exposed to a radio frequency (RF) electromagnetic field (EMF). It is expressed in watts per kilogram (W/kg) and is measured as the power absorbed by tissue per unit mass. SAR values are usually averaged over the whole body or a particular body tissue. While the SAR is determined at the highest certified power level, the actual SAR level of the device in operation can be well below the maximum value. To measure the SAR, a mobile phone handset should be placed at the head in a talk position, and the value is measured at the highest location of absorption rate in the entire head. The SAR value is affected by the conductivity and relative permittivity of human body tissues and can describe the possible biological effects of RF fields.(Miller et al. 2019; Ochbelagh Dariush Rezaei, Abdollah Borhanifar, and Asadi Asadollah n.d.; Salem n.d.)

High-energy RF field exposure can cause thermal effects in biological tissues, resulting in non-thermal effects and generating high SAR values. The effect of dielectric values of human body on SAR is frequency-dependent and influenced by the orientation of the human body. Different countries have their regulations for occupational exposure and general public exposure to radiofrequency electromagnetic radiation, based on the limits recommended by international organizations such as ICNIRP. Mobile phone handsets and satellite phone handsets operating in close proximity to the human body are required to undergo mandatory SAR compliance testing or evaluation in some countries. However, comparisons between different measurements cannot be made without information on the averaging volume used, and a single SAR value does not give complete information about the amount of radiofrequency exposure. While a lower SAR value may indicate lower exposure to radiofrequency energy, it is important to use specific absorption rate values as a tool for checking the maximum possible exposure from a particular model of mobile phone handset, and to follow safety guidelines set by the Federal Communications Commission.(Pandey 2022b, 2022a; Usha Rani, Srinivasa Baba, and Gundala 2018)

Calculations of Specific Absorption Rate (SAR) : Hossain, Faruque, and Islam **2015**; Khalatbari et al. **2006**; Wessapan and Rattanadecho **((2012** SAR calculations are affected by various factors, including the frequency of the electromagnetic waves, the distance from the source of radiation, and the skin depth of the tissue being exposed. The SAR values can be calculated using mathematical models that take into account the dielectric properties of the human body tissues.

The skin depth, which is the distance at which the intensity of the electromagnetic waves is reduced to $\frac{1}{e}$ of its original value, is also an important factor in SAR calculations. The skin depth depends on SAR calculations require sophisticated mathematical models that take into account various factors, such as the frequency of the electromagnetic waves, the distance from the source of radiation, and the skin depth and density of the tissue being exposed.

The specific absorption rate (SAR) is a measure of the rate at which energy is absorbed by a tissue when it is exposed to an electromagnetic field. It is defined as:

$$SAR = \frac{\Delta E}{\Delta t}\frac{1}{m} \qquad \text{.......................... (1)}$$

Where ΔE is the energy absorbed by the tissue in a time interval Δt, and m is the mass of the tissue.

Assuming that the electromagnetic field is uniform and the tissue is isotropic, the absorbed power density can be expressed as:

$$p = \frac{\sigma E^2}{2} \qquad \text{......................(2)}$$

Where σ is the electrical conductivity of the tissue, E is the magnitude of the electric field, and E^2 represents the power density of the electromagnetic field.

Since power density is energy per unit time and volume, it can be expressed as:

$$E^2 = \frac{P}{\rho V} \qquad \text{......................(3)}$$

where P is the total power of the electromagnetic field, ρ is the density of the tissue, and V is the volume of the tissue.

Substituting value of E^2 in equation (2) from equation (3) we get:

$$p = \frac{\sigma P}{2\rho V} \qquad \text{......................(4)}$$

Multiplying both sides of this equation by the volume V, we obtain the energy absorbed by the tissue in a time interval Δt :

$$\Delta E = \frac{\sigma P \Delta t}{2\rho}$$

Finally, substituting this expression for ΔE in the definition of SAR, we get:

$$SAR = \frac{\sigma P}{2\rho}\frac{1}{m}$$

Substituting E^2 from the earlier equation, we get:

$$SAR = \frac{\sigma E^2 V}{2}\frac{1}{m}$$

Simplifying this expression, we get:

$$SAR = \frac{\sigma E^2}{2\rho}$$

Thus, we have derived an expression for SAR in terms of the electrical conductivity, electric field, and density of the tissue. The electric field is calculated using the formula:

$$E = \sqrt{\frac{P}{4\pi r^2}}$$

Where P is the power of the tower and r is the distance from the tower.

Standard values

The standard values of conductivity and skin depth at frequency 2450 MHz, 3500 MHz and 6000 MHz for biological materials of density 1850 kg/m3 (blood), 3490 kg/m3 (muscle), and 1042 kg/m3 (bone) are:(Hossain, Faruque, and Islam 2015; Usha Rani, Srinivasa Baba, and Gundala 2018)

Frequency (MHz)	Blood		Muscle		Bone	
	σ (S/m)	Skin depth (mm)	σ (S/m)	Skin depth (mm)	σ (S/m)	Skin depth (mm)
2450	0.7	1.1	0.8	0.9	0.02	11.7
3500	0.7	0.13	1.03	0.09	0.27	0.26
6000	0.7	0.029	0.62	0.018	0.3	0.064

Table (1)

Note: These values are approximate and can vary based on factors such as temperature and composition of the biological material.

The standard value of time-varying electric fields for EMF radiation at different frequencies are:

The standard value of time-varying electric fields for EMF radiation with a frequencies 2450 MHz, 3500 MHz and 6000 MHz are 27.5 V/m, 27.5 V/m and 61.4 V/m respectively for general public exposure.

It's important to note that these values may vary depending on the specific regulations and standards set by different countries or organizations.

SAR (Specific Absorption Rate)

The SAR values are calculated based on the given parameters using the formula:

$$SAR = \frac{\sigma E^2}{2\rho}$$

Where σ is the conductivity, E is the electric field, and ρ is the density of the tissue.

The electric field is calculated using the formula:

$$E = \sqrt{\frac{P}{4\pi r^2}}$$

Where P is the power of the tower and r is the distance from the tower.

Here is a table of SAR (Specific Absorption Rate)

Distance (m)	SAR For BLOOD (W/kg)			SAR For MUSCLE (W/kg)			SAR For BONE (W/kg)		
	2450 MHz	3500 MHz	6000 MHz	2450 MHz	3500 MHz	6000 MHz	2450 MHz	3500 MHz	6000 MHz
1	156.5	154.7	146.7	0.204	0.407	1.105	0.38	0.55	0.94
10	0.002	0.0018	0.0013	0.002	0.016	0.147	0.00038	0.00055	0.00094
20	0.00022	0.00017	0.00012	0.001	0.005	0.037	0.000095	0.000138	0.000235
30	0.000087	0.000066	0.000047	0.0005	0.002	0.016	0.000042	0.000062	0.000105
40	0.000048	0.000035	0.000024	0.0003	0.001	0.009	0.000024	0.000035	0.00006
50	0.000031	0.000022	0.000015	0.0002	0.001	0.005	0.000015	0.000022	0.000038

Note: The above table is based on the Table (1)

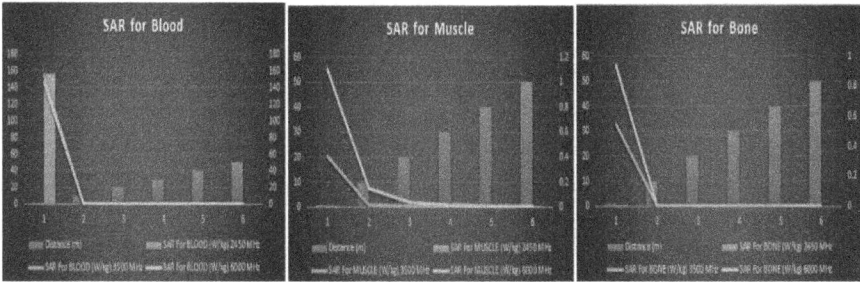

Discussion

The table provided shows the specific absorption rate (SAR) values for blood, muscle, and bone tissue at different distances from a radiofrequency (RF) source for various frequencies (2450 MHz, 3500 MHz, and 6000 MHz). SAR is a measure of the rate at which energy is absorbed by the body per unit mass of tissue exposed to an RF field. It is expressed in watts per kilogram (W/kg).

The data in the table suggests that the SAR values decrease with increasing distance from the RF source. At a distance of 1 meter, the SAR values for blood and muscle tissues are significantly higher than the values for bone tissue, which has a lower water content and therefore absorbs less RF energy.

At a distance of 10 meters, the SAR values for all tissue types decrease significantly, with values in the range of 0.0013 W/kg to 0.002 W/kg for frequencies of 2450 MHz and 3500 MHz. At 20 meters, the SAR values decrease even further, with values ranging from 0.00012 W/kg to 0.001 W/kg.

The data also shows that the SAR values increase with increasing frequency. For example, at a distance of 1 meter, the SAR values for blood tissue at 6000 MHz are almost 6 times higher than the values at 2450 MHz. Similarly, the SAR values for muscle tissue at 6000 MHz are more than 2.5 times higher than the values at 2450 MHz.

Overall, the data in the table suggests that the SAR values for tissues exposed to RF radiation decrease with increasing distance from the source and with decreasing frequency. It is important to note that the SAR values in the table represent exposure levels above the recommended limits set by the International Commission on Non-Ionizing Radiation Protection (ICNIRP), and therefore caution should be taken to minimize exposure to RF radiation.

Conclusion and Recommendation

Based on the data presented in the SAR table, we can draw several conclusions and recommendations:

SAR values decrease with increasing distance from the RF source. This means that the closer one is to an RF source, the higher the exposure levels and potential health risks.

SAR values increase with increasing frequency. This means that higher frequency RF radiation, such as that used by 5G networks, may pose higher risks to human health than lower frequency RF radiation.

At a distance of 1 meter from the RF source, SAR values for blood and muscle tissues are higher than those for bone tissue. This is because tissues with higher water content absorb more RF energy.

The SAR values shown in the table are above the recommended limits set by the ICNIRP. It is therefore important to minimize exposure to RF radiation and follow any guidelines or regulations that may be in place in your location.

Further research is needed to better understand the potential long-term health effects of exposure to RF radiation.

In light of these conclusions, it is recommended that individuals take steps to reduce their exposure to RF radiation whenever possible. This can include using hands-free devices for mobile phones, keeping mobile phones away from the body when not in use, and avoiding prolonged exposure to RF radiation from other sources. It is also important to stay informed about any guidelines or regulations that may be in place in your location regarding exposure to RF radiation. Finally, further research is needed to better understand the potential health risks of exposure to RF radiation, particularly at higher frequencies.

References

Hossain, M I, M R I Faruque, and M T Islam. 2015. "Analysis on the Effect of the Distances and Inclination Angles between Human Head and Mobile Phone on SAR." Progress in biophysics and molecular biology 119(2): 103–10.

Khalatbari, S., Dariush Sardari, Ali Akbar Mirzaee, and Hassan Ali Sadafi. 2006. "Calculating SAR in Two Models of the Human Head Exposed to Mobile Phones Radiations at 900 and 1800 MHz." PIERS Online 2(1): 104–9.

Miller, Anthony B et al. 2019. "Risks to Health and Well-Being From Radio-Frequency Radiation Emitted by Cell Phones and Other Wireless Devices." Frontiers in public health 7: 223.

Ochbelagh Dariush Rezaei, Abdollah Borhanifar, and Asadi Asadollah. "(PDF) Thermal Effects of Mobile Phone on Tissue." https://www.researchgate.net/publication/242581722_Thermal_Effects_of_Mobile_Phone_on_Tissue (June 28, 2022).

Pandey, Shivshankar Prasad. 2022a. "Does Mobile Tower Radiation Affect Birds?" Shodh Samiksha Aur Mulyankan 1(7): 12–19. http://www.ugcjournal.com/assets/authors/EMF_Radiation.pdf (August 5, 2022).

———. 2022b. "Use of Smartphones Causes Permanent Health Issues." World Journal of Pharmacy and Pharmaceutical Science 11(8): 382–89. https://storage.googleapis.com/journal-uploads/wjpps/article_issue/1659174800.pdf (August 5, 2022).

Salem, N M. Thermal Effects of Photon-Phonon Interaction on a Simple Tissue.

Usha Rani, M., V.S.S.N. Srinivasa Baba, and Srivalli Gundala. 2018. "Analysis of SAR in Human Blood, Bones and Muscles Due to Mobile Waves at 900MHz,1800MHz and 2400MHz." International Journal of Applied Engineering Research 13(3): 2125.

Wessapan, Teerapot, and Phadungsak Rattanadecho. 2012. "Numerical Analysis of Specific Absorption Rate and Heat Transfer in Human Head Subjected to Mobile Phone Radiation: Effects of User Age and Radiated Power." Journal of Heat Transfer 134(12).

***Department of Chemistry,
Government Mahamaya College Ratanpur (C.G.)
**Department of Physics,
Government Mahamaya College Ratanpur (C.G.)**

16. Effect of Climatic Changes on Living Organism including Plants, Animals and Human Beings

Dr Dhanendra Kumar Agnihotri[1],
Pravin Kumar Agnihotri[2]

Abstract

In the next decades, the world population will continue to be confronted with environmental changes to our food system, health management, agricultural products and their yield with nutrient quality and other things. Due to climatic changes, extremely high temperature and drought condition accelerates the evaporation of soil water and soil moisture, less decomposition of microbial activities in soil and loss of organic matters and soil nutrients in soil texture. An area's climatic affects the types of plants that can grow there. Plant growth is dependent on precipitation and temperature. If the precipitation and temperature level is too high or low, it greatly effects on plants and human life both.

The effect of climatic changes on plants, animal and human beings may be affected by e.g. interference with enzyme systems, changes in cellular chemical constituents and physical structure, retardation of growth and development due to metabolic changes as well as tissues degeneration.

The International Food Policy Research Institute (IFPRI), Global Food Policy 2022 report has warned that climatic change may push 90 million indian towards hunger by 2030. It has listed a decline in agricultural production and disruption in food supply chain, reason for future crisis.

Keywards : Climatic Changes, Agricultural Crops and their yield, Plants, Animals and Human beings life

Introduction

This article provides a comprehensive review of various reports, documents and related literature related to impact of climatic changes on agricultural crops and crop productivity. Agricultural field is affected by the emission of greenhouse gases (GHG) such as carbon dioxide, nitrous oxide and methane. These emissions mostly come from the tillage practices, fossil fuels, coal and agricultural synthetic fertilizer as well as farm animal's manure affected agricultural sector (Jones et al., 2012).

Climate changes refer to long term changes in climate including overage temperature and precipitation. Earth climate is changing and this is causing great concern. The changes place in the atmosphere have become one of the serious threats that world faces today. Human activities have the potential to disturb the balance of natural system and cause warming of the plant to an unprecedented extent. Some of these outlines are increasing the greenhouse gases emission to an extent that natural system is now not able to assimilate these gases. As a result, climate change has started endangering biodiversity, food and fresh water supply, impacting human health worldwide especially in developing countries like India due to low adaptive capacity.

The effects of climatic changes to be it natural or human induced vary from environment and environmental security to violation of human rights. While the effects of climatic change are multidimensional, its most significant outcome has been observed as human displacement.

The effects of climate change can vary from affecting livelihood of people to food scarcity and increase in natural disaster etc. this discussion is a legal inquiry of the problems which arise because of climatic change, it explores the implications of climate change that leads to human misery and examines the scope and extent to which they are addressed in the legal ordering. The effects of climate change are very grave and the problems which arise because of climate change leads to large scale violation of human rights. This study elaborates and highlighting the significant impacts of climate change and the inadequate attempt of global communities and the nation states in addressing the problems of human rights.

A climatic change is taking a toll on India's agricultural production and productivity. Intergovernmental panel on climate change (IPCC) has projected that by the end of 21st century temperature in India is likely to increase by 3-4^{0}C which would lead to a loss of 5-20% in net agricultural revenues (Kumar et al., 2020).

The causes of climatic change can be divided into two categories-

(A) Natural Cause : There are a number of natural factors responsible for climate change such as continental drift, volcanoes, ocean and earth's tilt.

(i) Continental Drift : The continents that we are familiar with today. Were formed landmass began gradually drifting apart, millions of year back. The drift also had an impact on the climate because it chanted the physical features of the landmass their position and the position of water bodies.

(ii) Volcanoes : When a volcano erupts it throws out large volumes of sulphur dioxid, water vapours, dust and ash into the atmosphere. The gases and dust particles can reach the stratosphere and partially block the incoming radiation leading to cooling. Sulphur dioxide combines with water to form tiny droplets of sulphuric acid. These droplets are so small that many of them can stay aloft for several years and are efficient rejector of sunlight and screen the ground from some of the energy that it would ordinarily receive from the sun.

(iii) Earth's Tilt : Earth is tilted at an angle of 23.5^0 is the perpendicular plane of its orbital path. For one half of the year when it is summer, the northern hemisphere tilts towards the sun. In the other half when it is winter, the earth is tilted away from the sun. If there was no tilt we would not have experienced seasons. Changes in the tilt of the earth can affect the severity of the seasons.

(iv) Ocean Current : Ocean currents have been known to change direction or slow down. Much of the heat that escapes from the oceans is in the form of water vapors the most abundant greenhouse gas on earth. Water vapours also contribute to the formation of clouds, which shade the surface and have a net cooling effect.

(B) Human Causes : All of us in our daily lives contribute little or more to this change in the climate.

(i). Utilization of high quantity of paper and timber in our office and school and manufacturing furniture's respectively.

(ii). Manufacturing the larger quantities of plastic and its materials as well as polythene which are non-degradable, thus this effects on directly our environment and atmosphere.

(iii). Consumption of high amount of diesel, petrol, coal for domestic and transportation which causes pollution and depletion of fossil fuels.

(iv). Many power plants are responsible for the emission of greenhouse gases and pollution.

Remarkable Observation :

Climatic changes are a threat to all living beings including plants, animals and human beings. Recent years have been the warmest since 1950, the year when regular instrumental records became available. Some important aspects of our lives can be affected through changes in climate-

Agriculture :

Climate change will affect agricultural yield directly because of alterations in temperature and rainfall and indirectly through changes in soil quality, pest and diseases. As the temperature rises a condition more favorable for pests such as grasshoppers to complete a number of reproduction cycles thereby increasing their population.

Climate changes alters the bioclimatic conditions during the growing period of plants directly or indirectly by causing shifts in spring and autumn leaf phenology that lead to changes in the timing and length of the growing period. Rising temperature lead to more frequent droughts, wildfires and invasive pest outbreaks leading to the loss of plant species. That has numerous detrimental effects including lowering productivity. Longer droughts and increased number of heat waves will stress plants causing them to be less productive. Due to enhance the climatic changes affects fruit crops in their different phases of growth and development such as flower and fruit shape and size, delay flowering and fruiting, delay in ripening, changes in color, low sugar contents, poor fruit taste quality, low fruit yield etc.

Weather :

A warmer climate will change rainfall and snowfall patterns, lead to increased droughts and floods cause melting of glaciers and polar ice sheets and results in accelerated sea-level rise. Rising warmth will lead to an increase in the level of evaporation of surface water, the air will also expand and this will increase its capacity to hold moisture. This is turn will affect water resources, forests and other natural ecological system, agriculture, power generation, infrastructure, tourism and human health.

Climate change makes many aspects of weather more extreme, especially heat waves, drought, rain intensity and storm size and their nature as well intensity. Global warming leads to an increase in extreme weather events such as heat waves, drought, cyclones, rainstorms etc.

Sea level Rise :

Coastal areas and small islands are the most threatened because of rises in sea level that global warming may cause. The heating of oceans and melting of glaciers and polar ice sheet is predicted to raise the average sea level by half a meter over the next century. Sea level rise could have a number of physical impacts on coastal areas. Including loss of land due to in urdation and erosion increased loading and salt water intrusion. Sea level rise poses a serious threat to coastal life around the world. Consequences include increased intensity of storm surges, flooding and damage to coastal areas. Finally, global warming is causing global means sea level to rise in two ways e.g. firstly glaciers and ice sheets worldwide are melting and adding water to the ocean, secondly, the volume of the ocean is expanding as the water warms. Sea level rise poses a serious threat to coastal life around the world. Consequences include increased intensity of storm surges, flooding and damage to coastal areas. In many cases, this is where large population centers are located, in addition to fragile wildlife habitat.

This declining trend in ocean productivity is expected to continue with productivity likely to decline by 5-10 percent by 2100. The decline will show regional variations. The tropical ocean NPP will decline more by 10-15 percent foe same emissions scenario. The flux of organic matter from the upper ocean into ocean interior will decrease because of increased stratification and reduced nutrient supply. The reduction in ocean productivity is due to the combined effects of warming, stratification, light, nutrients and predation.

Health :

Climate change is impacting human lives and health in a variety of ways. It threatens the essential ingredients of good health like clean air, safe drinking water, nutritional food supply and safe shelter and has the potential to undermine decades of progress in global health. Between 2030-2050, due to climatic change is expected to cause approximately 250000 additional deaths per year from malnutrition, malaria, diarrhoea and heat waves alone. Increase in temperature will directly affect human health by increasing cases of heat stress. Fluctuation in the climate especially in the temperature, precipitation and humidity can influence biological organism and the process linked to the spread of infectious diseases. Climate change is the single biggest health threat facing humanity and health professional worldwide are already responding to the health harms caused by this unfolding crisis. On the basis of this matter, human health can be affected by disruptions of physical, biological and ecological systems including disturbances originating here and elsewhere. The health effects of these disruptions includes increase respiratory and cardiovascular disease, injuries and premature deaths related to extreme weather events, changes in the prevalent and geographical distribution of food and water-borne illnesses and other infectious diseases and threats to mental health.

The Intergovernmental Panel on Climate Change (IPCC) has concluded that to avert catastrophic health impacts and prevent millions of climate change related deaths, the world must limit temperature rise 1.5^0C. Past emissions have already made a certain level of global temperature rise and other changes to the climate inevitable. Global heating of even 1.5^0C is not considered safe; however, every additional tenth of a degree of warming will take a serious toll on people's lives and health.

Marine Life :

As ocean water in the tropics become warmer due to climate change, the damage to coral reels seems to be increasing. These corals are very sensitive to changes in temperature of water, which causes bleaching. Zooplanktons, small organism that float on the sea surface are declining in numbers, reducing the number of fish and sea birds that feed on these organisms. Ranging temperatures increase the risk of irreversible loss of marine life and coastal ecosystem. Today widespread changes have been observed, including damage to coral reefs and mangroves that support ocean life and migration of species to higher latitudes and altitudes where the water could be cooler. Latest estimates from the United Nation Educational Scientific and Cultural Organization warn that more than half of the world's marine species may stand on the brink of extinction by 2100. At a 1.1^{0}C increase in temperature today, an estimated 60 percent of the world's marine ecosystem have already been degraded or are being used unsustainably. A warming of 1.5^{0}C threatens to destroy 70-80 percent of coral reefs and a 2.0^{0}C increase means a nearly 95 percent loss of marine diversity, but no return in own natural habitats.

Forest and Wild Life :

Percent loss ants, animals as well as human beings in the natural environment are very sensitive to change in climate. Animals are concerned in national parks and wildlife sanctuaries to provide them safety but no park boundary or conservation low car protect an ecosystem from climate change. Climate change can modify a disturbance regime that affects forest ecosystem structure and function. The change in forest structure and function are disrupted when disturbances exceed their natural ranges of variations e.g. Fires, insect outbreaks, wind storm and throws are an integral part of ecosystem dynamics in forests around the globe. A gradual enhance in temperature will alter the regeneration and growth of some species. Regeneration of tree species is affected by low soil moisture and competition with other species during the seedling stage as the temperature increase. Climatic variability and change results degeneration of the forest resources to emission of carbon dioxide in the atmosphere and affecting the forest resources and its ability to deliver its ecosystem services.

Conclusion :

Risk of climatic change is less with the right use of resources: Intergovernmental Panel on Climate Change (IPCC) has said in its report that if the existing resources are used strategically by removing policy barriers, then the risk of climatic change can be reduced. The Panel has said in its report that there should be a commensurate effort to deal with the threat of climate change, or to reduce the emission of greenhouse gases. Along with this, there are many practical and effective options to solve these problems. Sometimes it is only of policy decisions, substantial capital and resources are available to rapidly reduce greenhouse gas emissions if existing policy constraints are addressed. This can significantly reduce the impact of hazards. The report has been approved during one week conference organized in Interlaken city (Switzerland), focuses on human damage and future damage. It states that the most affected by climate change will be the vulnerable people and vulnerable ecosystem. IPCC chairman Hosung Lee said that mainstreaming effective and equitable climate action would not only reduce harm to nature and mankind, but would also bring wider benefits. The report also said that we need to take ambitious action to ensure a livable earth and a sustainable future (IPCC, 2018).

Energy Conversion Rate far from 1.5⁰C Target :

Limiting temperature rise to 1.5⁰C by the end of the century is critical to tackling the climate threat. This is possible only when the world moves rapidly towards adopting clean energy from fossil fuels. This is called energy conversion. However, the report suggests that there is no proper progress in the matter. On the basis of this report, global energy transformation has lost its way due to the impact of global crises (www.livehindustan.com date 31, March, 2023 page number 01).

Ten Thousand Gigawatts by 2030 of Clean Energy needed :

The reports of Berlin Energy Transition Dialogue states that to achieve the 1.5⁰C target, energy conversion should take place at the rate of one thousand Gigawatts annually, which is currently limited to three thousand Gigawatts by 2030. It is necessary to have ten thousand Gigawatts of clean energy. Only China, America, European Union are moving closer to this goal to some extent (www.livehindustan.com date 31, March, 2023 page number 01).

Quadruple the Investment have to extend for the Technologies :

The report says the world urgently needs major investment to accelerate the energy transition. There is an investment of 1.3 trillion American dollars in 2022 in the technologies related to this. But to meet the 1.5^0C target, it would have to increase fourfold. That is, it will have to be taken up to about five trillions American dollar. According to this reports, the cumulative investments by 2030 should be forty four trillions American dollars (www.livehindustan.com date 31, March, 2023 page number 01).

Literature Cites

IPCC (2018). Summary for Policymaker in Global Warming of 1.5^0C. An IPCC special report on the impacts of Global Warming of 1.5^0C above Pre-industrial level and related Global Greenhouse Gas Emission Pathways, in the Context of Strengthening the Global Response to the Threat of Climate Change and Sustainable Development. Editors: Masson-Delmotte, P., Zhai, H.O., Porter, D. and Shuklaet, P.R.

Jones, H.P., Hole, D.G. and Zavaleta, E.S. (2012). Harnessing nature to help people adapt to climate change. Nat. Clim. Changes. 2(7): 504-509.

Kumar, S., Mishra, A. K., Pramanik, S., Mamidanna, S. and Whitbread, A. (2020). Climate risk, Vulnerability and Resilience: Supporting Livelihood of Smallholders in Semiarid India. Land Use Policy 97, 104729. Doi: 10.1016/j.landusepol.2020.104729

www.livehindustan.com date 31, March, 2023 Page number 01.

[1]**Assistant Professor, Department of Botany' G overnment PG College, Hasanpur, Amroha, UP email : agnihotri.drdk@gmail.com**
[2]**Librarian, Kothiwal Dental College and Research Center, Moradabad, UP**

17. Photoluminescence Study of Synthesized Nontoxic Phosphor for Sustainable Environment

Shashank Sharma*,[1], Sanjay Kumar Dubey[2]

Abstract

A variety of inorganic compounds known as silicates has grown to be more popular as a result of their superior chemical resistance and transparency to visible light, which make them suitable for a wide range of uses. They are more expressively researched because to their excellent thermal and chemical stability, inexpensive price, and strong near-ultraviolet absorption. $Ca_2MgSi_2O_7:Eu^{2+}$, Dy^{3+} phosphor was synthesized by high-temperature solid-state reaction technique. This structure is a member of melilite group and revealed tetragonal, Akermanite structure with a space group P^-421m. The excitation spectrum shows a broad absorption band at 200–400nm with 365nm wavelength single broad emission peak situated at 505nm was obtained. The prepared $Ca_2MgSi_2O_7:Eu^{2+},Dy^{3+}$ phosphors were characterized using photoluminescence excitation and emission spectra. Prominent green colour emission was obtained under ultraviolet excitation.

1. Introduction

Light exhibits remarkable behaviour in the diverse applications of material science and nanotechnology, and as a result, cross-cutting concerns are inevitably growing in importance as the world becomes more networked and dependent on renewable energy in the twenty-first century. One of the most important and fundamental components of the green ecosystem that offers further innovation for human consumption is the new phrase "Material Diversity". The fact that photoluminescence analysis only needs a minimal amount of the sample (nearly 20 mg), and does not require the sample to be in solution form for powdered phosphor materials gives it a similar advantage over other spectroscopic methods. With the use of this technique, materials can be investigated quickly. This method was also used to create Eu^{2+} doped and Dy^{3+} codoped di calcium magnesium di silicate phosphors, and the properties of the powder were examined with and without the addition of a flux such H_3BO_3.

It is generally agreed that Eu^{2+} is a most common emission centre in persistent phosphor hosted by the $4f^7 \rightarrow 4f^65d^1$ transition [1-3]. Matsuzawa et al., it was stated that Eu^{2+} ions served as electron traps ($Eu^{2+} + e \rightarrow Eu^+$) while Dy^{3+} ions served as hole traps (Dy^{3+} + hole $\rightarrow Dy^{4+}$). Between the lower energy state (ground) and higher energy state (excited) state of Eu^{2+} ions, Dy^{3+} ions serve as deep hole trap levels [4,5]. Silicates are highly transparent to visible light and possess great chemical resistance, they are a desirable class of inorganic materials that are employed in a variety of applications [6]. Because they have good near-UV absorption, high thermal and chemical stability, are inexpensive, and have excellent water resistance [4]. Akermanite phosphors serve their purpose in production because of their excellent physical and chemical stability properties. A calcium magnesium silicate phosphor would be a fantastic by product from the manufacturing of optical devices for the lighting industries [7,8]. In the current work, we describe the high-temperature solid-state synthesis method used to produce the bright green-emitting $Ca_2MgSi_2O_7$:Eu^{2+}, Dy^{3+} phosphor, as well as its characterisation and luminous properties. On the basis of photoluminescence (PL), optical properties were also examined, with excitation and emission being thoroughly discussed.

2. Experimental Studies

Sample Preparation

In our study, the prepared samples with stoichiometric ratio of $Ca_2MgSi_2O_7$:Eu^{2+}, Dy^{3+} were synthesized via conventional high-temperature solid-state synthesis route (shown in fig.1). Initially, all raw reagents such as $CaCO_3$ (99.99%), MgO (99.99%), SiO_2 (99.99%) and H_3BO_3 (99.99%) of Hi-media (AR grade) as well as rare earth ions Eu_2O_3 (99.99%) and Dy_2O_3 (99.99%) were used in present research investigations. Very little amount of boric acid [H_3BO_3] was used as a flux. Before being transferred to a silica crucible, the precursor chemical reagents were completely crushed in an hour in an agate crusher and pestle. Then the mixture was presintered at $950°C$ and subsequently fired at $1150°C$ in high-temperature muffle furnace for 2h in a weak reducing atmosphere with liberation of gaseous products. The weak reducing atmosphere have produced by using activated charcoal [4]. To transform Eu^{3+}

into Eu^{2+} is the task of decreasing atmosphere. Further grinding into a fine powder was used to produce the finished product. The finished phosphor was produced as a white powder and stored in an airtight container for further characterisation studies including photoluminescence spectra.

The chemical reaction of this process is given as follows:

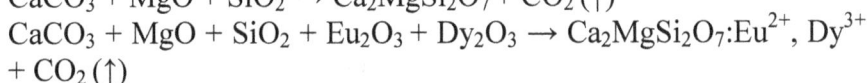

$$CaCO_3 + MgO + SiO_2 \rightarrow Ca_2MgSi_2O_7 + CO_2 (\uparrow)$$
$$CaCO_3 + MgO + SiO_2 + Eu_2O_3 + Dy_2O_3 \rightarrow Ca_2MgSi_2O_7:Eu^{2+}, Dy^{3+} + CO_2 (\uparrow)$$

Sample Characterization

By using the solid-state reaction technique, the $Ca_2MgSi_2O_7:Eu^{2+}$, Dy^{3+} powder sample was thoroughly prepared. It was presintered at 950°C and then fired at 1150°C in a high-temperature muffle furnace for two hours in a weak reducing atmosphere. The measurement of the Photoluminescence (PL) excitation & emission spectra were carried out using a Spectrofluorophotometer (SHIMADZU, RF-5301 PC) with a Xenon lamp as the excitation source.

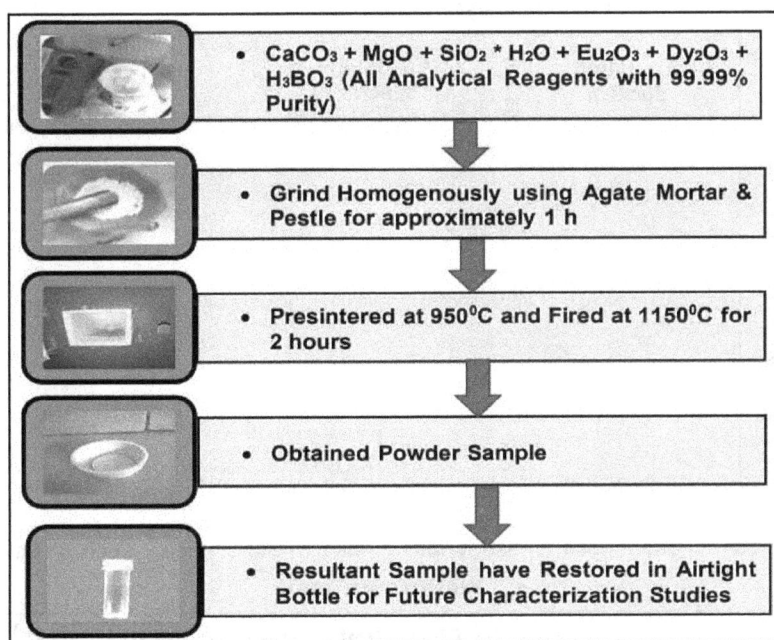

- $CaCO_3 + MgO + SiO_2 * H_2O + Eu_2O_3 + Dy_2O_3 + H_3BO_3$ (All Analytical Reagents with 99.99% Purity)

- Grind Homogenously using Agate Mortar & Pestle for approximately 1 h

- Presintered at 950°C and Fired at 1150°C for 2 hours

- Obtained Powder Sample

- Resultant Sample have Restored in Airtight Bottle for Future Characterization Studies

Fig. 1. Material Synthesization Process

2. Results and Discussion
Photoluminescence Spectra

The photoluminescence approach has become a primary way in a variety of materials chemistry domains thanks to advancements in nanoscience. When photons are absorbed under the stimulation of external energy, a substance will produce light on its own, a process known as photoluminescence. To examine luminescence characteristics of materials, such as their excitation and emission spectra, photoluminescence is a contactless, non-destructive method [9]. Jiang et al. reported that the possible sites for incorporating Eu^{2+} in $Ca_2MgSi_2O_7$ lattice are Ca^{2+} sites, or the Mg^{2+} sites or the Si^{4+} sites, Mg^{2+} (0.58 Å) and Si4+ sites (0.26 Å) are small, but Ca^{2+} (1.12 Å) is equal to the size of Eu^{2+} (1.12 Å). So, Eu^{2+} ions hardly incorporate into tetrahedral $[MgO_4]$ and $[SiO_4]$ and only incorporate into $[CaO_8]$ anions complexes in host [10]. $Ca_2MgSi_2O_7:Eu^{2+}$, Dy^{3+} is known as an efficient phosphor with good stability, which also shows green emission with great stability and persistency [4,11].

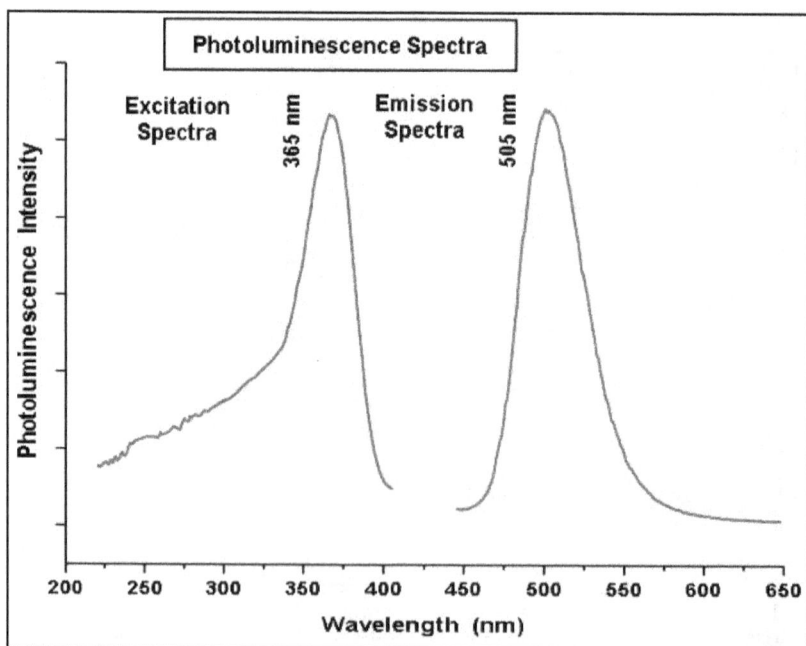

Fig. 2. Excitation and emission spectra of synthesized $Ca_2MgSi_2O_7:Eu^{2+}$, Dy^{3+} Phosphor

The excitation and emission spectra of $Ca_2MgSi_2O_7$: Eu^{2+}, Dy^{3+} phosphor prepared was shown in Figure 2. The broadband emission spectra centered at 505 nm (Green region) observed under the ultraviolet excitation of 365 nm correspond to the Eu^{2+} emission arising due to transitions from sublevels of $4f^6 5d^1$ configuration to $^8S_{7/2}$ level of the $4f^7$ configuration but with Eu^{2+} occupying different lattice sites. Since the crystal field can greatly affect the $4f^6 5d^1$ electron states of Eu^{2+}, it suggests that the crystal field is not changed much with the compositional variation [4, 12-13]. The emission spectra are identical in shape and the bands differ only in intensities. After stimulation by UV light, ground states of Eu^{2+} stimulation occurs as a result of electron and hole pairs generation from the ground state 4f to excited 4f5d state. Some free holes transported into the conduction band are captured by the Dy^{3+} traps [14]. Our results strongly imply that the popular "hole transfer" models.

Material Diversity and Environmental Protection

During the 21st century, scientific and technological progress have been closely linked to national advancement, and in recent years, this connection has gotten even stronger. In order to understand the chain mechanisms of material analysis, a large area of bio material engineering researches physics, chemistry, and the methods of innovative material modelling. This field applies fundamental ideas to luminescence behaviour. Human resources that placed a higher importance on mental and spiritual purity than on material success. In order to maintain a clean and natural environment, our brand-new, state-of-the-art optical device system, which is made of rare earth minerals, has the ability to absorb and control environmental pollution sources. When linked with business operations, it helps build a balanced industrial framework that has greater potential, better utilises the readily available natural nanomaterial resources, and upholds the planet's environmental sustainability.

Materials consider the diversity of habitats as well as human society. Rare-earth doped nanophosphors have shown to be a very interesting issue in a number of technological and environmental application sectors. Many applications for white LEDs with phosphor modifications are made possible by their exceptional key properties, including their long operational lifetime, clean energy, higher brilliance, improved luminous efficiency, chemical stability, compactness, and environmental friendliness.

Light sensors are used to get physical information about an object without physical contact or manipulation. Recently, communication has become a part of our daily lives. An abundance of nano sensor materials detects circumstances, and communication keeps the weather updated. One of the most inventive and cutting-edge is silicate-based nanomaterials, and it has been designed to give a quick overview of the potential uses of a fast communication network system.

Using silicate-based nano-sensor optical devices, which are noise-free and noise-free, the transmission of higher frequency, faster, and better transmitted messages has been expedited via this channel. The materials utilised to make electronics with this phosphor are more eco-friendly and energy-efficient. As a result, research and development in the domain of nanostructured silicate-based nanomaterials is extensive and diverse and has been growing rapidly over the past several years on a global scale.

4. Conclusions

In a summary, biomaterials and biodiversity have the same conservative components. It makes reference to the variety of human existence and the overall energetic exchanges that take place. It is a fundamental part of humanity's eco-friendly, sustainable behaviour. It plays a number of crucial ecological tasks related to precipitation, climate change, environmental adaptation, and dealing with new pests. From the results presented here, it can be concluded that $Ca_2MgSi_2O_7:Eu^{2+}, Dy^{3+}$ phosphors were prepared easily by via the solid-state reaction route. The broadband PL emission peaks exhibited maximum intensity of photoluminescence signals centered at 505 nm show efficient emission colour in green region, which is the most sensitive to the human eyes. Observed under the ultraviolet excitation of 365 nm correspond to the Eu^{2+} emission arising due to transitions from sublevels of $4f^65d^1$ configuration to $^8S_{7/2}$ level of the $4f^7$ configuration but with Eu^{2+} occupying different lattice sites. No emission peaks of Eu^{3+} were observed in the spectra. This suggests that under the reducing environment, all of the Eu^{3+} ions in the matrix had been converted to Eu^{2+} ions. This synthesized material is Eco-friendly and non-toxic. Moreover, near UV-LED conversion phosphor, medication delivery, white light emitting phosphor, long-lasting phosphor, tissue engineering, bone material, cancer illness detection, image processing of computer science, etc. are among the advantageous characteristics for applications.

Acknowledgements

Authors are gratefully acknowledged to Dept. of physics, Dr. Radha Bai, Govt. Navin Girls College Mathpara Raipur (C.G.) India, providing the facility of muffle furnace and other essential research equipment's in present investigations. We are also heartily and thankful to Dept. of physics, Pt. Ravishankar Shukla University, Raipur (C.G.), India for providing us the facility of Photoluminescence (PL) analysis.

References

1. Blasse, G. (1968). Fluorescence of Eu^{2+}-Activated Alkaline-Earth Aluminates. *Philips Res. Reps.*, *23*, 201.
2. Yamazaki, K., Nakabayashi, H., Kotera, Y., & Ueno, A. (1986). Fluorescence of Eu^{2+}- activated binary alkaline earth silicate. *Journal of the Electrochemical Society*, *133*(3), 657.
3. Dubey, S. K., & Sharma, S. (2020). A Brief Review to Study of Preparation and Photoluminescence (PL) Properties to Finding Possibilities of Divalent Europium Doped Barium Magnesium Silicate Based Phosphors. *IJSRED*, *9*, 12.
4. Sharma, S., Dubey, S. k., Diwakar, A. K. (2021). Luminescence investigation on $Ca_2MgSi_2O_7:Eu^{2+}$, Dy^{3+} phosphor. *International Journal of Materials Science*, 2, 8-15.
5. Matsuzawa, T., Aoki, Y., Takeuchi, N., & Murayama, Y. (1996). A new long phosphorescent phosphor with high brightness, $SrAl_2O_4:Eu^{2+}$, Dy^{3+}. *Journal of the Electrochemical Society*, *143*(8), 2670.
6. Lin, L., Yin, M., Shi, C., & Zhang, W. (2008). Luminescence properties of a new red long-lasting phosphor: Mg_2SiO_4: Dy^{3+}, Mn^{2+}. *Journal of Alloys and Compounds*, *455*(1-2), 327-330.
7. Sharma, S., & Dubey, S. K. (2021). The significant properties of silicate based luminescent nanomaterials in various fields of

applications: a review. *International Journal of Scientific Research in Physics and Applied Sciences*, 9(4), 37-41.

8. Dubey, S. K., Sharma, S., Pandey, S., Diwakar, A. K. (2021). Luminescence Characteristics of monoclinic ($Ba_2MgSi_2O_7:Dy^{3+}$) phosphor. *North Asian International Research Journal of Sciences, Engineering & I.T.*, 7(11), 45-55.

9. Jiang, L., Chang, C., Mao, D., & Feng, C. (2003). Concentration quenching of Eu^{2+} in $Ca_2MgSi_2O_7$: Eu^{2+} phosphor. *Materials Science and Engineering: B, 103*(3), 271-275.

10. Singha, A., Dhar, P., & Roy, A. (2005). A nondestructive tool for nanomaterials: Raman and photoluminescence spectroscopy. *American journal of physics, 73*(3), 224-233.

11. Yen WM, Weber MJ. Inorganic phosphors: compositions, preparation and optical properties. CRC press, 2004

12. Shi, C., Fu, Y., Liu, B., Zhang, G., Chen, Y., Qi, Z., & Luo, X. (2007). The roles of Eu^{2+} and Dy^{3+} in the blue long-lasting phosphor $Sr_2MgSi_2O_7$: Eu^{2+}, Dy^{3+}. *Journal of luminescence, 122*, 11-13.

13. Lin, L., Zhonghua, Z. H. A. O., Zhang, W., Zheng, Z., & Min, Y. I. N. (2009). Photo-luminescence properties and thermo-luminescence curve analysis of a new white long-lasting phosphor: $Ca_2MgSi_2O_7$: Dy^{3+}. *Journal of Rare Earths, 27*(5), 749-752.

14. Jia, W., Yuan, H., Lu, L., Liu, H., & Yen, W. M. (1999). Crystal growth and characterization of Eu^{2+}, Dy^{3+}: $SrAl_2O_4$ and Eu^{2+}, Nd^{3+}: $CaAl_2O_4$ by the LHPG method. *Journal of Crystal Growth, 200*(1-2), 179-184.

[1]**Department of Physics,
Dr. C. V. Raman University, Kota
Bilaspur (Chhattisgarh) India, 495113**
[2]**Department of Physics,
Dr. Radha Bai, Govt. Navin Girls College,
Raipur (Chhattisgarh) India, 492001**
*Corresponding Author:: shashanksharma1729@gmail.com

18. Bioplastics – Facile and Ecofriendly Substitute to Conventional Plastics

Ritu Saharan

Abstract

In recent years, intense use of plastics in various fields have raised economic and environmental complications. When plastics are burnt, toxic gases that are detrimental to human health are frequently produced. Due to excessive use of plastic products, the landfill problem has ascended which is the foremost environmental issue. Plastics accumulation in ocean, sea and other water bodies causes water pollution and harm to aquatic organisms. Furthermore, plastics are non-biodegradable in nature. It persists in the natural world for a long time and severely affect the eco-system. Due to these drawbacks of plastics, scientists and researchers are seeking for a sustainable substitute to plastics which should be eco-friendly, less toxic, biodegradable, inexpensive etc. This sustainable, facile and ecofriendly substitute is bioplastic. Bioplastics are produced from biomass viz. corn, sugar, potatoes, maize, etc. Use of bioplastics do not cause any type of pollution in the environment. In food and catering sectors they are used as a packaging material. There is a widespread opportunity of biodegradable plastics owing to their ecofriendly nature. Several investigations have been going on in this arena to enhance the quality and to reduce the processing cost of bioplastics so that these materials can be affordable and accessible by society for their effective use in day-to-day life.

Keywords : bioplastics, eco-friendly, biomass, biodegradable, sustainable

Bioplastics –Facile and Ecofriendly Substitute to Conventional Plastics

Population growth has rapidly increased the uses of several types of plastic materials to fulfill the essential needs of human beings (Amin et al. 2019). Plastics have wide-ranging applications and have become an essential component of our everyday lives because of their broad range of properties. So, demand of plastics is very high due to their attractive and numerous uses in household and in the

185

industries etc. (Albuquerque and Malafaia 2018; Alotaibi 2018). Each year several thousand metric tons of plastic products are produced globally. Various products like water bottles, disposable cups, food packing, grocery bags, toys, cutlery, carrier bags etc. are all made of plastics. LDPE, HDPE and PVC are some of the most commonly available plastic polymers in the packaging industry (Lestari et al. 2020). Plastics have become widely produced substances that find implementation in a variety of industries from grocery bags to plastic cutlery, food packaging, production of toys, bottles, in building and construction and electronics etc. (Napper and Thompson 2019). But wide range use of plastics in different sectors have raised economic and environmental problems. The soil is harmed by these substances. Toxic gases that are harmful to human health are often produced when plastics are burnt. The foremost environmental issue is the landfill problem which arises due to intense use of plastic products. Assemblage of plastics in ocean, sea and other aquatic bodies causes water pollution and harm the aquatic organisms (Li et al. 2016).

There are two types of plastics as-

Thermoplastic or Thermo-softening : Thermoplastic are plastics that can be molded easily upon heating. They are hard and rigid. They cannot be bent. Examples- PVC, Polythene, Toys, Water Bottles, etc.

Thermosetting or Permanent : Thermosetting are plastics that cannot be molded easily upon heating. Examples- Plastics used in electrical switches, plugs, sockets, floor tiles etc.

Plastics possess several properties, i.e., Plastic can be molded in to various shape and size. Plastics are highly durable. The specific gravity of plastics is much less, which makes it a light-weight materials (Nikolaivits et al. 2021). Plastics are unreactive, cheaper and highly durable. Manufacturing process of plastics part is budget friendly. Plastics are easily available. These have good physical properties such as tensile strength, hardness, resistance to heat and temperature. Plastics find usefulness in everyday life such as in food packaging, kitchen, factories, bucket, electronics, and industrial machinery, textiles, etc. (Gilsdorf et al. 2020).

Besides these properties, advantages and applications, plastic products

have severe drawbacks as these products are non-biodegradable. They persist in the natural world for a long time and severely affect the eco-system. Recycling and combustion of plastics produces harmful gases and residue that pollute the air, water and soil etc. and also causes ozone layer depletion, greenhouse gases production, melting of oceans, etc. (Scalenghe 2018). Many animals consumed plastic products which results in choking of throat and ultimately their death. The bulk plastics are extracted from fossil resources which are limited and non-renewable in nature. As a result of extreme manufacture of plastic materials, these natural habitats are exhausting in a very fast proportion (Skogen et al. 2018).

Due to these drawbacks of plastics, we need an alternative of plastics which is eco-friendly, degradable, less toxic and economically viable.

Bioplastic – An Ecofriendly Alternative to conventional Plastics

Bioplastics are an alternative to traditional plastics. Bioplastics are produced from biomass viz. corn, sugar, potatoes, maize, etc. Compostable bioplastics break down into harmless natural and safe compounds (Moshood et al. 2022).

Bioplastics are usually categorized into different types such as-

Starch-based Bioplastics

These bioplastics are derived from starch-based sources such as potato, corn, wheat etc. (Hern-andez-Jaimes et al. 2017). Starch is widely used raw material for making bioplastics. Starch based bioplastics materials are easily available and the most promising because of their abundance and easy to process. Banana peel contains high amount of starch, which is about18.5% (Gadhave et al. 2018; Ismail et al. 2016).

Cellulose-based Bioplastics

These type of bio plastics are produced using cellulose esters & cellulose derivatives. Cellulose is a polymer of glucose units wherein these units are linked by beta-1,4-glycosidic bonds. Cellulose is found in the cell wall of all plants, green algae and in the membranes of most fungi (Kharb J, Saharan R 2022).

Protein-based Bioplastics

These types of bioplastics are synthesized using casein, milk, wheat gluten etc. (protein source). The use of soy protein-based plastics provides some complications due to their high cost and water sensitivity (Tian et al. 2018).

Bio-derived Polyethylene

Polyethylene is synthesized by fermentation of sugarcane, corn etc. Bio derived polyethylene is similar to traditional polyethylene both chemically and physically. It does not decompose but it can be recycled. It is used in caps for food packaging, bottles, trays, etc. (Zhang D and Dumont 2017)

Aliphatic Polyesters

The acyclic bio polyesters are Poly lactic acid, polyhydroxya-lkanoates, poly-3-hydroxybutyrate etc.

(a) Poly lactic Acid (PLA)

Poly lactide plastics are the most important bioplastics in the global world. Poly lactic acid (PLA) is a clear plastic produced from cane sugar. Enzymes are used to break starch in the plants. This lactic acid is polymerized and converted into mulch film called poly lactic acid. Currently, PLA is available in granulated form to produce several grades of films, drink containers, cups, bottles, etc. (Nazrin et al. 2020).

(b) Poly-3-hydroxy Butyrate

The poly-3-hydroxybutyrate (PHB) is a polyester, synthesized by bacterial processing of glucose and waste water.

(c) Polyhydroxyalkanoates (PHA)

PHA based plastics (Albuquerque and Malafaia 2018) possess the chemical and physical properties comparable to polyethylene, polypropylene and polyesters.

Advantages of Bioplastics

There are several features of bioplastic which enable them as a facile and eco-friendly substitute to the harmful and nonbiodegradable traditional plastics (Saharan R and Kharb J, 2022). These features are-

Eco-friendly

Bioplastic contains less or no toxins. Biodegradable polymers in the presence of microorganisms and enzymes degrade in to carbon dioxide, water and biomass.

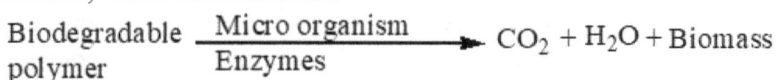

$$\text{Biodegradable polymer} \xrightarrow[\text{Enzymes}]{\text{Micro organism}} CO_2 + H_2O + Biomass$$

Bioplastic Resources Availability
Bioplastic is made from renewable resources which are easily affordable, available and inexpensive.

Recyclable
Bioplastics are degradable plastics, which can be decomposed by micro-organisms (soil degradation) and easily recyclable.

Energy Efficient
Bioplastics are energy efficient as lesser energy is required for their production as compared to conventional plastics.

Independence
Bioplastics are made up of renewable resources- sugarcane, corn, soy and other plant products (Tian et al. 2018) and do not depend upon non renewable petroleum based sources as compared to traditional plastics which are produced from petroleum.

Application of Bioplastics
Bioplastic products have been used in large variety of sector such as-

In Food Packaging
Biodegradable plastics present a huge variety of packaging applications alike conventional plastics. Bioplastic packaging possibilities consist of nursery products, bags, toys and clothes. Other sectors involved drinking cups, disposable cutlery, straws, stirrers, plates, lids and containers. It is seen that the bioplastic materials utilized in food packaging, protect the food from the environment and retains the food quality (Sanyang et al. 2016). After their use they can be reused again. These contains organic materials and can be composted. Bioplastics are widely used in packaging purpose like disposable cutlery, thermos-formed coffee cup lids, injection molds and food containers of all shapes and sizes (Marichelvam et al.2019).

In electronic Industries
Bioplastics supports to keep the products durable and light weight. They are used to produce more energy efficient devices. Bioplastic products are employed in electronics sector like keyboard elements, touch screen computer casings, a mouse for a laptop and loud speaker (Bozo E et al. 2021).

In agricultural Economy
Mulch foils made of bio-decomposable materials and flowerpot manufactured from bioplastics are used in the agricultural economy

and the gardening locality. These are mainly used because of their suitable lifespan and the surety that these materials are biodegradable in the soil. Plant pots used for flowering and vegetable plants are made by bioplastics, can be composted with kitchen rubbish and gardening (Ghimire S et al. 2020).

Medical Products

Now-a-days, medical professionals use the bioplastics in hospitals and surgeries. It is convenient to robust and sterile them. Bioplastics remain in operating place till healing the tissue and dissolving it into patient's body without appearing marks behind. Biodegradable plastics are also used for making medical devices. For example- tacks, pins, screws, syringe which are used during reconstructive surgery and bones healing. Surgeons use non-poisonous biodegradable polymer sutures in heart operations and other process. These can be easily sterilized and the sutures remain firm and unaffected until the surrounding tissue has healed. The sutures are metabolized at fast rate in the body and dissolved (Moshood TD et al. 2022).

Sanitary Products

Bioplastics are used in the production of sanitary products because of their specific characteristics. These materials are breathable and permit water vapor to permit, but they are water- resistant at the same time. Foils are manufactured from soft bioplastic and are used as diaper foil, and as disposable gloves.

Catering Products

Catering products pertain the group of decomposable plastics. Disposable crockery, cutlery, pack foils for straws and hamburgers made up of bioplastics are being used widely (Nanda S et al. 2022).

Conclusion

Bioplastics are a boon for the next generation where unique feature of biodegradability make them more useful compared to conventional plastics. The demand for sustainable and eco-friendly products has increased due to threatening issues such as global warming and environmental pollution. To overcome these issues, bioplastics are considered as a healthy solution. There is a wide scope of biodegradable plastics in future in regards of their ecofriendly properties. Bioplastics do not cause any type of pollution in the environment. They can be used in food and catering sectors as a packaging material.

In future their application in packaging sector can be seen. These bioplastics can serve as green and sustainable substitute to the synthetic plastics. Explorations have been going on in this area to enhance the quality and economic viability of bioplastics so that these products can be afforded by mankind and can be used more efficiently in everyday life.

References

Albuquerque PB, Malafaia CB (2018) Perspectives on the production, structural characteristics and potential applications of bioplastics derived from polyhydroxyalkanoates. Int J Biol Macromol 107(Part A):615-625. https://doi.org/10.1016/ j.ijbiomac. 2017.09.026

Amin MR, Chowdhury MA, Kowser MA (2019) Characterization and performance analysis of composite bioplastics synthesized using titanium dioxide nanoparticles with corn starch. Heliyon 5(8):e02009. https://doi.org/10.1016/j.heliyon.2019.e02009

Bozo E et al. (2021) Bioplastics and Carbon-Based Sustainable Materials, Components, and Devices: Toward Green Electronics. ACS Applied Materials & Interfaces, 13, 41, 49301-49312 https://doi.org/ 10.1021/acsami.1c13787

Gadhave RV, Das A, Mahanwar PA, Gadekar PT (2018) Starch based bio-plastics: The future of sustainable packaging. Open J Polym Chem 8:21-33. https://doi.org/10.4236/ojpchem.2018.82003

Ghimire S, Flury M, Scheenstra EJ, Miles CA (2020) Sampling and degradation of biodegradable plastic and paper mulches in field after tillage incorporation. Sci Total Environ 703:135577. https://doi.org/10.1016/j.scitotenv.2019.135577

Gilsdorf RA, Nicki MA, Chen EY-X (2020) High chemical recyclability of vinyl lactone acrylic bioplastics. Polym Chem 11(30):4942-4950. https://doi.org/10.1039/D0PY00786B

Hern-andez-Jaimes C, Meraz M, Lara VH, Gonz-alez-Blanco G, Buendia-Gonz-alez L (2017) Acid hydrolysis of composites based on corn starch and trimethylene glycol as plasticizer. Rev Mex Ing Quim 16(1):169-178.

Ismail NA, Tahir SM, Yahya N, Wahid MFA, Khairuddin NE, Hashim I, Rosli N, Abdullah MA (2016) Synthesis and characterization of biodegradable starch-based bioplastics. Mater Sci Forum 846:673-678. https://doi.org/10.4028/www.scientific.net/MSF.846.673

Kharb J, Saharan R (2022) Sustainable Biodegradable Plastics and their Applications: A Mini Review. IOP Conf Ser Mater Sci Eng 1248:012008 https://doi.org/10.1088/1757-899X/1248/1/012008

Lestari, R.A.S.; Kasmiyatum, M.; Dermwan, K.; Aini, A.N.; Riyati, N.; Putri, F.R. Bioplastics from jackfruit seeds and rice. *IOP Conf. Ser. Mater. Sci. Eng.* **2020**, 835, 120-35. 10.1088/1757-899X/835/1/012035

Li WC, Tse HF, Fok L (2016) Plastic waste in the marine environment: a review of sources, occurrence and effects. Sci Total Environ 566-567:333-349. https://doi.org/10.1016/j.scitotenv.2016.05.084

Marichelvam MK, Jawaid M, Asim M (2019) Corn and rice starch-based bio-plastics as alternative packaging materials. Fibres 7 (32):1. https://doi.org/10.3390/fib7040032

Moshood TD, Nawanir G, Mahmud F, Mohamad F, Ahmad MH, Ghani AA (2022) Biodegradable plastic applications towards sustainability: a recent innovations in the green product. Clean Eng Technol 6:100404 https://doi.org/10.1016/j.clet.2022.100404

Nanda S, Patra BR, Patel R, Bakos J, Dalai AK (2022) Innovations in applications and prospects of bioplastics and biopolymers: A review. Environ Chem Lett 20:379-395. https://doi.org/10.1007/s10311-021-01334-4

Napper IE, Thompson RC (2019) Environmental deterioration of biodegradable, oxo-biodegradable, compostable and conventional plastic carrier bags in the sea, soil, and open-air over a 3-year period. Environ Sci Technol 53 (9):4775-4783. https://doi.org/10.1021/acs.est.8b06984

Nazrin A, Sapuan SM, Zuhri MYM (2020) Mechanical, Physical and Thermal Properties of Sugar Palm Nanocellulose Reinforced Thermoplastic Starch (TPS)/Poly (Lactic Acid) (PLA) Blend Bionanocomposites. Polymers 12(10):2216. https://doi.org/10.3390/polym12102216

Nikolaivits E, Pantelic B, Azeem M, Taxeidis G, Babu R, Topakas E, Fournet M B, Nikodinovic-Runic J (2021) Progressing plastics circularity: A review of mechano-biocatalytic approaches for waste plastic (re)valorization. Front Bioeng Biotechnol 9:696040. https://doi.org/10.3389/fbioe.2021.696040

Saharan R, Kharb J (2022) Exploration of Bioplastics: (A Review). Orient J Chem 38(4):840-854. https://doi.org/10.13005/ojc/380403

Sanyang ML Sapuan SM, Jawaid M, Ishak MR, Sahari J (2016) Effect of plasticizer type and concentration on physical properties of biodegradable films based on sugar palm (arenga pinnata) starch for food packaging. J Food Sci Technol 53:326-336. https://doi.org/10.1007/s13197-015-2009-7

Scalenghe R (2018) Resource or waste? A perspective of plastics degradation in soil with a focus on end-of-life options. Heliyon 4 (12):00941. https://doi.org/10.1016/j.heliyon.2018.e00941

Skogen K, Helland H, Kaltenborn B (2018) Concern about climate change, biodiversity loss, habitat degradation and landscape change: Embedded in different packages of environmental concern? J Nat Conserv 44:12-20. https://doi.org/ 10.1016/j.jnc.2018.06.001

Tian H, Guo G, Xiang A, Zhong WH (2018) Intermolecular interactions and microstructure of glycerol-plasticized soy protein materials at molecular and nanometer levels. Polym Test 67 197-204. https://doi.org/10.1016/J.POLYMERTESTING.2018.03.002

Zhang D, Dumont M. J. Advances in polymer precursors and bio-based polymers synthesized from 5-hydroxymethylfurfural *J. Polym. Sci. A Polym. Chem.* 2017, *5* (9), 1478-1492. https://doi.org/10.1002/pola.28527

**Department of Chemistry,
University of Rajasthan, Jaipur, Rajasthan, India,
email : ritu.saharan84@gmail.com**

19. Applications of Stemcells in Modern Medical Treatments

Dr.P.Veena

Abstract

Stem cells are important for living organisms for many reasons. In the 3- to 5-day-old embryo, called a blastocyst, the inner cells give rise to the entire body of the organism, including all of the many specialized cell types and organs such as the heart, lung, skin, sperm, eggs and other tissues. In some adult tissues, such as bone marrow, muscle, and brain, discrete populations of adult stem cells generate replacements for cells that are lost through normal wear and tear, injury, or disease. Given their unique regenerative abilities, stem cells offer new potentials for treating diseases such as diabetes, and heart disease. However, much work remains to be done in the laboratory and the clinic to understand how to use these cells for cell-based therapies to treat disease, which is also referred to as regenerative or reparative medicine.Laboratory studies of stem cells enable scientists to learn about the cells' essential properties and what makes them different from specialized cell types. Scientists are already using stem cells in the laboratory to screen new drugs and to develop model systems to study normal growth and identify the causes of birth defects. The various stem cells are based upon their origin and ability to differentiate. Stem cells are revolutionizing medicine because of their potential to regenerate damaged tissue that is otherwise unable to be repaired. Bone marrow transplantation is one of the most widespread uses of stem cells today, and it helps with the treatment of some cancers. Ongoing research can help popularize stem cells for the treatment of other chronic illnesses. With stem cell therapy, the progression of autoimmune diseases can be slowed down and regressed, and even stopped completely. The success rate of the treatment is proportional to the patient's age, the duration of the disease and the patient's condition. Stem cell transplants are most often used to help people with leukemia and lymphoma. They may also be used for neuroblastoma and multiple myeloma. In recent years, stem cell therapy has shown promising results in HIV management, and it can have a major impact on the future of HIV treatment and prevention. The idea behind anti-HIV hematopoietic stem/progenitor cell (HSPC)-directed gene therapy is to genetically engineer patient-derived (autologous) HSPC to acquire an inherent resistance to HIV infection. COVID-19 is harmful and increases the risk of secondary infection, and effective treatment remains challenging owing to fibrosis and severe inflammation and infection. Sometimes our immune system can severely damage ourselves in disease. In the past, many researchers have conducted various studies on the immunomodulatory properties of stem cells.

Keywords : Stemcells, Neuroblastoma, Leukemia, lymphoma

Introduction

Stem cells are specialized human cells that can develop into many different types of cells in the body. In biology, a stem cell is an undeveloped cell of an organism capable of giving rise to indefinitely more cells of the same type. Stem cells can also become certain other kinds of cells through a process called differentiation. Stem cells serve as a body repair system and can generate healthy cells to replace those affected by the disease.

There are two main types of stem cells: embryonic stem cells, which come from embryos, and adult stem cells, which come from fully developed tissues such as the brain, skin, umbilical cord tissue and bone marrow. A third type of human engineered stem cell (Induced pluripotent stem cells) are adult stem cells that have been changed in a lab to be more like embryonic stem cells. There are several different types of stem cells, including:

Types of Stem Cells

Researchers categorize stem cells, according to their potential to differentiate into other types of cells.Embryonic stem cells are the most potent, as their job is to become every type of cell in the body.The classification includes

Totipotent : These stem cells can differentiate into all possible cell types. The first few cells that appear as the zygote starts to divide are totipotent.

Pluripotent : These cells can turn into almost any cell. Cells from the early embryo are pluripotent.

Multipotent : These cells can differentiate into a closely related family of cells. Adult hematopoietic stem cells, for example, can become red and white blood cells or platelets.

Oligopotent : These can differentiate into a few different cell types. Adult lymphoid or myeloid stem cells can do this.

Unipotent : These can only produce cells of one kind, which is their own type. However, they are still stem cells because they can renew themselves. Examples include adult muscle stem cells.Embryonic stem cells are considered pluripotent instead of totipotent because they cannot become part of the extra-embryonic membranes or the placenta.

How can Stem Cells be used?

MSCs are widely used in various stem cell treatments due to their self-renewable, differentiation, anti-inflammatory, and immunomodulatory properties. In-vitro (performed in a laboratory setting) and in-vivo (taking place in a living organism) studies have supported the understanding mechanisms, safety, and efficacy of MSC therapy in clinical applications.

Stem Cell Therapeutics

Stem cell therapeutics refers to the use of stem cells for the treatment or prevention of diseases or disorders. Stem cells are a type of cell that have the ability to differentiate into many different types of cells, and they have the ability to self-renew, meaning they can divide and produce more stem cells.

Tissue Regeneration

Tissue regeneration is probably the most important use of stem cells.Until now, a person who needed a new kidney, for example, had to wait for a donor and then undergoatransplant.There is a shortage of donor organs but, by instructing stem cells to differentiate in a certain way, scientists could use them to grow a specific tissue type or organ.

Stem Cell Cancer Treatment

It is also known as peripheral blood cell transplant. In stem cell cancer treatment, the doctor uses transplanted 'stem cells' to treat certain types of cancers. Cancers like myeloma, leukemia, and lymphoma can be treated through this process. Stem cell transplants do not usually work against cancer directly. Instead, they help you recover your body's ability to produce stem cells after treatment with very high doses of radiation therapy, chemotherapy, or both. However, in multiple myeloma and some types of leukemia, the stem cell transplant may work against cancer directly. This happens because of an effect called graft-versus-tumor that can occur after allogeneic transplants. Graft-versus-tumor occurs when white blood cells from your donor (the graft) attack any cancer cells that remain in your body (the tumor) after high-dose treatments. This effect improves the success of the treatments.

Cardiovascular Disease Treatment

Researchers are using stem cells in two important ways to improve cardiac health. First, they are turning stem cells into "heart muscle in a dish." If patients have genetic causes of heart disease, their stem cell-derived heart muscle also will have this disease and this heart muscle can be used to discover new drugs. Second, stem cells offer ways to replace damaged heart tissue. Using cellular therapy, researchers hope to repair or replace heart tissue damaged by congestive heart failure and heart attacks. Unlike the treatments listed above, cellular therapy could provide a durable treatment for heart deficiencies, rather than symptom-focused treatment.

Brain Disease Treatment

Doctors may one day be able to use replacement cells and tissues to treat brain diseases, such as Parkinson's and Alzheimer's. In Parkinson's, for example, damage to brain cells leads to uncontrolled muscle movements. Scientists could use stem cells to replenish the damaged brain tissue. This could bring back the specialized brain cells that stop the uncontrolled muscle movements. Researchers have already tried differentiating embryonic stem cells into these types of cells, so treatments are promising.

Cell Deficiency Therapy

Scientists hope one day to be able to develop healthy heart cells in a laboratory that they can transplant into people with heart disease. These new cells could repair heart damage by repopulating the heart with healthy tissue. Similarly, people with type I diabetes could receive pancreatic cells to replace the insulin-producing cells that their own immune systems have lost or destroyed. The only current therapy is a pancreatic transplant, and very few pancreases are available for transplant.

Blood Disease Treatments

Doctors now routinely use adult hematopoietic stem cells to treat diseases, such as leukemia, sickle cell anemia, and other immunodeficiency problems.

Hematopoietic stem cells occur in blood and bone marrow and can produce all blood cell types, including red blood cells that carry oxygen and white blood cells that fight disease. Mesenchymal stem cells (MSCs) are a type of adult stem cell in many body tissues, including bone marrow, fat tissue, and muscle. MSCs can differentiate into bone, cartilage, and fat cells.

MSCs have shown promise as a regenerative therapy for various diseases and conditions. In preclinical and clinical studies, MSCs have been shown to have anti-inflammatory and immune-modulatory effects invoking a positive immune response. They have been used to treat human diseases, including autoimmune diseases, degenerative neurological conditions, spinal cord injuries, joint pain, and other diseases affecting the human condition.

One of the key benefits of using MSCs for stem cell therapy is that they can be easily obtained from various sources and expanded in the laboratory. MSCs also have a low risk of immune rejection, as they are less immunogenic than other stem cells.

Overall, using MSCs for stem cell therapy holds great promise for treating various diseases and conditions. While more research is needed to fully understand these cells' potential and develop safe and effective treatments using MSCs, early results are encouraging. MSCs have the potential to be a valuable tool in the field of regenerative medicine.

Umbilical Cord Blood

The blood of newborn babies normally has large numbers of stem cells. After birth, the blood that's left behind in the placenta and umbilical cord (known as **cord blood**) can be taken and stored for later use in a stem cell transplant. Cord blood can be frozen until needed. A cord blood transplant uses blood that normally is thrown out after a baby is born. After the baby is born, specially trained members of the health care team make sure the cord blood is carefully collected. The baby is not harmed in any way.

Even though the blood of newborns has large numbers of stem cells, cord blood is only a small part of that number. So, a possible drawback of cord blood is the smaller number of stem cells in it. But this is partly balanced by the fact that each cord blood stem cell can form more blood cells than a stem cell from adult bone marrow. Still, cord blood transplants can take longer to take hold and start working. Cord blood is given into the patient's blood just like a blood transfusion.

List of Diseases that can be Treated with Stem Cells

Scientists have recognised the potential of stem cells and with advancements in regenerative medicine, scientists have been making attempts to its usage to individuals of all ages. Over 40,000 transplantations around the world have been performed to save thousands of lives. Stem cells obtained from **cord blood** are known to treat 80+ diseases and you'll find an FDA-approved list of diseases treated by stem cells further in this article. Numerous life-threatening diseases such as sickle-cell anaemia and malignancies have been approved for stem cell treatment. Let us know more!

List of Diseases can be Cured with Stem Cells

The full list of FDA-approved cord blood treatments is as follows:

Category of Diseases	Name of the Diseases
Leukemias	• Acute Lymphoblastic Leukemia • Acute Myelogenous Leukemia • Acute Biphenotypic Leukemia • Acute Lymphoblastic Leukemia Acute Undifferentiated Leukemia • Acute Myelogenous Leukemia (AML)

	• Chronic Lymphocytic Leukemia • Juvenile Chronic Myelogenous Leukemia Refractory Anem • Refractory Anemia with Excess Blasts • Juvenile Myelomonocytic Leukemia • Chronic Myelomonocytic Leukemia
Lymphomas/Malignancies	• Hodgkin's Lymphoma
Solid Tumors/Malignancies	• Neuroblastoma • Retinoblastoma • Medulloblastoma
Anaemias	• Congenital Dyserythropoietic Anaemia • Aplastic Anaemia • Fanconi Anemia • Paroxysmal Nocturnal Hemoglobinuria
Blood Disorders or Inherited Red Cell Abnormalities	• Blackfan-DiamondAnaemia • Beta Thalassemia Major (Cooley's Anaemia) • Pure Red Cell Aplasia • Sickle Cell Disease
Inherited Platelet Abnormalities	• Glanzmann Thrombasthenia • Congenital Thrombocytopenia
Inherited Immune Disorders or Immunodeficiencies	• SCID (X-linked) • SCID (ADA-SCID) • SCID with absence of normal B cells and T cells • Omenn Syndrome

	• Kostmann Syndrome • Bare Lymphocyte Syndrome • Ataxia-Telangiectasia • DiGeorge Syndrome • Common Variable Immunodeficiency • Lymphoproliferative Disorders • Leukocyte Adhesion Deficiency • Wiskott-Aldrich Syndrome • Acute Myelofibrosis • Myeloproliferative disorders • Polycythemia Vera • Agnogenic Myeloid Metaplasia • Essential Thrombocythemia
Phagocyte Disorders	• Neutrophil Actin Deficiency • Chronic Granulomatous Disease • Chediak-Higashi Syndrome • Reticular Dysgenesis
Inherited Immune and Other System Disorders	• Cartilage-Hair Hypoplasia • Pearson's Syndrome • Gunther's Disease • Hermansky-Pudlak Syndrome • Systemic Mastocytosis • Shwachman-Diamond Syndrome
Bone Marrow Cancers or Malignancies	• Plasma Cell Leukemia • Multiple Myeloma • Waldenstrom's Macroglobulinemia
Inherited Metabolic Disorders	• Hurler's Syndrome • Mucopolysaccharidoses • Scheie Syndrome • Sanfilippo Syndrome • Hunter's Syndrome

• Morquio Syndrome
• Maroteaux-Lamy Syndrome
• Sly Syndrome
• Mucolipidosis II
• Adrenoleukodystrophy
• Metachromatic Leukodystrophy
• Krabbe Disease
• Metachromatic Leukodystrophy
• Gaucher Disease
• Pelizaeus-Merzbacher Disease
• Sandhoff Disease
• Niemann-Pick Disease
• Tay-Sachs Disease
• Lesch-Nyhan Syndrome
• Wolman Disease
• Osteopetrosis

How Life Cell Comes to Rescue?

We bring in good tidings from the medical field that more than 40 diseases including autism, spinal cord injury, diabetes type I and knee cartilage repair are under clinical trials for umbilical cord blood stem cell treatment. Let us have a glance at medical conditions that are under clinical trials for cord blood stem cell treatment. It highlights the greater possibilities of diseases treated by stem cell therapy.

Before referring to the chart below, we want to highlight autologous and allogeneic. Autologous eligibility means therapy or transplantations done with the stem cells of the donor itself and allogeneic eligibility means therapy or transplants done with the matching stem cells from other family members including siblings.

Diseases or Rare Conditions	Autologous	Allogeneic
Cerebral Palsy	☐	☐
Crohn's Disease	☐	☐
Congenital Heart Defects	☐	☐
Autism	☐	☐

Acquired Hearing Loss	☐	☐
Eczema	☐	☐
Diabetes	☐	☐
Parkinson's	☐	☐
Stroke	☐	☐
Brain Injury	☐	☐
Alzheimer's	☐	☐
Cartilage Injury	☐	☐
Heart Disease	☐	☐
Lupus	☐	☐
Cleft Palate Repair	☐	☐
Multiple Sclerosis	☐	☐
Rheumatoid Arthritis	☐	☐
Spinal Cord Injury	☐	☐
Wound Healing	☐	☐
Amyotrophic Lateral Sclerosis (ALS)	☐	☐

Current uses of stem cells to treat diseases and injuries which are under clinical trials:

It's a lifetime comfort that you can attain access to your baby's preserved umbilical stem cells at any time. A broad range of rare conditions such as Autism Spectrum Disorder (ASD), related to brain development, makes parents worrisome. With LifeCell's stem cell banking program, you can benefit from a secure and healthy family future. Preserving stem cells of a newborn is not only helpful for the child, moreover, it benefits the other members of your family as well as the community. Opt for the private or community stem cell banking program and keep your near and dear ones well protected from the misfortune of rare diseases.

Treatment of Autoimmune Diseases
With stem cell therapy, the progression of autoimmune diseases can be slowed down and regressed, and even stopped completely. The success rate of the treatment is proportional to the patient's age, the duration of the disease and the patient's condition. Most common autoimmune diseases

Rheumatoid Arthritis

Rheumatoid arthritis (RA) is an autoimmune disease caused by the immune system attacking the joints. This attack leads to inflammation in the joints with pain, redness, swelling and increased temperature. Rheumatoid arthritis is a chronic disease and tends to begin in 30s.

Systemic Lupus Erythematosus (SLE)

Lupus is caused by the immune system's perception of many tissues and organs of the body as foreign. It affects a great deal of organs, including the skin, joints, kidneys, brain and heart. Joint pain, weakness and skin rashes are the most common symptoms.

Diabetes

The pancreas produces insulin, a hormone that helps regulate blood sugar levels. In Type 1 diabetes, the immune system attacks and destroys insulin-producing cells in the pancreas. As a result, insulin cannot be produced in the body, which leads to high blood sugar levels. High blood sugar damages various organs and tissues such as blood vessels, heart, kidneys, eyes and nerves.

Hashimoto

In Hashimato's disease, the thyroid gland is affected and thyroid hormone production is reduced. Its symptoms include weight gain, intolerance to heat and cold, fatigue, hair loss, and goiter (enlargement of the thyroid gland).

Psoriasis

Skin cells normally grow and shed when they are no longer needed. Psoriasis causes skin cells to multiply very quickly. Excess skin cells produced create plaque or patchy red rashes on the skin covered with white scales.

Sjogren Syndrome

In Sjögren syndrome, the immune system attacks joints and lachrymal and salivary glands. The most important symptoms of Sjogren syndrome are joint pain, dry eye and mouth.

Familial Mediterranean Fever (FMF)

Familial Mediterranean fever is a genetic autoimmune disease that causes recurrent fever and painful inflammation of the abdomen, lungs and joints. Joint pain, swelling, skin rashes and muscle pain are among other important symptoms. Familial Mediterranean fever is caused by a gene mutation that transmits from parents to children.

Ankylosing Spondylitis

Ankylosing spondylitis is an autoimmune disease affecting the spine. Spine bones (vertebrae) adhere to each other, creating movement limitation in the spine. These changes may be mild or severe and result in a hunched posture.

Behcet's Disease

Behçet's disease is an autoimmune rheumatic disease characterized by sores in the mouth or genital region, redness and swelling of the eyes, inflammation of the joints, skin and digestive system problems.

Multiple Sclerosis (MS)

Multiple sclerosis is a disease that occurs when the immune system attacks the protective myelin sheath surrounding nerve cells. Damage to the myelin sheath affects the transmission of messages between the brain and the body. This damage leads to symptoms such as drowsiness, weakness, balance problems and difficulty in walking.

Celiac Disease

Hypersensitivity to gluten, which is a protein that exists in cereal products such as barley, wheat, and rye, is seen in celiac patients. The immune system, which attacks gluten, also damages the wall of the small intestine and causes inflammation. Diarrhea, abdominal pain, nausea, vomiting are among the symptoms of this disease.

covid-19 Long-term steroid therapy for chronic inflammation following COVID-19 is harmful and increases the risk of secondary infection, and effective treatment remains challenging owing to fibrosis and severe inflammation and infection. Sometimes our immune system can severely damage ourselves in disease. In the past, many researchers have conducted various studies on the immunomodulatory properties of stem cells.

By priming the immune system and providing cytokines, chemokines, and growth factors, stem cells can be employed to build a long-term regenerative and protective response. This review addresses the latest trends and rapid progress in stem cell treatment for Acute Respiratory Distress Syndrome (ARDS) following COVID-19.

Human immunodeficiency virus (HIV) infection is a major global public health issue. Despite this, the only treatment available in mainstay is antiretroviral therapy. This treatment is not curative, it needs to be used lifelong, and there are many issues with compliance and side effects. In recent years, stem cell therapy has shown promising results in HIV management, and it can have a major impact on the future of HIV treatment and prevention. The idea behind anti-HIV hematopoietic stem/progenitor cell (HSPC)-directed gene therapy is to genetically engineer patient-derived (autologous) HSPC to acquire an inherent resistance to HIV infection. Multiple stem-cell-based gene therapy strategies have been suggested that may infer HIV resistance including anti-HIV gene reagents and gene combinatorial strategies giving rise to anti-HIV gene-modified HSPCs. Such stem cells can hamper HIV progression in the body by interrupting key stages of HIV proliferation: viral entry, viral integration, HIV gene expression, etc. Hematopoietic stem cells (HSCs) may also protect leukocytes from being infected. Additionally, genetically engineered HSCs have the ability to continuously produce protected immune cells by prolonged self-renewal that can attack the HIV virus. Therefore, a successful treatment strategy has the potential to control the infection at a steady state and eradicate HIV from patients. This will allow for a potential future benefit with stem cell therapy in HIV treatment.

Conclusion :

We conclude that ongoing research on stem cell therapies gives hope to patients who would normally not receive treatment to cure their disease. Stem cells have a bright future for the therapeutic world by promising stem cell therapy. We hope to see new horizon of therapeutics in the form of bone marrow transplant, skin replacement, organ development, and replacement of lost tissue such as hairs, tooth, retina and cochlear cells.

References :
1. C.S. Potten, Stem Cells. 1997 London: Academic Press.
2. S. Avasthi, R. N. Srivastava, A. Singh and M. Srivastava "Stem cells: Past, Present, Future – a review article", Internaet J. Med. Update, 2008, 3(1):22-30.
3. Understanding Stem Cells, An overview of the Science and Issues from the National Academics, The National Academics, Advisers to the Nation on Sciences, Engineering and Medicine.
4. A. Charles and Jr. Goldthwaite Regenerative Medicine. Department of Health and Human Services. Report, August 2006.
5. ISSCR, International Society for stem cell research, Guidelines for the Clinical Translation of Stem Cells. 2008.
6. A. R. Chapman, S. Mark, Frankel, and M. Garfinkel, "Stem Cell Research and Applications: Monitoring the Frontiers of Biomedical Research", American Association for the Advancement of Science, 1999.
7. J.A Thomson, E.J. Eldor , S.S Shapiro, M.A Waknitz , J.J Swiergiel, V.S Marshall ,J.M Jones , "Embryonic stem cell lines derived from human blastocysts". Science, 1998, 282 (5391): 1145–7.
8. K. Takahashi, S. Yamanaka, "Induction of pluripotent stem cells from mouse embryonic and adult fibroblast cultures by defined factors". Cell, 2006, 126 (4): 663–76.
9. "Good news for alcoholics". Discover Magazine. March 2007. http://discovermagazine.com/2007/mar/good-news-for-alcoholics.

Department of zoology,
TSWRDC Warangal East
Warangal Telangana
email : veenachalla2012@gmail.com

20. Synthesis and Characterization of New O, O'-BIS(α-Naphthyl, β-Naphthyl, and 2,3,5-Trimethylphenyl) Dithiophosphate Complexes of Antimony (III)

Mukhtyar S. Saini,[1]
Aran Kumar[2,]
Jaya Dwivedi[3]

Abstract

The reactions of O, O'(α-naphthyl, β-naphthyl, and 2,3,5-trimethylphenyl) dithiophosphate with antimony trichloride, $SbCl_3$, and various chlorodioxstabines, OGOSbCl, in toluene in different stichometry molar ratio are facile and resulted into cyclic and spirocyclic dithiophosphate complexes of the type [{α-$C_{10}H_7O$-, β-$C_{10}H_7O$-, or $(CH_3)_3C_6H_2O)_2PS_2$}$_n$SbCl$_{3-n}$] Where n =1 or 2) and [(α-$C_{10}H_7O$-, β-$C_{10}H_7O$-, or $(CH_3)_3C_6H_2O)_2PS_2SbO(CH_2)_nO$](where n = 2 or3) respectively. in 1:1 and 2:1 stichometry molar ratio resulted in complexes of the type [(α-$C_{10}H_7O$-, β-$C_{10}H_7O$-, or $(CH_3)_3C_6H_2O)_2PS_2SbCl_2$] or{α-$C_{10}H_7O$-, β-$C_{10}H_7O$-, or $(CH_3)_3C_6H_2O)_2PS_2$}$_2$SbCl] (Where n = 1 or 2). These complexes have been characterized by elemental analyses, C, H, S, and Sb, have been further characterized by some IR and NMR (^{1}H, ^{31}P, and ^{13}C) spectroscopic studies which indicate trigonal bipyramidal and pseudo octahedral geometry around the Antimony.

Keywords : α-Naphthyl; β-Naphthyl; 2,3,5-trimethylphenyl; dithiophosphates; antimony trichloride , chlorodioxstabines.

Introduction

Acylic dithiophosphate, $(RO)_2PS_2X$, and cyclic dithiophosphate ligands, $OGOPS_2X$, (R = Me, Et, Pr^n, Pr^i or Bu^t, G = -$CH_2CMe_2CH_2$-,-$CH_2CEt_2CH_2$-, -CMe_2CH_2CHMe- or -CMe_2CMe_2-; X = H, Na or NH_4) occupy an only one of its kind site as resourceful chelating ligands [1-3]. These ligands be evidence for bidentate [4-10], monodentate [11- 13] and also bridging mode of bonding with metals and metalloids [14]. Various dithiophosphato derivatives find universal applications in agriculture[15], industries such as extreme pressure oil additives [16], heat stabilizers for polymers [17], hydraulic fluid additives [18], extraction[19], analytical [20] and also show biologiocal activities [21].

A literature survey revealed that a substantial amount of work has been done with the dialkyl and alkylidene ligands and very little in a row is available on the derivatives of O, O'-bis(α-naphthyl, β-naphthyl, and 2, 3, 5-trimethylphenyl) dithiophosphate Ligands. [22-25]. Recently, some metal complexes with the α-naphthyl, β-naphthyl, and 2, 3, 5-trimethylphenyl) dithiophosphate Ligands have been synthesized and characterized [26-32]. Utilities of some derivatives of α-naphthyl, β-naphthyl, and 2, 3, 5-trimethylphenyl) dithiophosphate Ligands in industries [33-35] and agriculture [36] have also been described.

Keeping in view antimony has remarkable therapeutic usefulness in patients with sharp promyelocytic leukemia (apl). a great number of metallic complexes display a pronounced antitumoral activity, which makes them of a high interest for applications in the behavior of different types of cancer[37]. practically all transition and main group metals have been tested for antitumoral properties, and interestingly, a number of them have been shown marginal to good activity towards standard animal tumors [38-43] Aran(2007) a selection of O, O', - "dialkyl dithiophosphoric acids, $[(RO)_2PS_2H]$,(where R = Me, Et, Pr^n, Pr^i or Bu^t), their cyclic comparable alkylene dithiophosphoric acids, $OGOPS_2H$, (where G = 1,2- and 1,3-glycols) and their ammonium and alkali metal salts have been" used for the

synthesis of a variety of complexes with antimony(III).[44-55]. But no antimony derivatives of O, O' (α-naphthyl, β-naphthyl, and 2,3,5-trimethylphenyl) dithiophosphate have been reported. Because of the attention-grabbing structural, industrial chemistry, and biological applications [56-60].

We reported herein the synthesis and characterization of some new complexes of antimony(III) with O, O'-bis(α-naphthyl, β-naphthyl, and 2, 3, 5-trimethylphenyl) dithiophosphate Ligands by using antimony trichloride and antimony glycolates (cycloalkylenedioxyethoxy/propoxystabines).

Experimental Materials and Methods

Moisture was carefully excluded throughout the experimental manipulations by using modified Schlenk techniques. Solvents were dried by standard methods before their use. Carbon and hydrogen contents were analyzed by microanalytical techniques at Regional Research Laboratory, Jammu. Sulfur was estimated as $BaSO_4$ (Messenger's method) and antimony was estimated iodimetrically. O, O'-bis(α-naphthyl, β-naphthyl, and 2, 3, 5-trimethylphenyl) dithiophosphate Ligands were prepared by literature methods [61-63]. Molecular weights were determined cryscopically in freezing benzene. IR spectra were recorded in KBr mulls in the range 4000–200 cm^{-1} on a Perkin Elmer- 377 spectrophotometer. The ^1H, ^{13}C, and ^{31}P NMR spectra were recorded on a Bruker DRX 300 (120 MHz) spectrometer using TMS as the internal reference for ^1H NMR and 85% H_3PO_4 as an external reference for ^{31}P NMR at the Regional Research laboratory Jammu

Synthesis of the Compounds

These complexes were prepared by the methods reported in the literature [64]-[72].

Synthesis of $[\alpha\text{-}C_{10}H_7O\text{-}, \beta\text{-}C_{10}H_7O\text{-}, \text{or} (CH_3)_3C_6H_2O)_2PS_2\}_nSbCl_{3-n}]$ **(Where n= 1or 2):**

For the synthesis of $[\alpha\text{-}C_{10}H_7O\text{-})_2PS_2SbCl_2]$ (1-2), $((CH_3)_3C_6H_2O\text{-})_2PS_2SbCl_2$ (3), around50 ml) toluene solution of $SbCl_3$ (0.22gm,1.0,mmol,) was taken in a 100 ml round bottom flask. To this solution, was added (~50ml) toluene suspension of the sodium salt of O, O'-bis (α-naphthyl, β-naphthyl) dithiophosphates ligand, $[(\alpha,\beta\text{-}C_{10}H_7O)_2PS_2Na]$ (0.40gm,1.0 mmol) and 2, 3, 5-trimethylphenyl) dithiophosphate Ligand (0.77gm,1.0mmol) in a dropwise manner, through a dropping funnel. Initially, no reaction was observed but after 15-25 minutes of refluxing, the color of the contents in the flask turned light orange and a small amount of precipitation of sodium chloride also took place.

As the color of the reaction mixture further deepened, the refluxing continued for 4 hours. Then the reaction mixture was brought to room temperature and sodium chloride formed during the reaction was filtered off through a G-4 Sintered glass disc. Subsequently, the excess solvent was evaporated under reduced pressure.

Final drying of the product in *vacuo* [(α-$C_{10}H_7O)_2PS_2SbCl_2$],(($CH_3)_3C_6H_2O$-)$_2PS_2SbCl_2$,(1-3)as yellow-colored sticky solid in 82. % yield. A similar methodology was applied for the synthesis of complexes (4-6).[(α-$C_{10}H_7O)_2PS_2SbCl$],(($CH_3)_3C_6H_2O$-)$_2PS_2SbCl$

The synthetic and analytical details are given in Table 1.4

Synthesis of α-$C_{10}H_7O$-,β-$C_{10}H_7O$-, or($CH_3)_3C_6H_2O$-) $_2PS_2\overline{SbO(CH_2)_nO}$ (7-9)

For the synthesis of the compound [(α,β-$C_{10}H_7O)_2PS_2SbO(CH_2)_2O$] (7-8), ($CH_3)_3C_6H_2O$-) $_2PS_2SbO(CH_2)_2O$] (9):

(~ 40 ml) a toluene solution of $\overline{OCH_2CH_2OSbCl}$ (0.21gm,1.0mmol) was taken in a 100 ml round bottom flask. To this solution, was added in a dropwise manner (~ 40ml) toluene suspension of the sodium salt of *O, O'*-bis (α-naphthyl) dithiophosphate ligand [(α-$C_{10}H_7O)_2PS_2Na$] (0.40gm,1.0 mmol) and [($CH_3)_3C_6H_2O$-)$_2PS_2Na$,(0.77gm,1.0mmol) an immediate reaction was observed which was indicated by the formation of a white precipitate of sodium chloride and turning of the color of contents in the flask orange-red.

As the color of the reaction mixture further deepened, the refluxing continued for 4 hours. Then the reaction mixture was brought to room temperature and sodium chloride formed during the reaction was filtered off through Sintered G4 glass disc. Subsequently, the excess solvent was evaporated under reduced pressure.

Final drying of the product in *vacuo* yielded [(α,β-$C_{10}H_7O)_2PS_2SbO(CH_2)_2O$](7-8), ($CH_3)_3C_6H_2O$-)$_2PS_2\overline{SbO(CH_2)_2O}$] *(9)* as yellow sticky solid in 80% yield. A similar methodology was applied for the synthesis of complexes (10-12). The synthetic and analytical details are listed in Table 1.4.

Results and Discussion

O, O'-dialkyl dithiophosphoric acids, [(RO)2PS2H],(where R =Me, Et, Prn, Pri or But)] and their cyclic analogous alkylene dithiophosphoric acids, OGOPS2H (where G=1,2 and 1,3-glycols) have been used for the synthesis of a variety of complexes with Antimony (III)[27-30]

The reactions of O, O'(α-naphthyl, β-naphthyl, and 2,3,5-trimethylphenyl) dithiophosphate with antimony trichloride, $SbCl_3$, and various chlorodioxstabines, OGOSbCl, in toluene in different stichometry molar ratio are facile and resulted into cyclic and spirocyclic dithiophosphate complexes of the type [{α-$C_{10}H_7O$-, β-$C_{10}H_7O$-, or $(CH_3)_3C_6H_2O)_2PS_2$}$_n$$SbCl_{3-n}$] Where n =1 or 2) and [(α-$C_{10}H_7O$-, β-$C_{10}H_7O$-, or $(CH_3)_3C_6H_2O)_2PS_2SbO(CH_2)_nO$](where n = 2 or3) respectively. For convenience, these reactions are divided into two parts.

(i) Reaction of O, O'- α-$C_{10}H_7O$-, β-$C_{10}H_7O$-, or $(CH_3)_3C_6H_2O)_2PS_2Na$ dithiophosphates ligands with $SbCl_3$ in 1:1 and 2:1 resulted into complexes of the type [(α-$C_{10}H_7O$-, β-$C_{10}H_7O$-, or $(CH_3)_3C_6H_2O)_2PS_2SbCl_2$] or {α-$C_{10}H_7O$-, β-$C_{10}H_7O$-, or $(CH_3)_3C_6H_2O)_2PS_2$}$_2SbCl$] (Where n = 1 or 2). As the reactions are a bit more sluggish than that of the antimony, the reaction mixture was refluxed for 4-5 hours to ensure the completion of the reaction. During the refluxing the color of the reaction contents changed to orange-yellow and precipitation of sodium chloride took place.

Scheme 1.1: Reactions of [(RO)$_2$PS$_2$Na] with SbCl$_3$.
Where R= α-naphthyl, β-naphthyl and 2, 3, 5-trimethylphenyl
(a)

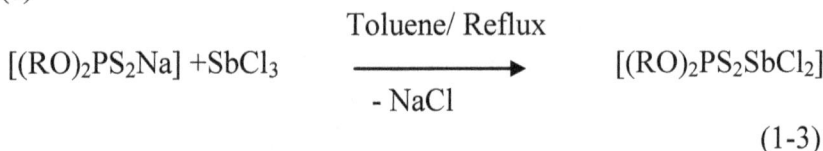

$$[(RO)_2PS_2Na] + SbCl_3 \xrightarrow[- NaCl]{Toluene/ Reflux} [(RO)_2PS_2SbCl_2]$$

(1-3)

(b)

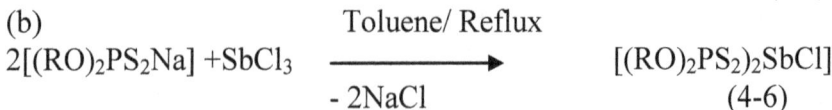

$$2[(RO)_2PS_2Na] + SbCl_3 \xrightarrow[- 2NaCl]{Toluene/ Reflux} [(RO)_2PS_2)_2SbCl]$$

(4-6)

(ii) Reaction of O, O'-(α-naphthyl, β-naphthyl, and 2,3,5-trimethylphenyl) dithiophosphates ligand with OGOSbCl in 1:1 resulted in complexes of the type α-$C_{10}H_7O$-, β-$C_{10}H_7O$-, or $(CH_3)_3C_6H_2O)_2PS_2SbO(CH_2)_nO$](where n = 2 or 3.), As the reactions are a bit simpler than that of the SbCl$_3$ and get completed in 3-4 hours of relaxation. During the refluxing the color of the reaction contents changed to orange-yellow and precipitation of sodium chloride took place.

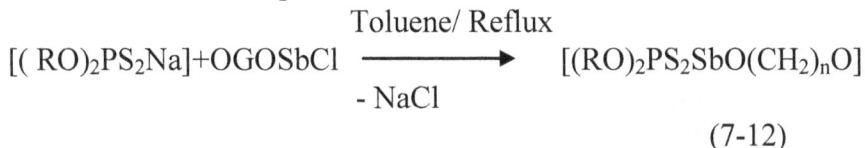

$$[(RO)_2PS_2Na] + OGOSbCl \xrightarrow[\text{- NaCl}]{\text{Toluene/ Reflux}} [(RO)_2PS_2SbO(CH_2)_nO]$$

(7-12)

Where G = $-CH_2CH_2-$ (7-10) or $-CH_2CH_2CH_2-$ (9-12).

Scheme 1.2: Reactions of the $[(RO)_2PS_2Na]$ with OGOSbCl,

Removal of sodium chloride, NaCl, and the evaporation of the solvent under reduced pressure results in the formation of the compounds as an orange-yellow sticky solid. in 78-83.5% yield.

The micro elemental analyses, particularly C, H, S, and Sb of all the complexes were found reliable to the molecular formula of the complexes. The molecular weight determination of the few represented compounds indicated the monomeric nature of these derivatives (Table 1.4) They have been further characterized by some other spectroscopical data like IR and NMR (^{1}H and ^{31}P).

These complexes were obtained in quantitative yield, soluble in common organic solvents like benzene, toluene, chloroform, acetone, and also in coordinating solvents like DMSO and DMF but they are sparingly soluble in the non-polar organic solvents *viz.* carbon tetrachloride. They appear to be susceptible to moisture but can be kept unbothered for a long time under an anhydrous atmosphere.

The compounds obtained were sufficiently pure but for the sake of extra purity, these were further washed with dried *n*-hexane or diethyl ether.

Infrared Spectra

IR spectra were recorded in the range 4000-200 cm^{-1} and the tentative assignments were made based on relevant literature reports[73-78.]The IR spectra of these complexes show the formation of a new sharp peak for the ν Sb-S bond in the region 470-460 cm^{-1} for complexes. The peak for ν Sb- Cl, ν Sb- O, and ν P-S was found in the region 352-347, 644-622, and 672-669 cm.$^{-1}$ Peaks for ν(P)-O-C, ν P-O-(C) and Aromatic ν (C-H) were observed in the region 1153-1152, 941-936 and 2950-2945 cm^{-1} for these complexes. The detailed data are given in Table 1.1

^{1}H NMR Spectra

The ^{1}H NMR spectra were recorded in CDCl$_3$ and the chemical shifts of –CH$_3$ attached to the benzene ring for compounds (3,6,9, and 12) of the liganad moiety were recorded at δ 2.32-2.33. A multiplet characteristic for ring protons was observed at δ 7.34-7.45 for compounds (1-12). The peaks for the ligand moiety in the above-said region, peaks for –OCH$_2$CH$_2$O– protons at δ 2.70-2.75 ppm for complexes (7-9) and–OCH$_2$– and –CH$_2$– protons at δ 2.62-2.70 and δ 4.2-4.4 were observed for complexes (10-12). The detailed ^{1}H NMR spectral data are given in Table 1.2

^{31}P NMR Spectra

^{31}P NMR spectra were recorded in DMSO. Spectra of all the complexes show a singlet in the range 81.5- 85.5 ppm which shows the symmetrical nature of the phosphorus nuclei and bidentate mode of binding for the newly synthesized ligand. The ^{31}P NMR spectral data of all these complexes are given in Table 1.2

^{13}C NMR spectral ^{13}C NMR spectral analysis of the above compounds. However, chemical shifts were observed for each carbon atom in these complexes has been shown in Table 1.3

Structural Features

Our efforts to get a single crystal for single-crystal X-ray analysis were unsuccessful. Therefore, it would not be possible to predict the precise structure of these complexes. However, the micro elemental analysis (C, H, S, and Sb) molecular weight determination and mass spectral studies have supported the formation of these complexes and their monomeric nature as well. The occurrence of a singlet with a downfield shift in ^{31}P NMR has favored the symmetric nature of complexes and equivalence of phosphorus nuclei in the molecule. Further, based on literature, a Ψ-trigonal bipyramidal (Ψ = lone pair of the electron at equatorial position) geometry around the antimony may be proposed for complexes (1-3 and 7-12). In the case of complexes (1-3), the antimony atom is bonded to two chlorine atoms in axial positions and two sulfur plus a stereochemically active lone pair of electrons in the equatorial positions (fig.1.1) whereas in the case of complexes (7-12) the antimony atom is bonded with two oxygen atoms of glycolate moiety and two sulfur atoms of dithiophosphate moiety and a lone pair of electrons (fig.1.2) based on the various spectroscopic studies, particularly ^{31}P and IR in case of complexes (4-6), a bidentate mode of bonding by the dithiophosphate ligand has been indicated. Therefore, a pseudo octahedral (oh) *geometry* may be assigned to the complexes (4-6), in which antimony is bonded to four sulfur atoms of two dithiophosphate ligands, one chlorine atom, and having a lone pair of electrons (fig,1.3).

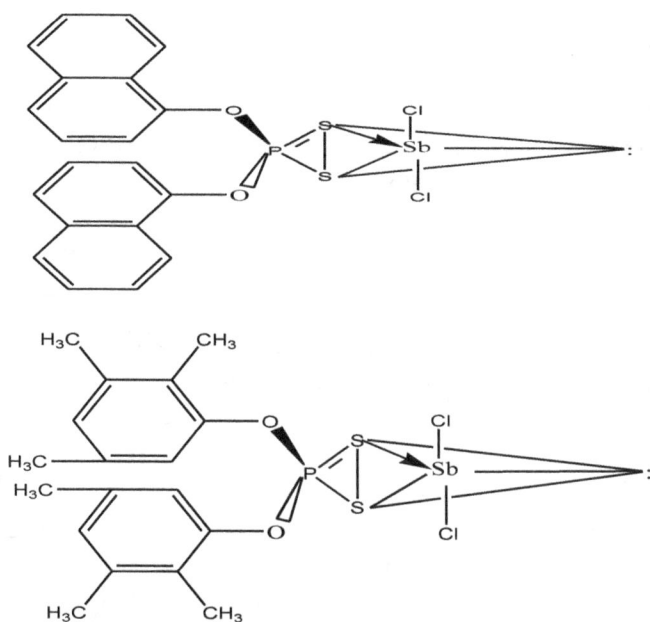

Figure 1.1: proposed trigonal bipyramidal structure of [(α-C₁₀H₇O-, β-C₁₀H₇O-, or (CH₃)₃C₆H₂O)₂PS₂SbCl₂].

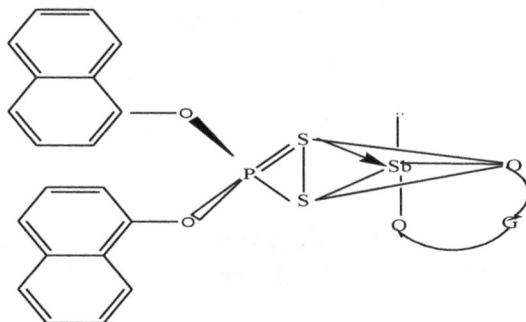

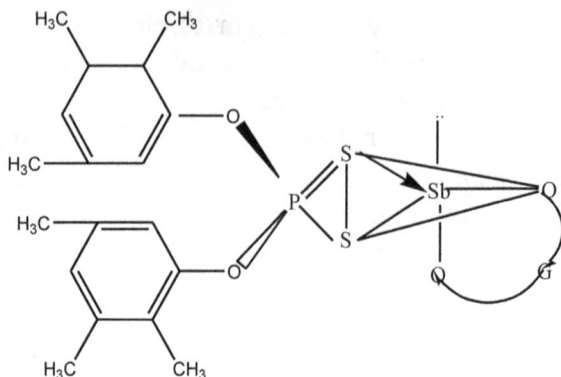

Figure1.2.: Proposed trigonal bipyramidal structure of [(α-$C_{10}H_7O$-, β-$C_{10}H_7O$-, or $(CH_3)_3C_6H_2O$))$_2PS_2SbO(CH_2)_nO$] (where n = 2 or 3).

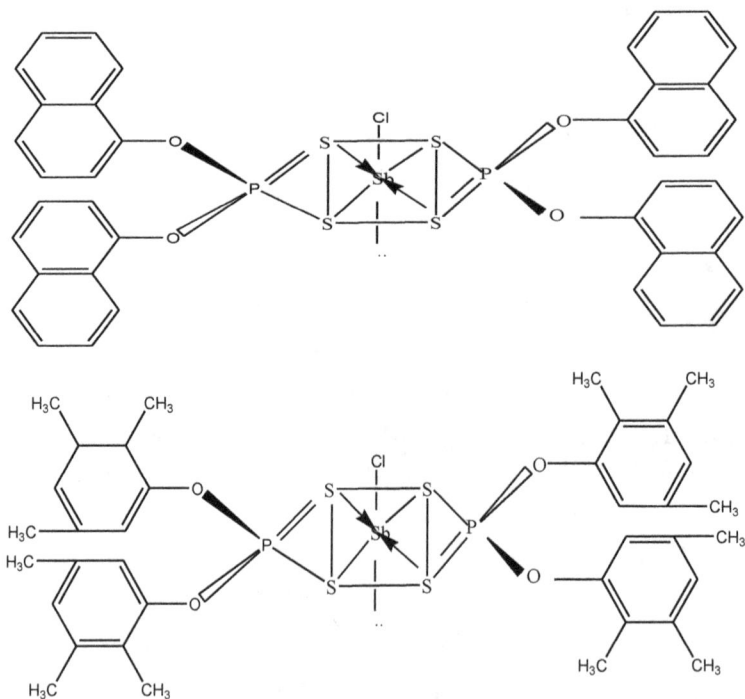

1.3.Figure: Proposed octahedral structure of the complexes of the type[{[(α-$C_{10}H_7O$-, β-$C_{10}H_7O$-, or $(CH_3)_3C_6H_2O)_2PS_2$}$_2SbCl$].

Table 1.1.IR spectral data of Antimony(III) O, O'- α-Naphthyl, β-Naphthyl, and 2,3,5-Trimethylphenyl) dithiophosphates. (in cm^{-1}).

S.No.	Compound No.	Aromatic vC-H	v(P)-O-C	vP-O-(C)	vP–S	vSb-S	Sb-Cl	vSb– O
1	[(α-C$_{10}$H$_7$-O)$_2$PS$_2$SbCl$_2$]	2950	1153s	936s	671 m	460,m	350,m	---
2	[(β-C$_{10}$H$_7$-O)$_2$PS$_2$SbCl$_2$]	2950	1152s	937s	672 m	468,m	345,m	---
3	[((CH$_3$)$_3$C$_6$H$_2$-O)$_2$PS$_2$SbCl$_2$]	2945	1153s	937s	672 m	470,m	352,m	---
4	[(α-C$_{10}$H$_7$-O)$_2$PS$_2$]$_2$SbCl	2947	1152s	937s	671 m	466,m	347,m	---
5	[(β-C$_{10}$H$_7$-O)$_2$PS$_2$]$_2$SbCl	2948	1152s	940s	669 m	465m	348,m	---
6	[((CH$_3$)$_3$C$_6$H$_2$-O)$_2$PS$_2$]$_2$SbCl	2950	1152s	941s	670 m	465m	351,m	---
7	[(α-C$_{10}$H$_7$-O)$_2$PS$_2$SbOCH$_2$CH$_2$O]	2950	1153s	936s	672m	462m	---	622,m
8	[(β-C$_{10}$H$_7$-O)$_2$PS$_2$SbOCH$_2$CH$_2$O]	2950	1152s	937s	670 m	469,m	---	632,m
9	[((CH$_3$)$_3$C$_6$H$_2$-O)$_2$PS$_2$SbOCH$_2$CH$_2$O]	2945	1153s	937s	671 m	470,m	---	642,m
10	[(α-C$_{10}$H$_7$-O)$_2$PS$_2$SbOCH$_2$CH$_2$CH$_2$O]	2947	1152s	937s	671 m	466,m	---	644,m
11	[(β-C$_{10}$H$_7$-O)$_2$PS$_2$SbOCH$_2$CH$_2$CH$_2$O]	2948	1152s	940s	669 m	465,m	---	641,m
12	[((CH$_3$)$_3$C$_6$H$_2$-O)$_2$PS$_2$SbOCH$_2$CH$_2$CH$_2$O]	2950	1152s	941s	670 m	466,m	---	640,m

Where s =Strong, b = broad, m = medium

Table 1.2. ^{1}H and ^{31}P NMR spectral data of Antimony(III) of O, O'-bis α-Naphthyl, β-Naphthyl, and 2,3,5-Trimethylphenyl dithiophosphates.

S.No	Compound	^{1}H NMR	^{31}PNMR
1	[(α-C$_{10}$H$_7$O)$_2$PS$_2$SbCl$_2$]	7.34-7.44, m, 14H (-C$_{10}$H$_7$);3.52,	84.5s
2	[(β-C$_{10}$H$_7$O)$_2$PS$_2$SbCl$_2$	7.34-7.45, m, 14H (-C$_{10}$H$_7$);3.52,	82.4s
3	[((CH$_3$)$_3$C$_6$H$_2$O)$_2$PS$_2$SbCl$_2$	2.33, s, 18H (-CH$_3$); 6.94-7.43, m, 12H (-C$_6$H$_2$);	81.5s
4	[(α-C$_{10}$H$_7$O)$_2$PS$_2$)$_2$SbCl]	7.35-7.44, m, 28H (-C$_{10}$H$_7$);3.52	85.5s
5	[(β-C$_{10}$H$_7$O)$_2$PS$_2$)$_2$SbCl]	7.34-7.42, m, 28H (-C$_{10}$H$_7$);	84.6s
6	[((CH$_3$)$_3$C$_6$H$_2$O)$_2$PS$_2$)$_2$SbCl]	2.33, s, 36H (-CH$_3$); 6.93-7.42, m, 8H (-C$_6$H$_2$)	83.6s
7	[(α-C$_{10}$H$_7$O)$_2$PS$_2$SbOCH$_2$CH$_2$O	7.35-7.44, m, 14H (-C$_{10}$H$_7$);2.75, s,4H(OCH$_2$-)	84.5s
8	[(β-C$_{10}$H$_7$O)$_2$PS$_2$SbOCH$_2$CH$_2$O	7.34-7.45, m, 14H (-C$_{10}$H$_7$);2.74, s,4H(OCH$_2$-)	82.4s
9	[((CH$_3$)$_3$C$_6$H$_2$O)$_2$PS$_2$SbOCH$_2$CH$_2$O	2.34, s, 18H (-CH$_3$); 7.34-7.43, m,12H (-C$_6$H$_2$); 2.70,s, 4H(OCH$_2$-)	81.5s
10	[(α-C$_{10}$H$_7$O)$_2$PS$_2$SbOCH$_2$-CH$_2$-CH$_2$O]	7.36-7.44, m, 14H (-C$_{10}$H$_7$);4.3, m, 2H(CH$_2$-);2.70,s, 4H (OCH$_2$-)	85.5s
11	[(β-C$_{10}$H$_7$O)$_2$PS$_2$SbOCH$_2$CH$_2$CH$_2$O]	7.35-7.42, m, 14H (-C$_{10}$H$_7$): 4.2.m,2H (-CH$_2$-); 2.62,s,4H(-OCH$_2$-)	84.6s
12	[((CH$_3$)$_3$C$_6$H$_2$O)$_2$PS$_2$]SbOCH$_2$CH$_2$CH$_2$O	2.33, s, 36H (-CH$_3$); 7.34-7.42, m, 8H (-C$_6$H$_2$),4.1,m,2H (-CH$_2$-); 2.65, s,4H (-OCH$_2$-)	83.6s

Where s = singlet, d = doublet, t = triplet, and m = multiplet

Table 1.3. ^{13}C NMR spectral data of Antimony complexes of -O, O'- α-Naphthyl, β-Naphthyl, and 2,3,5-Trimethylphenyl dithiophosphates.in CDCl$_3$ (δ ppm).

S.no	Ligand/(gm) mmol	Metal salt(gm)/ mmol SbCl$_3$/ OG'OSbCl	M.R.	Ref. T	Product/ (Color/M.pt/yield %)	Analyses Calc./ (Found) Sb	S	Cl
1	[(α-C$_{10}$H$_7$-O)$_2$PS$_2$Na] 0.40gm,1.0 mmol	SbCl$_3$ 0.22gm,1.0,mmol,	1:1	4.0	(α-C$_{10}$H$_7$-O)$_2$PS$_2$SbCl$_2$ Orange yellow sticky solid ,78%	21.2 (21.0)	11.1 (11.0)	12.3 (12.1)
2	[(β-C$_{10}$H$_7$-O)$_2$PS$_2$Na] 0.40gm,1.0mmol	SbCl$_3$,0.22 gm,1.0 mmol	1:1	4.0	(β-C$_{10}$H$_7$-O)$_2$PS$_2$SbCl$_2$ Orange yellow sticky solid ,78%	21.2 (21.1)	11.1 (10.9)	12.3 (12.2)
3	[((CH$_3$)$_3$C$_6$H$_2$O)$_2$PS$_2$Na] 0.77gm,1.0mmol	SbCl$_3$,0.22 gm,1.0 mmol	1:1	4.0	((CH$_3$)$_3$C$_6$H$_2$O)$_2$PS$_2$SbCl$_2$ Orange yellow sticky solid, 81.8%	21.8 (21.5)	11.4 (11.2)	12.7 (12.5)
4	[(α-C$_{10}$H$_7$-O)$_2$PS$_2$Na] 0.80gm,2.0 mmol	SbCl$_3$,0.22 gm,1.0 mmol	2:1	4.0	[(α-C$_{10}$H$_7$-O)$_2$PS$_2$]$_3$SbCl] Orange yellow sticky solid , 86.7%	22.6 (22.4)	11.9 (11.7)	6.5 (6.4)
5	[(β-C$_{10}$H$_7$-O)$_2$PS$_2$Na] 0.80gm,2.0 mmol	SbCl$_3$,0.22 gm,1.0 mmol	2:1	4.0	[(β-C$_{10}$H$_7$-O)$_2$PS$_2$]$_2$SbCl] Orange yellow sticky solid , 86.7%	22.6 (22.5)	11.9 (11.5)	6.5 (6.3)
6	[((CH$_3$)$_3$C$_6$H$_2$O)$_2$PS$_2$Na] 0.77gm,2.0mmol	SbCl$_3$,0.22 gm,1.0 mmol	2:1	4.0	[((CH$_3$)$_3$C$_6$H$_2$O)$_2$PS$_2$]$_2$SbCl] Orange yellow sticky solid , 73.8%.	23.2 (23.1)	12.2 (12.0)	6.7 (6.5)
7	[(α-C$_{10}$H$_7$-O)$_2$PS$_2$Na] 0.40gm,1.0 mmol	OCH$_2$CH$_2$OSbCl,0.21gm,1.0mmol.	1:1	4.5	(α-C$_{10}$H$_7$-O)$_2$PS$_2$ SbOCH$_2$CH$_2$O Orange yellow sticky solid, 80.3%	21.6 (21.4)	11.3 (11.2)	----
8	[(β-C$_{10}$H$_7$-O)$_2$PS$_2$Na] 0.40gm,1.0 mmol	OCH$_2$CH$_2$OSbCl,0.21gm,1.0mmol	1:1	4.5	(β-C$_{10}$H$_7$-O)$_2$PS$_2$ SbOCH$_2$CH$_2$O Orange yellow sticky solid, 80.3%	21.6 (21.3)	11.3 (11.1)	----
9	[((CH$_3$)$_3$C$_6$H$_2$O)$_2$PS$_2$Na] 0.77gm,1.0mmol	OCH$_2$CH$_2$OSbCl,0.21gm,1.0 mmol	1:1	4.5	((CH$_3$)$_3$C$_6$H$_2$O)$_2$PS$_2$ SbOCH$_2$CH$_2$O Orange yellow sticky solid, 83.3%	7.4 (7.3)	16.2 (16.0)	----
10	[(α-C$_{10}$H$_7$-O)$_2$PS$_2$Na] 0.40gm,1.0 mmol	OCH$_2$CH$_2$CH$_2$OSbCl 0.23gm 1.0 mmol	1:1	4.5	[(α-C$_{10}$H$_7$-O)$_2$PS$_2$]$_2$Sb OCH$_2$CH$_2$CH$_2$O] Orange yellow sticky solid ,77.1%	22.2 (22.0)	11.7 (11.5)	----
11	[(β-C$_{10}$H$_7$-O)$_2$PS$_2$Na] 0.40gm,1.0 mmol	OCH$_2$CH$_2$CH$_2$OSbCl 0.23gm,1.0 mmol	1:1	4.5	[(β-C$_{10}$H$_7$-O)$_2$PS$_2$]$_2$Sb OCH$_2$CH$_2$CH$_2$O Orange yellow sticky solid ,77.1%	22.2 (22.1)	11.7 (11.4)	----
12	[((CH$_3$)$_3$C$_6$H$_2$O)$_2$PS$_2$Na] 0.77gm,1.0mmol	OCH$_2$CH$_2$CH$_2$OSbCl 0.23gm,1.0 mmol	1:1	4.5	[((CH$_3$)$_3$C$_6$H$_2$O)$_2$PS$_2$]$_2$Sb OCH$_2$CH$_2$CH$_2$O Orange yellow sticky solid ,86.5%	21.7 (21.3)	11.4 (10.9)	----

Table 1.4. Synthetic and analytical data of Antimony(III) O, O'-α-Naphthyl, β-Naphthyl, and 2,3,5- Trimethylphenyldithiophosphates.

S.no	Ligand/(gm) mmol	Metal salt/(gm)/ mmol SbCl3/ OC'OSbCl	M.R. T	Ref.	Product/ (Color/M-pt/yield %)	Analysis Calc./ (Found)		
						Sb	S	Cl
1	[(α-C$_{10}$H$_7$O)$_2$PS$_2$Na] 0.40gm,1.0 mmol	SbCl$_3$ 0.22gm,1.0,mmol,	1:1	4.0	(α-C$_{10}$H$_7$O)$_2$PS$_2$SbCl$_2$ Orange yellow sticky solid ,78%	21.2 (21.0)	11.1 (11.0)	12.3 (12.1)
2	[(β-C$_{10}$H$_7$O)$_2$PS$_2$Na] 0.40gm,1.0mmol	SbCl$_3$ 0.22 gm,1.0 mmol	1:1	4.0	(β-C$_{10}$H$_7$O)$_2$PS$_2$SbCl$_2$ Orange yellow sticky solid ,78%	21.2 (21.1)	11.1 (11.0)	12.3 (12.2)
3	[((CH$_3$)$_3$C$_6$H$_2$O)$_2$PS$_2$Na] 0.77gm,1.0mmol	SbCl$_3$ 0.22 gm,1.0 mmol	1:1	4.0	((CH$_3$)$_3$C$_6$H$_2$O)$_2$PS$_2$SbCl$_2$ Orange yellow sticky solid ,81.8%	21.8 (21.5)	11.4 (11.2)	12.7 (12.5)
4	[(α-C$_{10}$H$_7$O)$_2$PS$_2$Na] 0.80gm,2.0 mmol	SbCl$_3$ 0.22 gm,1.0 mmol	2:1	4.0	[(α-C$_{10}$H$_7$O)$_2$PS$_2$]$_3$SbCl Orange yellow sticky solid ,86.7%	22.6 (22.4)	11.9 (11.7)	6.5 (6.4)
5	[(β-C$_{10}$H$_7$O)$_2$PS$_2$Na] 0.80gm,2.0 mmol	SbCl$_3$ 0.22 gm,1.0 mmol	2:1	4.0	[(β-C$_{10}$H$_7$O)$_2$PS$_2$]$_3$SbCl Orange yellow sticky solid, 86.7%	22.6 (22.5)	11.9 (11.5)	6.5 (6.3)
6	[((CH$_3$)$_3$C$_6$H$_2$O)$_2$PS$_2$Na] 0.77gm,2.0mmol	SbCl$_3$ 0.22 gm,1.0 mmol	2:1	4.0	[((CH$_3$)$_3$C$_6$H$_2$O)$_2$PS$_2$]$_3$SbCl] Orange yellow sticky solid, 73.8%.	23.2 (23.1)	12.2 (12.0)	6.7 (6.5)
7	[(α-C$_{10}$H$_7$O)$_2$PS$_2$Na] 0.40gm,1.0 mmol	OCH$_2$CH$_2$OSbCl 0.21mmol,1.0mmol	1:1	4.5	(α-C$_{10}$H$_7$O)$_2$PS$_2$ SbOCH$_2$CH$_2$O Orange yellow sticky solid, 80.3%	21.6 (21.4)	11.3 (11.2)	-----
8	[(β-C$_{10}$H$_7$O)$_2$PS$_2$Na] 0.40gm,1.0 mmol	OCH$_2$CH$_2$OSbCl 0.21gm,1.0mmol	1:1	4.5	(β-C$_{10}$H$_7$O)$_2$PS$_2$ SbOCH$_2$CH$_2$O Orange yellow sticky solid, 80.3%	21.6 (21.3)	11.3 (11.1)	-----
9	[((CH$_3$)$_3$C$_6$H$_2$O)$_2$PS$_2$Na] 0.77gm,1.0mmol	OCH$_2$CH$_2$OSbCl 0.2 gm,1.0 mmol	1:1	4.5	((CH$_3$)$_3$C$_6$H$_2$O)$_2$PS$_2$ SbOCH$_2$CH$_2$O Orange yellow sticky solid, 83.3%	7.4 (7.3)	16.2 (16.0)	-----
10	[(α-C$_{10}$H$_7$O)$_2$PS$_2$Na] 0.40gm,1.0 mmol	OCH$_2$CH$_2$CH$_2$OSbCl 0.23gm,1.0 mmol	1:1	4.5	[(α-C$_{10}$H$_7$O)$_2$PS$_2$Sb OCH$_2$CH$_2$CH$_2$O] Orange yellow sticky solid, 77.1%	22.2 (22.0)	11.7 (11.5)	-----
11	[(β-C$_{10}$H$_7$O)$_2$PS$_2$Na] 0.40gm,1.0 mmol	OCH$_2$CH$_2$CH$_2$OSbCl 0.23gm,1.0 mmol	1:1	4.5	[(β-C$_{10}$H$_7$O)$_2$PS$_2$]Sb OCH$_2$CH$_2$CH$_2$O Orange yellow sticky solid, 77.1%	22.2 (22.1)	11.7 (11.4)	-----
12	[((CH$_3$)$_3$C$_6$H$_2$O)$_2$PS$_2$Na] 0.77gm,1.0mmol	OCH$_2$CH$_2$CH$_2$OSbCl 0.23gm,1.0 mmol	1:1	4.5	[((CH$_3$)$_3$C$_6$H$_2$O)$_2$PS$_2$]Sb OCH$_2$CH$_2$CH$_2$O Orange yellow sticky solid, 86.5%	21.7 (21.3)	11.4 (10.9)	-----

References :
1. V.K.Jain, B Varghese, Synthesis and characterization of pentamethylcyclopentadienyl rhodium(III) dialkyldithiophosphate complexes, the single crystal structure of [Cp*RhCl{S₂P(OEt)₂}]. J. Organomet. Chem, 584, 159. 1999.
2. V.K. Jain, V.S. Jakkal, "Synthesis and characterization of areneruthenium(II) dialkyldithiophosphate complexes: single-crystal structure of [Ru{SSP(OEt)₂}(Z6-p-cymene)(PPh₃)][BPh₄]." J. Organomet. Chem,515, 81, 1996.
3. P.U. Jain, P. Munshi, M.G Walawalker, S.P. Rath, K.K Rajak, G.K Lahiri,. Ruthenium dithiophosphates: synthesis, x-ray crystal structure, spectroscopy, and electrochemical properties. Polyhedron. 19, 801,2000.
4. A.A.S El-Khady, Y.P Singh, R Bohra, G.Srivastava, R.C. Mehrotra, "Synthesis and spectra studies of mixed acetodibutyltin dialkyl (or alkylene) dithiophosphates and crystal structure of dibutyltin bis(neopentylene)". Main Group Met. Chem., 14, 305, 1991.
5. B.W. Liebich, M. Tomassini, Bis (O, O-diethyl dithiophosphato) diphenyltin. Acta Cryst. B34, 944, 1978.
6. M.-A. Munoz-Hernandez, R.Cea-Olivares, S. Hernandez-Ortega, "Synthesis and characterization of oxa and thio metallocances substituted Vanadium(III) Dithiophosphates with phosphorodithioate ligands and crystal and molecular structure of1,3,6-trithia-2-arsocane dimethyl phosphorodithioate". Inorg. Chim. Acta, 253, 31,1996.
7. V.K.Jain, B.Varghese, Synthesis and characterization of pentamethylcyclopentadienylrhodium(III) dialkyldithiophosphate complexes, the single-crystal structure of [Cp*RhCl{S₂P(OEt)₂}]. J. Organomet. Chem, , 584, 159,1999.
8. A.A.S. El-Khady, Y.P Singh, R.Bohra, G.Srivastava, R.C. Mehrotra, "Synthesis and spectra studies of mixed acetodibutyltin dialkyl (or alkylene) dithiophosphates and crystal structure of dibutyltin bis(neopentylene)". Main Group Met. Chem., 14, 305. 1991
9. B.P.Singh, G. Srivastava, R.C. Mehrotra, "Synthesis and reactions of triorganotin dialkyldithiophosphates". J. Organomet. Chem., 171, 35,1979

10. P.G. Garcia, R. Cruz-Almanza, R. Toscano, R. Cea-Olivares, "Synthesis, characterization and x-ray structure of stannocanes substituted with a cyclic dithiophosphate ligand X(CH2CH2S)2SnnBu[S2- POCH2C(Et)2CH2O], (X= O, S): a study about the conformational tendencies and the relationship with the anomeric effect of the stannocane rings. J. Organomet. Chem. ,598, 160,2000.

11. J.E. Drake, C. Gurnani, M.B. Hursthouse, M.E.Light, M. Nirwan, and R. Ratnani, "Triethyl ammonium salt of O, O'-bis(p-tolyl)dithiophosphate, [Et3NH](+)[(4-MeC6H4O) (2)PS2" (-),Journal of Chemical Crystallography, (36, (10), 627-630,2006.

12. I. Haiduc, Phosphoric acid derivatives of Tin(II). Crystal and molecular structure of (O, O-diethyl dithiophosphate) triphenyl tin(IV) derivative at 138K. A unique monodentate behavior. Inorg. Chem. 18, 3507-3511,1980.

13. S.L. Lawton, C.J. Fuhrmeister, R.G. Hass, C.S. Jarman, F.G. Lohmeyer, Inorg. Chem. 13 ,135, 1974.

14. T.Ito, H. H. Igarashi, "the crystal structure of metaldithiophosphate I: Zinc diethyl dithiophosphate". Acta Crystallogr. Sec. B., 25, 2303-2309,1969.

15. Xie Q, Luo N, Li J, Jing X ,"Youj Haux. Ditolyldithiophosphato derivatives of phosphorus(III) and phosphorus(V)" Chem Abstr ,117:26650w ,1992.

16. Julio Zukerman-SchpectorEdward R.T. Tiekink Stereochemical activity of lone pairs of electrons and supramolecular aggregation patterns based on secondary interactions involving tellurium in its 1,1-dithiolate, structures Coordination Chemistry Reviews, 46–76. 2010.

17. J. A. Ejk. C. R. Ringwood, U. S. Pat.4, 010,138; Chem. Abstr., , 86, 122403e,1977

18. A. M.Barnes, K. D. Bartle, Thio, A. Tribology International, 389-395. 2001.

19. G. A. Marinkina, I. L.Kotlyarevskii, I. S. Levin, "Thermal decomposition of isooctyl hydrogen dithiophosphate and search for selective extraction of arsenic(III)."Zh. Prikl., Khim. 1977, 50, 427-428; Chem. Abstr.1977. 86,146568p

20. N. A.Ulakhovich, G. K. Budhnikov, I. V Postnova, N. K. Shakukurova, "Extraction polarograpic determination of mercury using zinc dithiophosphate".Zabad Lab. 1980,46, 587-591; Chem. Abstr., 93, 125128z,1980

21. M. Jain, S. Gaur, V.P. Singh, R.V. Singh, Appl. Organometal. Chem. 18 , 73,2004.

22. Seema. Maheshwari, John E. Drake, Kavita Kori, Mark Edward Light, and Raju. Ratnani, "Synthesis and spectroscopic characterization of tris(O,O '-ditolyl dithiophosphato) arsenic/antimony/bismuth(III) compounds: Crystal structures of [As{S2P(OC6H4Me-m)(2)}(3)]center dot 0.5C(6)H(14), [Sb {S2P(OC6H4Me-m)(2)}(3)] and [Bi{S2P(OC6H4Me-m)(2)} (3)]".Polyhedron28, (4), 689-694. (doi:10.1016/ j.poly. 2008.12.017). ,(2009),

23. Vimal K. Jain, Satyajeet Chaudhury, Anima Vyas, and Rakesh Bohra Synthesis and characterization of methylplatinum(II)O, O'-dialkyl dithiophosphates. Crystal structure of [PtMe{S2P(OPri)2}(AsPh3)] J. Chem. Soc., Dalton Trans., 1207-1211, 1994.

24. A.M. Barnes, K.D. Bartle, Thibon, Kanerva, L Tupasela, O. Jolanki an examination of the reactivity of zinc di-alkyl-di-thiophosphate to its use AS AN.VRA,TRIBOL INT, 34(6), 389-395;R ,2001.

25. Vimal K. Jain, Satyajeet Chaudhury, Anima Vyas, and Rakesh Bohra Synthesis and characterization of methylplatinum(II)O, O'-dialkyl dithiophosphates. Crystal structure of [PtMe{S2P(OPri)2}(AsPh3)] J. Chem. Soc., Dalton Trans., 1207-1211, 1994.

26. *W.F. Tabor, P.M. Williamson* Chemistry of arsenic, antimony and bismuth compounds, U.S. Patent 3,549,533, Chem. Abstr. 74 , , 7813,1970, 1971

27. I. Haiduc. Nitrogen, phosphorus, arsenic, antimony, and bismuth, Coord. Chem. Rev., , 158, 3,1997.

28. R. F. Makens, H. H. Vaughan, and R. R. Chelberg H.P.S. Chauhan, G. Srivastava, R.C. Mehrotra Mixed halide dialkyl dithiophosphate derivatives of arsenic(III) and antimony(III), Anal. Chem., 27, 1062, 1955

29. H.H. Farmer, H.F. Tompkins, B.W. Malone Antimony(III) diorganophosphoro and diorgano phospinodithioates S. African *Pat.*, 6 802089,1968.

30. D.Bryan Sowerby, Ionel Haiduc, Marius Salajan Anamaria Barbul-Rusu, Antimony(III) diorganophosphoro and,diorganophospinodithioates::Inorganica Chimica Acta, 87-96,1983.

31. *R. K. Gupta, A. K. Rai, R. C. Mehrotra*, V. K. Jam, B. F. Hoskins and E. R. T.Tiekin Synthesis and reactions of diaryl antimony (III) amides Inorg. Chem.,*24, 3280. 1985*

32. S. K. Hadjikakou, C.D. Antoniadis, N. Hadjiliadis, M. Kubicki J. Binolis Karkaounas. Synthesis and characterization of new water-stable antimony(II I) complex with pyrimidine-2-thione and in vitro biological study. Inorg Chim Acta 358: 2861–6. 2005.

33. C. Silvestru, A. Bara. Socaciu, I. Haiduc."Chemistry of arsenic, antimony, and bismuth compounds Anticancer Res. 10. 803,1990.

34. G.C. Wang, J, Xiao, Y, Lu, JS, Li, J.R. Cui, R.Q Wang, "Synthesis, crystal structures and in vi to antitumor activities of some aryl antimony derivatives of analogs of dimethyl cantharimide" J Organomet Chem 689: 1631–8. 2004.

35. G.C . Wang, Y.N Lu, J. Xiao, L . Yu, H.B. Song, J.S. Li, Synthesis, Crystal structure and in vitro antitumor act it is of some organoantimony aryl hydroxamates. J Organomet Chem 690: 151–6. 2005.

36. J.Kanazawa, H.Kubo, R Sato. "Gas-liquid chromatography of organophosphorus pesticides". Agri. Boil. Chem., 29, 43-56,1965

37. B. Desoize, Metals, and metal compounds in cancer treatment. Anticancer Res; 24: 1529–44. 2004.

38. M. Gielen, editor. Metal-based antitumor drugs. London: Freund Publishing House Ltd; 1988.

39. B.K. Keppbereditor, Metal complexes in cancer chemotherapy. Weinheim Germany: VCHp1–8,1993.

40. Köpf–Maier P. Complexes of metals other than platinum as antitumor agents. Eur J Clin Pharmacol; 47: 1–16. 1994

41. CFJ. Barnard, S.P. Fricker, O.J. Vaughan, "Medical applications of inorganic chemicals. In Thompson D, editor. Insights into specialty inorganic chemicals. Cambr edge: Royal Society of Chemistry; 35–60. 1995.
42. P.J. Sadler, Z. Guo, Metal complexes in medicine: design and mechanism of action. Pure Appl Chem; 70: 863–71. 1998.
43. Z . Guo, P.J. Sadler. Metals in medicine. Angew Chem Int Ed Engl38: 1512–31. 1999.
44. I. Haiduc.   Nitrogen, phosphorus, arsenic, antimony, and bismuth, Coord. Chem. Rev., 158, 325. 1997.
45. R. F. Makens, H. H. Vaughan, and R. R. Chelberg H.P.S. Chauhan, G. Srivastava, R.C. Mehrotra Mixed halide dialkyl dithiophosphate derivatives of arsenic(III) and antimony(III), Anal. Chem. 27, 1062, 1955,
46. *W.F. Tabor, P.M. Williamson* Chemistry of arsenic, antimony and bismuth compounds, U.S. Patent 3,549,533, 1970, Chem. Abstr. 74 7813. (1971).
47. H.H. Farmer, H.F. Tompkins, B.W. Malone Antimony(III) diorgano phosphoro- and diorgano phospinodithioates S. African *Pat.*, 6 802089,1968.
48. D.Bryan Sowerby,   Ionel Haiduc,   Marius Salajan Anamaria Barbul-Rusu,   Antimony(III)   diorganophosphoro- and,diorganophospinodithioates::Inorganica Chimica Acta, 87-96. 1983.
49. *R. K. Gupta, A. K. Rai, R. C. Mehrotra*, V. K. Jam, B. F. Hoskins, and E. R. T. Tiekink.Synthesis and reactions of diaryl antimony (III) amides Inorg. Chem.,*24, 3280. 1985.*
50. R. Karras, Y. P. Singha & A. K. Raia, O, O'-dialkyl dithiophosphate complexes of diphenyl antimony (iii) vol, phosphorus, sulfur, and silicon and the related elements, 45145-150, 1989,
51. Rajesh K. Gupta, A.K. Rai, R.C. Mehrotra Vimal K. Jain Cyclic o,o-alkylenedithiophosphates of phenyl-arsenic and -antimony, Inorg.Chim.Acta, ,88 " 201-207,1984.
52. S .K.Hadjikakou, C.D. Antoniadis, N . Hadjiliadis, M . Kubicki, J.Binolis, S. Karkaounas "Synthesis and characterization of new water-stable antimony(II I) complex with pyrimidine-2-thione

and in vitro biological study".Inorg Chim Acta 358: 2861–6. 2005.

53. I . I Ozturk, S.K Hadjikakou, N . Hadjiliadis, N. Kourkoumelis, M. Kubicki, M . Baril, "Synthesis, structural characterization, and biological studies of new antimony (III) complexes with thiones. The influence of the solvent on the geometry of the complexes" Inorg Chem; 46: 8652–61. 2007.

54. Xu S, Guo G, Wang J, Huang Y. Effects of potassium antimonyl tartrate on proliferation and apoptosis in vitro of human gastric cancer. Disi Junyi Daxue Xuebao; 25: 1464–6. 2004.

55. M. Salerno, A.G. Suillerot, "Resistance to arsenic-and antimony based drugs". Bioinorg Chem Appl; 1: 189–98. 2003.

56. C.Silvestru, A. Bara. Socaciu, I. Haiduc, "Chemistry of arsenic, antimony and bismuth compounds" Anticancer Res. 10803. 1990.

57. Wang GC, Lu YN, Xiao J, Yu L, Song HB, Li JS, et al. Synthesis, Crystal structure and in vitro antitumor activities of some organoantimony aryl hydroxamates. J Organomet Chem 690: 151–6. 2005.

58. Carraher CE Jr, Nass MD, Giron DJ, Cerutis DR. Structural and biological characterization of antimony(V) polyamines. J Macromol Sci Chem; 19: 1101–20. 1983.

59. S K Hadjikakou, CD Antoniadis, N.Hadjiliadis M. Kubicki, J . Binolis, S . Karkaounas, Synthesis and characterization of new water-stable antimony(III) complex with pyrimidine-2-thione and in vitro biological study. Inorg Chim Acta 358: 2861–6. 2005.

60. I. I. Ozturk, S.K. Hadjikakou, N. Hadjiliadis, N. Kourkoumelis, M . Kubicki, M . Baril, "Synthesis, structural characterization, and biological studies of new antimony (III) complexes with thiones. The influence of the solvent on the geometry of the complexes" Inorg Chem 46: 8652–61, 2007.

61. U. N. Tripathi, G. Srivastava, R. Bohra, and R. C. Mehrotra R. Gupta O, O'-alkylene dithiophosphate derivatives of iron (II) and iron (III) Polyhedron, ll, 1187, Ph.D. thesis, Rajasthan University, Jaipur, (9). 1992.

62. L. H. Pingolet. . Willemse, J. A. Crass, J. J. Steggarda and C. P. Keijers, in. J. D. Dunitz Synthesis and spectral studies of nickel (II), palladium (II   Topics Current Chem. (Ed.), Structure and Bonding, 56, 91,1975.

63. S.K.Pandey, G.Srivastava and R.C.Mehrotra S.E.Nefedov, I.L.Eremenko, A.A.Pasynskii, A.I.Yanovskii Spectroscopic properties of inorganic and organometallic compounds Transition Met. Chem., 18, 31. 365, 1993.

64. Simerpal Kour, Bhawana Gupta, Romesh Chander, Sushil Kumar Pandey, O, O'-Ditolyldithiophosphates of Zinc(II), Cadmium(II) and Mercury(II)   Main Group Metal Chem. 32, 4,195–202.2011.

65. A.M Barnes, K.D. Bartle, Thibon, Kanerva, L. Tupasela, O. Jolanki an examination of the reactivity of zinc di-alkyl-di-thiophosphate to its use AS AN... VRA, TRIBOL INT, 34(6), pp. 389-395; R 2001.

66. W.F. Tabor, P.M. Williamson Chemistry of arsenic, antimony and bismuth compounds, U.S. Patent 3,549,533, Chem. Abstr. 74 (1971). 7813,1970.

67. I. Haiduc.   Nitrogen, phosphorus, arsenic, antimony, and bismuth, Coord. Chem. Rev., , 158, 3,1997

68. R. F. Makens, H. H. Vaughan, and R. R. Chelberg H.P.S. Chauhan, G. Srivastava, R.C. Mehrotra Mixed halide dialkyl dithiophosphate derivatives of arsenic(III) and antimony(III), Anal. Chem., 27, 1062, 1955.

69. H.H. Farmer, H.F. Tompkins, B.W. Malone Antimony(III) diorganophosphoro- and diorganophospinodithioates S. African Pat., 6 802089 (1968)

70. D.Bryan Sowerby, Ionel Haiduc, Marius Salajan Anamaria Barbul-Rusu, Antimony(III) diorganophosphoro-and,diorganophospinodithioates::Inorganica Chimica Acta, 87-96,1983,

71. R. K. Gupta, A. K. Rai, R. C. Mehrotra, V. K. Jam, B. F. Hoskins and E. R. T.Tiekin   Synthesis and reactions of diaryl antimony (III) amides Inorg. Chem.,24, 3280. 1985.

72. S. K. Hadjikakou, C.D. Antoniadis, N. Hadjiliadis, M. Kubicki, J. Binolis, S . Karkaounas, Synthesis and characterization of new

water-stable antimony(III) complex with pyrimidine-2-thione and in vitro biological study. Inorg Chim Acta 358: 2861–6. 2005.

73. C. Silvestru, L. Silaghi-Dumitrescu, 1. Haiduc, M.J. Begley, M. Nunn, and D.B. Sowerby, Diphenylantimony(III) diphenylphosphine and diphenylmonothiophosphinate: synthesis, spectra, and crystal structure *J. Chem. Soc., Dalton Trans., 1031,1986.*

74. Seema. Maheshwari, John E. Drake, Kavita Kori, Mark Edward. Light, and Raju .Ratnani, Synthesis and spectroscopic characterization of tris(O,O '-ditolyl dithiophosphato) arsenic/antimony/bismuth(III) compounds: Crystal structures of [As{S2P(OC6H4Me-m)(2)}(3)]centerdot 0.5C(6)H(14), [Sb{S2P(OC6H4Me-m)(2)}(3)] and [Bi{S2P(OC6H4Me-m)(2)}(3)]. Polyhedron, 28, (4), 689-694. (doi:10.1016/j.poly.2008.12.017). 2009.

75. W.F. Tabor, P.M. Williamson Chemistry of arsenic, antimony and bismuth compounds, U.S. Patent 3,549,533, 1970, Chem. Abstr. 74 7813 ,1971.

76. G. H. Sin and S. G. Ryom, Hwahak Kwa Hwahak Knogop. Mixed halide dialkyl dithiophosphate derivatives of arsenic(III). 1974, 17 ,234,chem..Abstr, ,82,124652,1975.

77. M.M. Glebova, O. K.;Sharaev, E. I. Tienyakova, B. A. Dolgoplosk, Vysokomolekul. Soedin. Seriya Synthesis and Spectroscopic characterization of bis(o.o'-ditolyl)[31] 37(7), (1995), 1145; Chem. Abstr., 125, 14337g,1996.

78. I. Haiduc. Nitrogen, phosphorus, arsenic, antimony, and bismuth, Coord. Chem. Rev.158, 3, 1997.

[1,2]**Department of Chemistry,**
Govt. G. M. Science College, Jammu, Jammu, India.
[3]**Department of Chemistry,**
Banasthali University, Jaipur, Rajasthan, India.

www.ingramcontent.com/pod-product-compliance
Lightning Source LLC
Chambersburg PA
CBHW050223270326
41914CB00003BA/544